# The Dark Historic Page

# THE DARK HISTORIC PAGE

## Social Satire and
## Historicism in the Novels of
## *ALDOUS HUXLEY*
### *1921–1939*

## Robert S. Baker

THE UNIVERSITY OF
WISCONSIN PRESS

Published 1982

The University of Wisconsin Press
114 North Murray Street
Madison, Wisconsin 53715

The University of Wisconsin Press, Ltd.
1 Gower Street
London WC1E 6HA, England

First printing

Printed in the United States of America

For LC CIP information see the colophon

ISBN 0-299-08940-1

Parts of this book have appeared previously in a somewhat different form in *Texas Studies in Literature and Language* 19, no. 1 (Spring 1977): 60–82 (published by the University of Texas Press); *Studies in the Novel* 9, no. 4 (Winter 1977): 537–63; and *Criticism* 16 no. 2 (Spring 1974): 120–35.

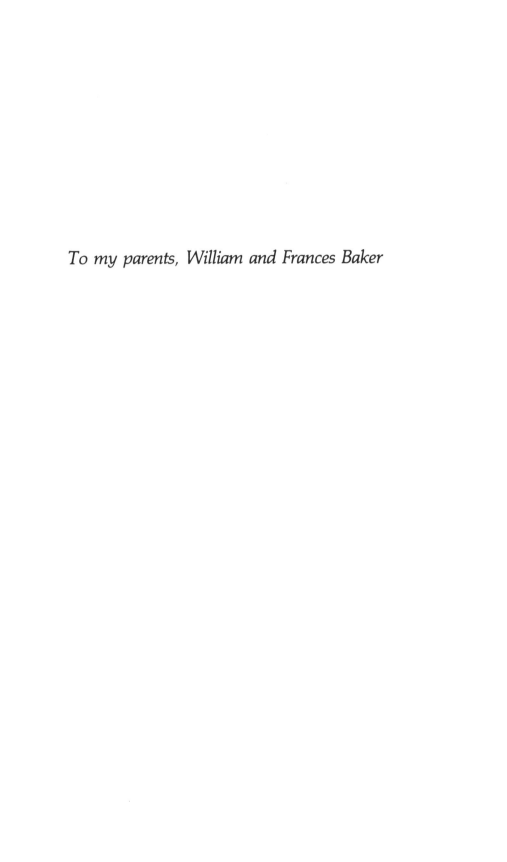

*To my parents, William and Frances Baker*

# Contents

# *Illustrations*

# Abbreviations

The editions of Huxley's novels and essay collections used in this study can be found at the beginning of the bibliography. The following convention has been employed when incorporating page references into the text. See Bibliography for list of first editions and editions used in this study.

| | |
|---|---|
| AF | *After the Fireworks* |
| AMS | *After Many a Summer Dies the Swan* |
| AR | *Along the Road* |
| AH | *Antic Hay* |
| BNW | *Brave New World* |
| BC | *Brief Candles* |
| CE | *Collected Essays* |
| CY | *Crome Yellow* |
| DL | *The Devils of Loudun* |
| DWW | *Do What You Will* |
| EM | *Ends and Means* |
| EG | *Eyeless in Gaza* |
| JP | *Jesting Pilate* |
| L | *Limbo* |
| MN | *Music at Night* |
| OM | *On the Margin* |
| OT | *The Olive Tree* |
| PCP | *Point Counter Point* |
| PS | *Proper Studies* |
| TV | *Themes and Variations* |
| TBL | *Those Barren Leaves* |
| TS | *Time Must Have a Stop* |
| TG | *Two or Three Graces* |

# The Dark Historic Page

# The Dark Historic Page:

## Romanticism and Historicism in Huxley's Social Satire

In 1939, as an insurgently fractious Europe moved steadily towards war, R. G. Collingwood advanced the thesis that history was gradually asserting its ascendancy as the preeminent science of man, declaring in his autobiography that "historical thought, whose constantly increasing importance had been one of the most striking features of the nineteenth century, would increase in importance far more rapidly during the twentieth; and that we might very well be standing on the threshold of an age in which history would be as important for the world as natural science had been between 1600 and 1900."[1] Two years earlier Aldous Huxley contended that "the sooner we convince ourselves that 'historicalness' is not a value and that what we allow circumstances to make us do has no necessary connection with what we ought to do, the better it will be for ourselves and for the world we live in. At the present moment of time the 'historical' is almost unmitigatedly evil. To accept the 'historical' and to work for it is to co-operate with the powers of darkness against the light" (*EM*, 69).

The meaning that Huxley, in this particular context, attached to the word "historical," while not identical to Collingwood's, is nevertheless closely related to it. Huxley's aversion for what E. M. Forster called the rationalized "sequences . . . fabricated by historians" derived in part from his reservations concerning the status of history as a science but attributable mainly to his sensitivity to the potentially ideological implication of such a positivistic faith in "historical thought." Unable to dispel the shadows cast by "the Weltanschauung of 1933"[2]—the year of Hitler's rise to power—and aware of the historicist element present both in the

[ 3 ]

elevation of history as a discipline grounded in empirically testable theory as well as the obstinate craving to reintroduce time-honored teleological biases into the study of history, Huxley found it increasingly difficult to view "historical thought" apart from its ideological and meta-historical assumptions.

Beginning with *Crome Yellow* in 1921, Huxley wrote a series of six novels that attempted to trace the fatalistic drift of English society in the wake of World War I and to explore the gradual acceleration of those historical and social currents within the narrowly doctrinaire channels of the ideologies of the 1930s. His endeavor to probe the prevailing political and cultural values of his contemporaries and to chart the transformation of the social turmoil of the twenties into the ideological fixities of the thirties resulted in a satiric vision whose emphasis was insistently psychological. It focused primarily on two related problems: first, what he regarded as his contemporaries' addiction to discernibly romantic concepts and aspirations; and second, their reliance on history as the principal source of meaning and value. The continuity of Huxley's fiction throughout the interwar period is apparent in the recurrence of motifs like the country estate; the repeated employment of imagery drawn from art history; and the reappearance of character types like the socialist or Marxist ideologue, the romantic visionary, the withdrawn aesthete, or the self-destructive sadomasochist. But the constant element that governs Huxley's social satire is his theory of "modern" romanticism that informs in large measure his systematic formulation of the course of modern history and appears and reappears in many guises and situations.

Five years after the end of World War II, Huxley again raised the issue of history, its publicly apprehended meaning and its ambiguous relationship to the private life of the individual: "The life of every individual occupies a certain position in time, is contemporary with certain political events and runs parallel, so to speak, with certain social and cultural movements. In a word, the individual lives surrounded by history. But to what extent does he actually live *in* history? And what precisely is this history by which individuals are surrounded and within which each of them does at least some of his living?" (*CE*, 221) The novels of the interwar period represent a sustained attempt to answer these two fundamental questions by tracing through the fabric of English society the various ideological threads of historicism and romanticism. Huxley's characters are not only caught up in the swirl of postwar history, but very often their lives are touched by the discipline itself. Indeed, his novels are crowded with historians, both amateur antiquarians or professional academics, all of whom are either obsessed with the past and determined to elicit meaning from it or, bemused by the absence of purpose or design, repudiate it entirely. *Crome Yellow*, Huxley's first novel, is carefully structured around the work of an amateur historian, whose "History of Crome" contributes substantially to the meaning of the narrative. In *Antic Hay* the protagonist is a teacher of history who resigns from his position and attacks his discipline as methodologically corrupt, while the final novel of the interwar period, *After Many a Summer Dies the Swan*, turns thematically on the activities and prejudices of two professional historians. This fascination with history, its methodological assumptions and procedures as well as their epistemological and political ramifications, pervades the novels and extends to Huxley's essays as well. Equally important, the meaning of history bears one aspect in novels like *Point Counter Point* or *Eyeless in Gaza* and a related yet slightly modified aspect in the essays of *Do What You Will* or *Ends and Means*. One measure of the difference between them lies with the aggressive urgencies of the conservative fictional satirist, as opposed to the guarded pragmatism of the political essayist. Yet the essays, despite their occasional flashes of hopeful rationalism, are essentially in agreement with the darker currents of pessimism that satirically energize the fiction. Huxley's philosophy of history, however, is so variously built into the novels that it cannot be separately stated apart from a multitude of related themes; it cannot in fact be fully comprehended if divorced from his theory of modern romanticism.

Huxley's depiction of a society numbed by the trauma of the Great War and given up to unvaryingly hedonistic aims, yet increasingly tempted to wayward forays in the direction of apocalyptic faiths and coercive ideologies, is inseparable from his criticism of historicism. He came to regard the postwar society of the twenties and thirties as a fundamentally historicist culture, in which Hegelian notions of idealist history, Wellsian and Shelleyan ideas of historical progress, and what Huxley regarded as Marxist "modern" romanticism combined to create a bewildering ideological landscape, one that he traced back to the intellectual excesses of the romantic period. All of these thematic categories intersect in Huxley's exploration of ideological historicism, an analysis of a set of interrelated ideas such as "historical process," "historical inevitableness," or, more fundamentally, the prevailing tendency "to regard historicalness as a value" (*EM*, 67–68).

In the twentieth century, historicism,[3] with its roots in the nineteenth century, has altered our perception of the past, inspiring on the one hand the violent ideologies of modern history while on the other encouraging a relativist rejection of absolute or trans-historical values. Historicism, however, eludes a single comprehensive formulation, especially, as Rolf Gruner has shown, a formulation free of inner contradiction.[4]

Throughout this study, I shall employ the word "historicism" to refer to the attempt to discover meaning in history apart from extra-historical consideration; that is, to view man as inseparably linked to time and dynamic-evolutionary change in a secular world where historical process has supplanted divine providence and the historical record has displaced apocalyptic revelation. I shall use the term "ideological historicism" when dealing with the endeavor to systemize the contingent and provisional phenomena of history into a teleological pattern that, while not necessarily appealing to trans-historical or metaphysical principles, does nevertheless attempt to reintroduce a sense of universal design into the flux of temporal experience. In this respect, the object of Huxley's satire is, broadly, to expose the failure of his society to make sense of the past, a failure all the more urgently pressing in the wake of the Great War. More narrowly, it is to dramatize his contemporaries' tendency to fabricate superficial historical explanations in order to escape the relativism inherent in historicist modes of perception.

In his study of the role of historical theory in modern literature, Harvey Gross claims that modern modes of perception and thinking are mainly, even exclusively, historicist: ". . . historicism is inescapable fact. Modern categories of knowing and understanding are historical; historical perceptions are the Kantian 'green glasses' with which we view the phenomenal world."[5] The belief that all personal, social, and cultural experience is dominated by change and is thus radically temporalistic, while offering an escape from the rigidly conceived values normally associated with a theologically oriented conception of the world, carries with it not only the logically consequent dangers of moral and intellectual skepticism but also the germ of the dogmatic ideologies of twentieth-century totalitarianism.

In modern literature the risks attendant on historicism have been frequently voiced. T. S. Eliot's Gerontion fears history, recoiling from its "cunning passages, contrived corridors" as a labyrinth in which man, blindly self-involved, wanders aimlessly. In Virginia Woolf's *Between the Acts,* Mrs. Swithin refuses to "believe in history," a menacing enigma that Joyce's Stephen Dedalus characterizes as "a nightmare" from which he is "trying to awake." In *Coming Up for Air,* George Orwell's protagonist observes that "the past is a curious thing. It's with you all the time, I suppose . . . yet most of the time its got no reality, it's just a set of facts that you've learned, like a lot of stuff in a history book." Joseph Conrad repudiates "the world's history" as a record of increasingly sophisticated violence, while in H. G. Wells's *The History of Mr. Polly,* history is defined as a set of "lists and dates" employed to inspire "pride of empire." Similarly, in E. M. Forster's *Howard's End* the "shows of history" are introduced only as sinister forces, incomprehensible and chaotic. In *Brave New World* the Director of Hatcheries admits that "when you're not accustomed to history, most facts about the past *do* sound incredible" (*BNW*, 36), while Mustapha Mond reaffirms Henry Ford's dictum that "history is bunk" (*BNW*, 38). In Mond's antiseptically contrived world, historical process has been terminated, the apocalyptic end of history having ushered in a static society where historicist values and modes of perception have been repudiated and where even individual biography has come under the control of social engineering and its trans-historical perspective. Mond's apocalyptic falling out of history is a more bizarre and systematically comprehensive endeavor to achieve what so many of Huxley's characters dream of, to "break out of contemporary history" (*CE*, 219) into a world of supra-historical experience—what Huxley refers to as "enclaves" of "non-historicity" or the "non-historical" (*CE*, 232). In the novels such privileged realms are either illusory fabrications or genuinely autonomous experiences of a nontemporal level of experience. In the fiction of the twenties and thirties, however, the former predominate and account for the pervasive "burrow" imagery, an incrementally developed motif that extends throughout all Huxley's interwar novels, while the "non-historical" is at most only reconditely hinted at until the appearance of *Eyeless in Gaza* in 1936.

Huxley's satires are populated not only by historians, museum-directors, antiquarians, and collectors but also by memoirists and autobiographers, all of whom are engaged in the task of making sense of the past, conferring meaning and purpose on the experience of temporal process or teasing a sense of design out of the random events of an individual life span. Theodore Gumbril, for example, composes a brief autobiographical essay at the outset of *Antic Hay*. In *Those Barren Leaves* Francis Chelifer writes a memoir central to the novel's structure, entitled *Fragments from the Autobiography of Francis Chelifer*. In a similar vein, Philip Quarles in *Point Counter Point* scrupulously records his ideas and observations in a notebook and attempts to write a personal memoir called "The Kitchen in the Old House," while his father Sidney Quarles, an amateur historian, compiles a mass of autobiographical fragments entitled "Memories and Reflections of Fifty [Years]." Similarly, in *Eyeless in Gaza* Anthony Beavis, fascinated by "historical facts," assembles a lengthy diary based on his sociological observations and his own daily experiences. Significant sections of *After Many a Summer Dies the Swan* consist of pages from the diaries of the Earl of Gonister. This motific repetition of memoir, diary, and autobiography is closely linked to the equally pervasive presence of prophecy and apocalyptic vision as Huxley's characters reach out to impose order on the future as well as on the past. But in Huxley's novels time is intractable, "the brute fact of becoming" (EM, 12) being susceptible neither to scientific analysis nor visionary illumination. Autobiography, in particular, beguiles Huxley's characters with its promise of order. The memoirist's impulse is not simply to record a life but to shape a text in which the arbitrary events of a lifetime take on a patterned significance. In this, especially in view of the fact that Huxley's autobiographers are romantic egoists (Francis Chelifer's autobiography, for example, is based on Wordsworth's *Prelude*), it is essential to undertake a brief schematic review of Huxley's philosophy of history and its relationship to romanticism.

In Huxley's novels the "dark historic page" (CY, 86), so feared by Sir Hercules Lapith, is inherently unfathomable. Huxley's historians and autobiographers inevitably fail in their implicit aim to master a historical record always fragmentary and incomplete and thus tend to either dissolve their anxieties in idealistic images of temporal transcendence or turn with fanatical devotion to an ideological faith in some teleological procession in which they are what they are in virtue of a role created for them in a vast cosmic drama. More often, however, they react with a cynical despair, repudiating history and preferring to see life's possibilities shrunk to the manageable scope of the modern romantic's "nonhistorical" enclave. The intertwined themes of time, history, and autobiography are inseparable from Huxley's avowed aim "to write a novel that shall be at once personal and social," in which the central character becomes "a social symbol, a paradigm of the whole life of the community."[6] His interest in "the novel of social history"[7] flows at least in part from his complementary fascination with analytic philosophy of history.

For a novelist Huxley exhibits a surprisingly comprehensive interest in a wide array of procedural problems connected with history, including what constitutes an historical fact, causality in history, the possibility of objectivity, the nature of historical generalizations or law explanations, and the role of holism in historical theory. In 1927 he argued that "one becomes more than ever suspicious of the generalizations of historians about the character and mentality of the men and women of past ages. For upon what are these generalizations based? Upon an originally inadequate documentation further reduced by the ravages of time to a random collection of literary and archeological odds and ends. As statements about the past such generalizations are therefore of dubious value" (OT, 134). Huxley's novels are filled with such "random" collections, assemblages of haphazardly gathered documents, paintings, and relics—ranging from the collections gathered and preserved within the estate of Crome to Mercaptan's collection of historical and aesthetic artifacts in *Antic Hay*, from the "Ethnographical Collection" of primitive art in

*Eyeless in Gaza* to the massive and confusedly diverse collections of Joseph Stoyte in *After Many a Summer Dies the Swan*. These accumulations of discrete and unrelated fragments are emblems of discontinuity, finding their literary counterparts in the fragmentary autobiographical texts scattered throughout the novels. They collectively testify to Huxley's belief that the failure to discover meaning in the past too often finds a counterpart in the inability to confer meaning upon the present.

For Huxley it is wiser to confront and even accept the relativistic diversity of history rather than rush to embrace the illusory historical hypotheses actively propounded or tacitly assumed by so many of his characters. Huxley's satirical attack is directed against a broad spectrum of historicist formulations, from antiquarian nostalgia and vaguely "Wellsian" notions of progress in *Crome Yellow* to the ideological historicism analyzed in *Ends and Means* and dramatized in *Eyeless in Gaza*. It also includes the romantic prophecy of Shelley and Wordsworth, satirized in *Those Barren Leaves*, and culminates in Huxley's rejection of historicism in all of its conflicting manifestations in *After Many a Summer Dies the Swan*.

Huxley's reservations concerning the validity of historical explanations stems from a conviction that "all classifications and theories are made after the event," but "reversing the historical process, we attack the facts forearmed with theoretical prejudice" in an effort to make the facts correspond to a predetermined "theoretical scheme" (*EN*, 60–61). The theoretical schemes propounded by Huxley's characters are invariably the result of such prejudice and as a consequence are uniformly escapist, deeply subjective, and often ideologically inspired. Their inability to come to terms with history is best contrasted with Huxley's metahistorical caution:

Generalized history is a branch of speculation, connected (often arbitrarily and uneasily) with certain facts about the past. Circumstances alter, each age must think its own thoughts. Not until there is a settled and definitive world order can there be such a thing as a settled and definitive version of human history. (*OT*, 134)

Huxley's provisional acceptance of historicist relativism and the necessity of each epoch "to think its own thoughts" is juxtaposed with the concept of a terminating perspective, a final stage of social and political stability inspiring a clarity of vision unattainable in the 1930s. Lurking behind this assertion is Huxley's belief that "history is not a science" (*DWW*, 29) as well as his aversion for "those 'deep' metaphysical hypotheses, in terms of which some modern German historians have so excitingly and so unjustifiably interpreted the course of past events" (*OT*,

130). This refusal to tolerate sweeping historical generalizations can be traced to Huxley's conviction that "social and historical philosophy" tends often to simplify events by underestimating the formidably entangled causal web in which they inhere and take on meaning.

"Sociologists and historians," he observes, "are inclined to talk altogether too glibly about the 'causes' of events, thoughts, and actions in the human universe. Now the human universe is so enormously complicated that to speak of *the* cause of any event is an absurdity" (PS, xv). The "facts of history," he argues, are inseparable from a rich complex of causes so formidably intricate that "historical facts are qualitatively functions of the causes to which they are attributed" (PS, xvi). For Huxley an historical or sociological fact is part of a field of interacting forces so entangled that the attempt to isolate simple causal sequences tends to falsify the nature of the events themselves. By 1929, however, Huxley's strictures regarding the explanatory power of "generalized history" had become more severe. In particular, he insisted that history, being a field of inquiry where controlled experimentation was hardly feasible, cannot achieve the level of precise observation characteristic of the sciences, a reservation directed at the speculative ambitions of ideological historicism: "there can be no crucial experiments in history, nor for that matter, any completely accurate observations. History is not a science" (DWW, 29). Historians who aspired to subsume the historical event to be explained under a law were he believed pursuing an unnecessary fiction, an impossible nomological ideal in the face of which Huxley adopted a position in line with many contemporary philosophers of history:[8] "there is no such thing as Historical Truth—there are only more or less probable opinions about the past, opinions which change from generation to generation" (DWW, 245).

Earlier in *Proper Studies* Huxley had raised the issue of historical causality by asking, "what is a cause?" His answer, in line with his consistent rejection of nomological explanations in history, was to define historical explanation as the attempt to locate events within a chronological pattern, as opposed to a strictly causal sequence: "the best any observor can do is to present the facts, and with them a few of the most *humanly significant* antecedents and accompaniments which seem to be invariably connected with the facts of that particular class" (PS, xvi—italics mine). This procedural recommendation is borrowed directly from David Hume, although Huxley makes no reference to Hume's work in *Proper Studies*. Hume's "regularity" theory of causation defines a cause as simply a factor both temporally antecedent to and regularly associated with a specific type of effect.[9] Such a conception of causation, with its stress on sufficient or necessary conditions, *can* lay the basis for a scientific (and deterministic) approach to causal explanations. But for Huxley it seems to involve a flexible empiricism, too tentatively exploratory to support or even encourage the idealistic categories of ideological historicism, much less the positivist ambitions of scientific history.

Huxley's reservations on the subject of causal laws in history places him with those contemporary philosophers who insist that history is autonomous, not a science but a discipline with its own unique methodology. Historical explanation, they argue, differs significantly from the law explanations of the sciences because historians are concerned with individual behavior, human actions which admit of "purposive or rational explanations"; what appear to be laws are really mere generalizations that are themselves "summaries of singular statements about a number of individuals."[10] Thus as Huxley conceived it, historical truth was at best a matter of "probable opinions," of which none could be considered "settled and definitive," and the sequence of events constituting history was too complicated to yield intellectually satisfying causal explanations. Historicism, the belief that whatever the limitations of historical inquiry, the collective human experience of temporal evolution was the final measure of significance, value, and meaning, was never accepted by him. Many of his characters, however, either succumb to it or fabricate various alternatives, including ideologically inspired theories of history that substitute for the authority of God the modern absolute of "historical necessity" (*EM, 67*).

Two commanding themes of Huxley's novels are the various ways in which what he calls "the archaeologist's will to historical truth" (*TV, 216*) is easily deflected from its ostensible aim and, more important, the price to be paid for such confusion in a secular society that essentially has only history to begin with. Huxley's response to the relativism inherent in a fundamentally historicist culture was, at least during the 1920s, to insist upon a set of related moral, epistemological, and aesthetic concepts derived from a variety of sources but exemplified principally in the work of artists and poets like Sir Christopher Wren, Chaucer, William Blake, or Piero Della Francesca. However, the context in which these ideas were developed lies with Huxley's tentative formulations concerning the erratic course of modern history as it extends back to what he regarded as the excesses and aberrations of the romantic period. He was acutely aware of the fallacies involved in historical periodization and on one occasion argued that there are as many versions of the eighteenth century as there are historians engaged in defining it.[11] Such reservations did not deter him from evolving a comprehensive theory of romanticism or from maintaining that beneath the apparent discontinuities of modern history, especially after the trauma of the Great War, lay a deeper continuity of social evolution, the roots of which lay in the "Romantic Revival" (*TBL*, 37).

As early as 1910 Huxley was busily engaged in what was to become an almost lifelong attack on romanticism and its major artists and poets. In a letter to his father, written during his second year at Eton, he boasted of completing "a gross caricature of Shelley,"[12] although eight years later he had adopted a more temperate and receptive attitude, arguing that "one's aim in leading the life of reason should be to combine the lyrical with the critical, to be simultaneously Shelley and the *Edinburgh Review*."[13] Huxley was never able to strike the desired balance between advocacy and protest where romanticism was concerned, and his first volume of essays, *On the Margin*, reveals a mind delighting in the classical restraint and ordered rationality of an artist like Sir Christopher Wren, who is pointedly praised at the expense of Shelley and Wordsworth. No one has systematically traced the evolution of the main components of Huxley's detailed and dialectically developed theory of romanticism, both in terms of what he rejected and what he valued in the work of poets like Blake, Wordsworth, Shelley, or Keats. Yet romanticism, "old" or "new," is both a persistent theme in Huxley's early novels and at the same time a broadly philosophical stance that he returns to denounce again and again in the essays from *On the Margin* (1923) to *Music at Night* (1931) and *The Olive Tree* (1936), in an effort to clarify his own somewhat mercurial perspective on a set of related ideas that he found alternately pernicious and yet richly exploitable.

The dangerous illusions of the "baroque, romantic" sensibility constitute a theme not merely delicately etched into the margins of the early essays but subtly woven into the very fabric of Huxley's vision, influencing the behavior of a number of characters strung out on a line that meanders through most of his interwar novels. Romanticism became increasingly important to Huxley, as both a sharply definable chronological period in English literary history and a perennial state of mind he identified with seventeenth-century baroque aesthetics and twentieth-century cubism. It lay at the source of his interpretation of modern history, providing a satirical framework for a cast of emblematic characters striving to find shelter under the wind-torn umbrella of historicism and romantic Prometheanism. In *Antic Hay* and *Those Barren Leaves*, Huxley differentiated between two contrasting yet related forms of romanticism, while in *Point Counter Point* and *Eyeless in Gaza* he continued to employ the romantic vatic tradition of prophecy and apocalyptic revelation as a recurrent satirical motif. However, in spite of his repudiation of romantic aesthetics, specific romantic concepts, particularly Blake's theory of the states (to be defined later) and Wordsworth's associational theory of memory, came to influence his own theory of the self or personality—to such a degree as to profoundly modify the ethical as well as psychological presuppositions of his thinking throughout the period from 1928 to 1939.

In *Jesting Pilate*, published in 1926, the year following *Those Barren Leaves*, Huxley observed that "the fire of Prometheus is put to the strangest uses" (*JP*, 286)—a judgment that could easily serve as an epigraph to the early novels, particularly to what Jerome Meckier has described as the "natural trilogy"[14] of *Crome Yellow* (1921), *Antic Hay* (1923), and *Those Barren Leaves* (1925). Huxley's critics have neglected the repeated references to prophecy and apocalypse in *Those Barren Leaves*, particularly as they pervade the novel's atmosphere, gradually adumbrating its central themes and linking it to *Antic Hay*, a work equally concerned with romantic Prometheanism. Huxley regarded romanticism as identical in style and substance with baroque painting and architecture, arguing that both modes were cultural aberrations from a norm established by artists like Sir Christopher Wren. In the early novels and essays, he consistently associated what he referred to in *Along the Road* (1925) as the "extravagant baroque, romantic style" (*AR*, 174) with a dead-end of philosophical and aesthetic extremes, a passion for theatrical display, and histrionic self-mythologizing. But Huxley's criticism of romanticism is only in part an aesthetic issue. Its primary significance lies with its historical implications; that is, with Huxley's interpretation of modern history and the intimate connection he saw between the restiveness of a postwar society that seemed to pursue, if not endorse, the fragile and fragmentary apocalypses of a Casimir Lypiatt or a Lilian Aldwinkle and the cultural roots of that society extending back to the formative experiences of the romantic period.

Sanford Marovitz has suggestively observed that ". . . even in his earliest fiction, Huxley's references to painting and artists generally do serve a distinctive thematic or satiric purpose."[15] Huxley's interest in art history, however, shaped his approach to the art of fiction to a greater degree than Marovitz recognized. The early novels are filled with references to painting, sculpture, and architecture—especially to romantic Prometheanism, prophecy and "revelation"—as well as to the major romantic poets, Blake, Wordsworth, Shelley, Keats, and Byron. Huxley's interest in romantic poetry and baroque architecture and condemnation of its underlying aesthetic and epistemological assumptions are inseparable from his endeavor to probe and anatomize the intellectual and psychological matrices of postwar culture. Once the significance of these allusions to romantic and baroque art are understood, particularly as they are used to inform specific symbolic settings, the issue of the aesthetic unity of the early novels can be placed on a more comprehensible footing.

In Huxley's novella *After the Fireworks*, published in 1930, Miles Fanning stands in the Villa Giulia facing the finest surviving example of Etruscan sculpture, "the Apollo of Veii." Repelled by the encroaching irrationality of a society that in his view had become increasingly debased, Fanning cherishes the Etruscan Apollo as "a lovely symbol of the small, the local, the kindly" (*AF*, 240), an aesthetically realized embodiment of an emotional and intellectual equipoise that Huxley believed modern European culture was neither capable nor desirous of achieving. Discovered in 1916, amid the violent upheavals of the Great War, the cryptically smiling terra-cotta statue became for Fanning (and, temporarily, for Huxley) an "apocalyptic voice of the past" (*AF*, 239), whose composed simplicity was an outward sign of the inner equilibrium of the Lawrencian "integrated man" (*AF*, 243). Huxley's characterization of Fanning, like that of Kingham in *Two or Three Graces* (1926) or Rampion of *Point Counter Point*, is in part dependent on his personal knowledge of D. H. Lawrence as well as his interpretation of Lawrence's ideas. Nevertheless, Fanning's analysis of contemporary European culture and endorsement of the countervailing values symbolized by "the unsplit Apollonian way" (*AF*, 245) can be traced to a wholly *Huxleyan* context, first evolved and clarified in the early essays and novels.

The Apollo of Veii is an especially revealing instance of Huxley's rejection of romantic idealism; indeed, the meaning of the Etruscan sculpture can only be fully grasped against the background of Huxley's sustained examination of the significance of "the Romantic Revival," its assimilation of the baroque impulse and its continuing influence in contemporary history in the form of "reverse romanticism." In *Those Barren Leaves*, using the sardonic Cardan as a mouthpiece, Huxley emphasized the inherent instability of the baroque-romantic style: "Romanticism, of which the seventeenth-century baroque is a queer sub-species, makes violent gestures; it relies on violent contrasts of light and shade, on stage effects; it is ambitious to present you with emotions in the raw" (*TBL*, 207). The baroque style, Huxley argues, thrives on distortion and illusion, spawning a host of "vision-inducing works created by the new generations of baroque sculptors and architects," but works that were formally atectonic and metaphysically deceptive. In *Along the Road* he condemned what he referred to as "the baroque style and the kindred romantic style" for their "mistrust of realism" (*AR*, 172), an accusation later directed at the "new romanticism" analyzed in *Music at Night*. However, the basis for Huxley's identification of romanticism with the baroque can be found in *On the Margin* (1923), a collection whose essays are more assiduously arranged than might at first appear. The twenty-seven essays intertwine sociopolitical, psychological, and aesthetic issues within a discursive structure governed by the careful placing of the introductory and concluding pieces. The opening essays, "Centenaries," "On Re-Reading Candide," and "Accidie," form a prefatory ensemble that raises issues more fully developed in the concluding ones, "Sir Christopher Wren," "Ben Jonson," and "Chaucer." Moreover, *On the Margin* is further unified by its references to the centenary of Shelley's death (1822) and the bicentenary of Sir Christopher Wren's (1723).

In "Centenaries," written while Huxley was in Italy (on the Viareggio, where as he notes Shelley's body was cremated), he described the function of a centenary as an occasion for historical as well as aesthetic reassessment, "that we may see precisely where, in relation to their achievement, we stand at the present time, that we may appraise the life still left in their spirit and apply to ourselves the moral of their example" (*OM*, 174–75). Huxley's assessment of Shelley, unlike his straightforward endorsement of Wren, is significantly ambivalent. Shelley is praised as a "literary innovator" but gently chided as the author of "strangely childish poetry" (*OM*, 2), while the essay "Sir Christopher Wren" is an enthusiastic endorsement of an artist whose work was perceived by Huxley as avowedly anti-romantic. Huxley felt a real philosophical allegiance for Wren's aesthetic, one that helped to form the main directions and stages of his thinking on romanticism and the major romantic poets. Accordingly, Shelley and Wordsworth on the one hand and Wren and Chaucer on the other are representatives of two contending aesthetics—the former rooted in "theories" that were "emotional on principle" (*OM*, 188) as a consequence of a specifically romantic faith in the existence of "inenarrable emotions" (*OM*, 157) and the latter characterized by an inherent rationality expressed in a classical aesthetic marked by "clarity, solidity of sense, and economy of forms" (*OM*, 197). Huxley argues that Wren created a body of work exemplifying "reason and order" united with a distrust of the "extravagance and excess (*OM*, 170) of the obscuring chiaroscuro of seventeenth-century baroque: "Wren, the restrained and dignified gentleman, stands out most clearly when we compare him with his Italian contemporaries. The baroque artists of the seventeenth century were interested in the new, the startling, the astonishing; they strained after impossible grandeurs, unheard-of violence." Such art was not only atectonic but inherently illusory: "The architectural ideals of which they dreamed were more suitable for embodiment in theatrical cardboard than in stone. And indeed, the late seventeenth and early eighteenth century was the golden age of scene-painting in Italy." Wren's art of "sober restraint" is "never theatrical," while his masterpiece, St. Paul's cathedral, is in essence "a country gentleman's house." If Wren's St. Paul's is a "monument of temperance and chastity," the work of his successors was "infected by a touch of the baroque *folie de grandeur*," as a consequence of which the "architects of the eighteenth century built houses in imitation of Versailles and Caserta—huge stage houses, all for show and magnificence and all but impossible to live in" (*OM*, 179–80). Mrs. Aldwinkle's Cybo Malaspina, as I shall show later, is such a huge stage house, a romantic palace of art associated with baroque theatricality and prophetic illusion.

While Wren is praised for a "restrained and dignified" art that stands out in relief against the murky background of the prevailing baroque of his Italian contemporaries, whom Huxley criticized for substituting for the integrated rationality of Renaissance classicism an avant-garde bias for "the new" and "the astonishing," he remains nevertheless an "artist of profoundly original mind" (*OM*, 178), whose "most characteristic quality . . . [is] rather moral than aesthetic" (*OM*, 178). What Huxley finds so morally commendable in Wren's work is a rejection of the triumphal sublimity of the baroque, an ornate and mannered theatricality that in Huxley's view had divested itself of everything human in the pursuit of extreme effects. For Huxley aberrations of taste reflect deeper aberrations of behavior. Accordingly, the fundamental discrepancy between the typical baroque facade and the inner form of the building was an aesthetic deception that he interpreted as morally and spiritually flawed.

Similarly, Chaucer's art is praised for its refusal to indulge itself in "vision-inducing" histrionics, its unwillingness to "go to nature as the symbol of some further spiritual reality" (*OM*, 206). Huxley's tendency to "prefer Chaucer as a poet to Keats" (*MN*, 239) lies with the former's "serenity of detachment," a poised acceptance of "the law of kind" (*OM*, 206)—that is, of nature and the empirical order—as well as a metaphysical sobriety that could not be found in the work of baroque architects like Bernini or Borromini, or poets like Shelley or Wordsworth. In *Point Counter Point* Huxley defined the baroque style as flamboyantly ambitious in its striving after dramatic effect but undermined by its exploitative duplicity: "High, impressive, the facade seems to belong to a great cathedral. But look more closely and you discover that it is only a screen. Behind the enormous and elaborate front there crouches a wretched little temple of brick and rubble and scabby plaster" (*PCP*, 346). For Huxley the failure of baroque art is not simply aesthetic but also and perhaps even primarily ethical, and it is important to note that the "baroque Italian churches with sham facades" suggestively evoked in this passage are introduced as aesthetic analogues to underscore the moral failure of Sidney Quarles.

The baroque-romantic style, then, while manifesting an expansiveness corresponding to its idealistic impulses, is ironically a perfect fusion of form and content, pointing to nothing beyond itself and celebrating its own egoistic aspirations rather than embodying, as in Wren's art, an attained vision. To return for a moment to the "beautifully sane" Apollo of Veii (*AF*, 240), a work praised by Huxley for its attainment of a similarly controlled formal reticence—the aesthetic expression of an ethical integrity—it is not surprising to find the achievement of the Etruscan sculptor drawn into the wake of Huxley's continuing quarrel with the baroque-romantic aesthetic. As an emblem of "the unsplit Apollonian way," it is not to be found, Fanning argues, "on the road that led to . . . Bernini" (*AF*, 242). Exhibiting a salutary disregard for the "supernatural" world sought alike by the romantic poet and the baroque artist, a world defined by Fanning as "so terribly baroque—altogether too Counter-reformation and Bernini" (*AF*, 246–47), the Apollo of Veii epitomizes the restrained but formal "solidity" that Huxley perceived in Wren, Piero della Francesca, or Alberti and that he valued as a moral as well as artistic merit. In this respect, Huxley's aesthetics are quite consistent. The baroque style is intrinsically hollow, a fragile shell precariously erected to disguise a moral-aesthetic void and thus "a lie and a sham" (*AR*, 179) that hopes to survive and persuade on the basis of its twitching, deliberately violent deformity. Indeed, "violent" is the word used most often by Huxley in his discussion of the baroque. Again, romanticism and the baroque are conflated by him in linking "Wagner and Bernini" as artists "who can turn what is false and theatrical into something almost sublime" (*AR*, 180). Almost—but not quite. Piero della Francesca and Alberti are praised in psychological terms resembling those used for Wren as "majestic without being at all strained, theatrical or hysterical" (*AR*, 181). And, like both Wren and the Etruscan Apollo, Piero is associated with "the resurrection of the classical ideal" (*AR*, 183), an aesthetic stressing "solidity" and "mass" that is again contrasted favorably to the theatrical vacancy of the baroque with its "spectacular Caravaggioesque light and shade" (*AR*, 184).

The Apollo of Veii, then, is not merely a variation on Lawrence's Pan or one of the African or West Pacific sculptures of *Women in Love*—although it may have drawn some of its inspiration from these sources. Just as Huxley was quite capable of linking Piero della Francesca's painting with ancient Egyptian sculpture, so the ancient Etruscan god is an artistic masterpiece in the manner of Wren's St. Paul's; like the latter, it is marked by a formal completeness as a surviving vestige of an older, saner culture that existed before "the great split that broke life into spirit and matter, heroics and diabolics, virtue and sin and all the other ac-

cursed antitheses" (*AF*, 241). According to Huxley, this split was especially aggravated by the romantic revival and the abandonment of the
classical-Renaissance aesthetic with its intensely rational yet balanced
synthesis of emotion and intellect. The rise of "anti-intellectual" aesthetic
doctrines "dates from the time of romanticism," as does, Huxley argues,
the appearance of "sublime inebriates" like Shelley, Wordsworth, and
Wagner, who along with their baroque precursors "were wild and emotional on principle" (*OM*, 187–88). Wren's art of resilient exactness and
balanced order, like the directly sensuous art of Chaucer, transcended
the "accursed antitheses" typical of the baroque-romantic aesthetic.

Equally important, Huxley defined romanticism as a movement based
on theories that were not only "emotional on principle" but attempted
the "conversion of emotions into intellectual terms" (*OM*, 156) and then
proceeded to erect "a whole cosmogony" (*OM*, 157) on what was a
demonstrably irrational basis. Such a judgment strikes at the very foundation of Wordsworth's *Prelude*, of the poet's attempt to record his emotional growth as, in M. H. Abrams' words, "an evangelist of a new
redemption"[16] and to describe his apocalyptic revelations in the valley of
the Gondo and on the summit of Snowdon—as well as his identification
of visionary imagination with "Reason in her most exalted mood." *The
Prelude*, as I will later show, plays a key role in *Those Barren Leaves*;
Huxley linked it with what he understood to be one of the defining traits
of the romantic sensibility, the "dangerous" faith in the subjective
resources of thought and feeling that lay at the basis of the romantic
theory of the imagination. However his general conception of romanticism was complicated by both his interpretation of painting and architecture of the baroque period and the appearance of what he termed
"new" or "inverse romanticism."

Miles Fanning's concept of a "great split" presupposes an earlier golden
age, one more satisfyingly harmonious in its reconciliation of contending
impulses than the unstable discord of "accursed antitheses" that underlies
modern society and that informs the structure and content of *Point
Counter Point* and *Eyeless in Gaza*. Huxley is deliberately vague on the
subject of this fall from an earlier state of psychological concord, but the
aesthetic context in which this idea was embedded profoundly influenced
his interpretation of modern history. By the time Huxley composed "The
New Romanticism," his conception of the romantic had evolved to subsume any artistic style or intellectual stance that, like the "extravagance
and excess" (*OM*, 179) characteristic of the baroque, could be described
as "extravagant and one-sided (that is to say . . . romantic)," while "modern romanticism" had come to mean the "romanticism of Shelley," only
"turned inside out" (*MN*, 212). The unrelieved egoism and the non-

human exclusiveness characteristic, respectively, of the older or Shelleyan romantic's assessment of the artist's stature and the ideally supernal beauty—broadly Platonic or mystical—that he attempted to incarnate in his art had been replaced by the radical assertion of the bankruptcy of nineteenth-century liberalism and the superiority of technology to the aesthetics of subjective idealism.

In "The New Romanticism" Huxley discerned in "the political doctrines elaborated by Lenin" the "exact antithesis of the revolutionary liberalism preached by Godwin and . . . Shelley." The latter he described as "democrats and individualists," their supreme political values repudiated by both "Mussolini" and "the Bolsheviks" (*MN*, 215), who in Huxley's view represented a further dialectical development of romanticism but in the direction of an inherently illiberal collectivist idealism. Huxley observed that "it is in the sphere of politics that the difference between the two romanticisms is most immediately apparent" (*MN*, 213). But he also stressed an epistemological bias against the "chaotically vital" (*MN*, 214) that, as shall be demonstrated shortly, was fundamental to his view of history and society. The new romanticism embraced practically everything Huxley rejected in modern English and European culture. He associated it with a deep and life-denying allegiance to collectivist ideologies and technological or materialist progress, as well as with a broad spectrum of psychological neuroses and sadomasochistic forms of behavior. Such a process of social decadence led Huxley to an odd—at least on the face of it—grouping of historical figures that included Hegel, Marx, Nietzsche, and the Marquis de Sade. Huxley's dramatization of reverse romanticism will be explored in greater detail in chapters two through five. For the present, it is enough to note that these two terms "old" and "new" romanticism bracket for Huxley the moral history of his era.

Such broadly conceived historical generalizations sound suspiciously like the kind of "generalized history" that Huxley later criticized in *The Olive Tree* as "speculative." But by "generalized history" Huxley meant one premised on nomological truths, not the more Humean endeavor to achieve "probable" opinions concerning "humanly significant" trends. The cultural movement from nineteenth-century "liberal" romanticism to its modern "reverse" counterpart is an inclusive development Huxley refers to as an "historical undulation," a cultural trend first defined in *The Olive Tree*, where he argued that "history pursues an undulatory course." These all-embracing undulations, he maintained, were in part the result of a "tendency displayed by human beings to react after a certain time, away from prevailing habits of thought and feeling towards other habits." He then adds that the "autonomous nature of psychological undulations is confirmed by the facts of history" (*OT*, 20). Huxley is claiming that collective trends engendered by shared cultural conventions occur throughout broad sections of time and appear as "autonomous" wholes. Moreover, they are intrinsically "psychological" because they are inspired by emotional and intellectual behavior and are attributable to individual actions, not vast impersonal forces. This purposive or individualistic emphasis was stressed by Huxley as a consequence of his belief in the relative freedom of "the individual will" (*EM*, 24) and his aversion for deterministic ideologies: "The course of history is undulatory, because (among other reasons) *self-conscious men and women* easily grow tired of a mode of thought and feeling which has lasted more than a certain time" (*OT*, 23—italics mine).

Huxley's theory of the undulatory course of history does not appreciably modify his more fundamental conviction that history exhibits a heterogeneity not merely inviting but in fact compelling skepticism. However, as a metaphorical evocation of historical process, it gave his social satire a plausible principle of explanation, both dynamic in form and panoramic in scope—while as a broad historical trend, it resisted the notion of a single cause. Huxley observed with approval that the attempt "to refer phenomena back to a first cause had ceased to be fashionable, at any rate in the West. The identities to which we try to reduce the complicated diversities around us are of a different order" (*EM*, 14). He regarded social whole, or the comprehensive undulations of history, as "complicated diversities" insusceptible of summation due to the presence "of many causes acting simultaneously," a process involving "intricate correlations and reduplicated actions and reactions" (*EM*, 15). This undulatory swirl of reduplicated action and reaction is related to one of the precipitating images of Huxley's novels, both connected with his concept of the interplay between modern history's two forms of romanticism and his speculations regarding the art of the novel, including his theory of the musicalization of fiction. It would appear Huxley tended to think most naturally in terms of dynamic motion and patterns of corresponding events or actions. This stress on both simultaneity and complicated diversity pervades the novels, affecting both their structure and their presiding themes. Despite his recurrent fascination with history and sociology, Huxley was primarily a satirist evolving a set of images, metaphors, and tentatively conceived tropes adequate to express his comprehension of social and historical process. It is not surprising, then, to discover that the evolution of these notions coincides with his practice as both novelist and literary critic.

The following three quotations reveal the subtle formal correspondences as well as the theoretical consistency of Huxley's speculations on the craft of fiction, modern history, and individual psychology. Often citing the first passage, his critics have overlooked the other two, yet when juxtaposed they demonstrate the degree to which Huxley's overriding obsession with the "complicated diversities" of a world of "intricate correlations" embraces both the form *and* content of his work. The first quotation, from Philip Quarles' notebook in *Point Counter Point*, is familiar to Huxley's readers:

A theme is stated, then developed, pushed out of shape, imperceptibly deformed, until, though still recognizably the same, it has become quite different. In sets of variations the process is carried a step further. Those incredible Diabelli variations, for example. The whole range of thought and feeling, yet all in organic relation to a ridiculous little waltz tune. . . . All you need is a sufficiency of characters and parallel, contrapuntal plots . . . More interesting, the modulations and variations are also more difficult. A novelist modulates by reduplicating situations and characters. He shows several people falling in love, or dying, or praying in different ways—dissimilars solving the same problem. (*PCP*, 408)

Such a theory of narrative technique is itself a variation on Huxley's undulatory metaphor of social and historical interaction referred to earlier, a connection that will become more apparent when Quarles's theory of contrapuntal form is compared to the following fugal evocation of the state of modern English culture:

The activities of our age are uncertain and multifarious. No single literary, artistic, or philosophic tendency predominates. There is a babel of notions and conflicting theories. But in the midst of this general confusion, it is possible to recognize one curious and significant melody, repeated in different keys and by different instruments in everyone of the subsidiary babels. It is the tune of our modern romanticism. (*MN*, 212)

The one melodic line within the "multifarious" tendencies of twentieth-century culture is a peculiar but representative "tune," developed in "different keys" and performed by "different instruments." Like the "same problem" that so many "dissimilars" attempt to resolve in Quarles's musical metaphor of narrative structure, Huxley posits an active matrix of social and historical factors. This matrix is not attributable to a single cause but suggestively adumbrated by a central "tendency" that does not "predominate" so much as undergo a protean series of modulations and developments. Furthermore, it does not exist apart from an interplay of cacophonic variations. As such, it is an even more apt description of novels like *Antic Hay*, *Those Barren Leaves*, or *Point Counter Point* because in this passage the "little waltz tune" referred to by Quarles is identified as "the tune of our modern romanticism," a melodic line embellished or varied by the characters of Huxley's novels, almost all of whom—as either "old" or "modern" romantics—exemplify a diverse range of romantic values and attitudes.

In the third passage Huxley's "Pyrrhonic" skepticism, with its epistemological distrust for the "intellectually vicious love of system and fixity" (*DWW*, 234) and its bias towards concepts based on dynamic motion and atomistic divisibility, insinuates itself into an attack on the idea of the unitary personality. He begins by claiming that the self is inherently discontinuous:

Men do not want to admit that they are what in fact they are—each one a colony of separate individuals, of whom now one and now another consciously lives with the life that animates the whole organism and directs its destinies . . . they pretend, in the teeth of the facts, that they are one person all the time, thinking one set of thoughts, pursuing one course of action throughout life. . . .

He then substitutes for such a monistic notion the by now familiar metaphor of fugue-like diversity:

My music, like that of every other living and conscious being, is a counterpoint, not a single melody, a succession of harmonies and discords. (*DWW*, 234)

Just as the "one . . . melody" of modern history is in reality a set of fluid variations derived from the intrinsically hollow idioms of the baroque-romantic sensibility, the "single melody" of the presumably enduring personality is in fact a "counterpoint" of discrete states, alternately discordant and harmonious. Huxley, however, is not stressing simple linearity. History is a succession of oscillating rhythms, the self is a succession of contrapuntal states, and the novel is a textual pattern evocative of a dynamic interplay of related but varied points of view. This emphasis on musical form between 1928 and 1931 reappears in the late thirties, when in *Ends and Means* Huxley claims that "every culture" is comprised of "arbitrary and fortuitous associations of behaviour-patterns, thought-patterns, feeling-patterns" that eddy and twist in the larger currents of historical process. Coming together for "long periods," only to succumb to "changing circumstances" and new arrangements or groupings, they are regarded so long as they last as "necessary, natural, right, inherent in the scheme of things," despite their "arbitrary and fortuitous" origins (*EM*, 22).

Huxley's stress on complicated patterns of contrapuntally related phenomena, whether in history, in the novel, or within the mind itself, precluded the gross overdetermination of experience that he associated with philosophical monism and certain aspects of Hegelian idealism. This chronic aversion for what he terms "spiritual onanism" (*DWW*, 42) and its pursuit of "system and fixity" lay behind much of his attack on Hegel and the "ferocious ideologies" of modern history. It also explains his emphasis on the role of psychological explanation in history. To understand the state, he argues, "we must do so as psychologists" (*EM*, 58), thereby avoiding the customary political and economic interpretations of contemporary history tending to falsify events that "are ultimately psychological in their nature" (*EM*, 99). His belief in the relative freedom of the will and his skeptical pluralism led to repeated attacks on the flights of speculative Hegelianism that he detected in Marxism, fascism, and most forms of modern nationalism, all of which depended upon the personification of collective abstractions. He argued that Hegel was "the man who elaborated an inappropriate figure of speech into a complete philosophy of politics" (*OT*, 95). In truth, nineteenth- and twentieth-century nationalism was neither created nor even significantly shaped by Hegel, but for Huxley Hegel was a convenient representative of both ideological historicism in general and specific ideologies like postwar Marxism and prewar Prussian nationalism.

In *The Olive Tree* he blamed Hegel for the modern tendency to view the state as an animate being, "an entity that possesses some kind of reality distinct from that of the individuals constituting the group" (*OT*, 44). "Reality," Huxley claims, "is a succession of concrete and particular situations" (*OT*, 99) too often obscured and distorted by the neo-Hegelian "language of historians" and their "elaborate systems of abstractions, ambiguities, metaphors and similes" (*OT*, 93). Huxley's own contrapuntal metaphor was intended to register his sense of the sheer complexity of events and, like his metaphor of historical undulations, to suggest an intricate and comprehensive trend or tendency that resisted oversimplified causal explanation and nonempirical generalizations. Hegelian notions that history is the objective manifestation of an immanent spirit unfolding itself according to a predetermined end ignored the contingency—indeed, the arbitrary randomness of events— that Huxley always insisted upon as characteristic of historical process.

Similarly, Huxley objected to Hegel's glorification of the state as the necessary condition and final goal for such a dialectical process, both the means and the end of human culture, criticizing Hegel as an ideologue who "opposed those who dared to apply ethical standards to the activities of nations" (*OT*, 97). Somewhat unfairly, he tended to view Hegel as the arch-priest of ideological historicism, where "in Hegelian language, the real is the rational—that what happens is ultimately the same as what ought to happen" (*EM*, 67). Historical events are guided by an "historical providence" (*EM*, 69), and all events are endowed with necessary significance: "they occur; they are therefore historical" (*EM*, 67). *Eyeless in Gaza*, Huxley's most comprehensively political novel, draws upon his frustration with what he regarded as a decade in which "for ever-increasing numbers of men and women, 'historicalness' is coming to be accepted as one of the supreme values" (*EM*, 68), a mode of perception that he believed fatefully conditioned the ideological conflicts within both Germany and Russia. Such a formulation of historical process he regarded as fundamentally aberrant, a unique distortion based on a belief in historical laws and "historical necessity" (*EM*, 67); and again Hegel is dismissed as the source of such an anomalous and sinister historicist faith: "Hegel and the contemporary philosophers of Fascism and dictatorial communism, are eccentrics in the sphere of political thought" (*EM*, 6).

In turning to the discretely individual, the "psychological facts" of history, Huxley saw in place of necessary laws validating the "historical mission" of Marxism or fascism a universal contingency that allowed for both human freedom and a limited degree of progress. But he also maintained that the overriding trait of modern politics and the animating bias of European history and ideology was "the lust for power" (*EM*, 19). The word "lust" was deliberately chosen in place of the customary "will" because Huxley linked Hegel, Nietzsche, and Marx with the Marquis de Sade, a grouping reflecting a tendency of the satirist to supplant the intellectual historian in an effort to create his own "Sadean sociology" (*CE*, 204)—a satiric typology that will serve his artistic purposes without too great a distortion of intellectual history. In *Point Counter Point*, *Eyeless in Gaza*, and *After Many a Summer Dies the Swan*, Huxley's interpretation of the course of modern history and the ascendency of the "new romanticism" took on an additional psychological dimension that can be traced back to a letter written to Julian Huxley in 1918, in which he linked "the spirit of Romanticism" with what he called "spiritual sadisme."[17] I shall show that sadomasochistic behavior is a pervasive motif in Huxley's novels, a symbol of social decadence and a psychological perversion that the novelist associated with death, baroque art, funerary practices, and anomic suicide. In *Ends and Means* he located the source of evil in "the individual will," in a connection between "progress and aggressiveness" that lay "in the depth of human psychology" (*EM*, 24). In a paragraph attacking Hegel, Marxism, and fascism, he observed that "a few moralists—of whom Nietzsche is the most celebrated and the Marquis de Sade the most uncompromisingly consistent—have denied the value of non-attachment" (*EM*, 6). Beginning with *Proper Studies* and continuing through *Do What You Will* and *Ends and Means*, Huxley attempted to define an ideal moral and psychological type free of "the narrow prison of . . . age and country," transcending history *and* ideological historicism. This culminated in the "non-attached" man, an idealized type whose opposite came increasingly to be identified in Huxley's mind with the Marquis de Sade. In this respect, de Sade takes his place with Shelley, Bernini, Wordsworth, and Hegel as part of the cultural and "psychological background" (*EM*, 98) of Huxley's satirical fiction.

If "Hegel's mistake was to imagine that nature was wholly rational" (*EM*, 253), de Sade took the opposite course, elaborating a "philosophy of meaninglessness carried to its logical conclusion" (*EM*, 270). In *The Triumph of Time*, Jerome Buckley observed that "the new English novelists, especially Virginia Woolf and Aldous Huxley, sought the materials of beauty or of irony in a social order they assumed to be futile and decadent."[18] Huxley rarely employed the word "decadent," but gazing through a somewhat Spenglerian mist, he perceived throughout his society ubiquitous traces of the sinister figure of de Sade, the proponent of "ultimate revolution" and prophet of universal pointlessness—a "philosophe" who denied human claims to importance and morality, and a psychotic whose violent impulses and voyeuristic stances were adopted by a number of Huxley's characters in *Point Counter Point, Eyeless in Gaza*, and *After Many a Summer Dies the Swan*. In redrawing the map of Eliot's *Waste Land*, the Marquis de Sade became for Huxley an important reference point. As the proponent of a systematically conceived cynicism, de Sade's ideas differ radically from the Humean skepticism of the life-worshipper of *Do What You Will* or the "Pyrrhonism" (*DWW*, 285) that Huxley himself advocated throughout the 1920s. De Sade's rejection of meaning did not encourage the skeptical and disciplined detachment Huxley valued but rather its opposite, a sensual materialism and a self-indulgent egotism derived from a belief that "sensation and animal pleasure alone possessed reality and alone were worth living for" (*EM*, 270). More important, in Huxley's view de Sade's "philosophy of meaninglessness" corresponded to the general anomic condition of European society in the wake of the Great War, when "the philosophy of meaninglessness came once more triumphantly into fashion" (*EM*, 274).

This observation in 1937 finds its precursor in Huxley's essay "Accidie," published sixteen years earlier in *On the Margin*, where conceding the presence of accidie throughout history, Huxley argued that the markedly intense anomie of the modern period had its origins in the willful, subjective obscurities of romanticism:

It is a very curious phenomenon, this progress of accidie from the position of being a deadly sin, deserving of damnation, to the position first of a disease and finally of an essentially lyric emotion, fruitful of much of the most characteristic modern literature. The sense of universal futility, the feeling of boredom and despair, with the complementary desire to be "anywhere, anywhere out of the world". . . . What is the significance of this fact? For clearly the progress of accidie is a spiritual event of considerable importance. How is it to be explained? (OM, 22–23)

Huxley's explanation was the course of European "history since 1789" (OM, 23). The "Romantic generation" created "a state of mind" that, given additional impetus by "the appalling catastrophe of the War of 1914" (OM, 25), continued into the twentieth century and culminated in a society whose increasing ennui and gradually dimming energy could best be emblematized by the Marquis de Sade. Accidie, Huxley claimed, was not mere lassitude but a "subtle and complicated vice." And just as this condition originated during the romantic period (in particular, with the French Revolution and its unattainable and insatiable aspirations), Huxley described the Marquis de Sade as a romantic "revolutionary," less violent than "his fellow-Jacobins" but nevertheless an author whose books "contain a kind of reductio ad absurdum of revolutionary theory" (EM, 271).

If Hegel was "the spiritual father of . . . Marxian theories of history" (TV, 203), de Sade, according to Huxley, was a more systematically nihilistic ideologue. In a letter to George Orwell, Huxley compared Orwell's vision of the future totalitarian state with his own dystopia and concluded that "the nightmare of Nineteen Eighty-Four is destined to modulate into the nightmare of a world having more resemblance to that which I imagined in Brave New World." The reason for this lay with the nature of what he referred to as "the ultimate revolution," or what in Do What You Will he called the "nihilist revolution" (DWW, 226). In the letter to Orwell, he maintained that the first hints of a philosophy of the ultimate revolution—the revoluton which lies beyond politics and economics and aims at the total subversion of the individual's psychology and physiology—are to be found in the Marquis de Sade, who regarded himself as "the continuator, the consummator, of Robespierre and Babeuf."[19] In the novels of the interwar period, especially Point Counter Point, Eyeless in Gaza, and After Many a Summer Dies the Swan, de Sade and sadism are linked with a number of related themes, including revolutionary romanticism, romantic prophecy, social accidie, and ideologies stressing progress and "the march of history." In Huxley's satire De Sade is an emblematic figure, "a mixture of escapist maniac and philosophe" who "lives in a world where insane phantasy alternates with post-Voltairean ratiocination" (CE, 203). Such a description applies to characters like Maurice Spandrell, whose behavior alternates between lucid intellectuality and irrational phantasy, or Lucy Tantamount, whose intellectual nihilism is inseparable from sadomasochistic eroticism. In the letter to George Orwell, Huxley stressed de Sade's role as an early representative of romantic nihilism and insisted that the revolution he associated with de Sade was psychological in essence, transcending "politics and economics."

In *Ends and Means* he described the society of the thirties as oscillating between Sadean cynicism and accidie on the one hand and ideological historicism on the other: "The 'heads' of pointlessness has its 'tails' idolatrous nationalism and communism. Our world oscillates from a neurasthenia that welcomes war as a relief from boredom to a mania that results in war being made" (*EM*, 125). Huxley felt de Sade's "strictly sexual perversion," his mania for "flogging actresses, sticking penknives into shop-girls, feeding prostitutes on sugar-plums impregnated with cantharides" inspired his philosophical disquisitions, "the theoretical justification of his erotic practices." Accordingly, de Sade "preaches violent revolution not only in the field of politics and economics, but (logical with the appalling logicality of the maniac) also in that of personal relations, including the most intimate of all, the relations between lovers . . . De Sade is the one completely consistent and thoroughgoing revolutionary of history" (*EM*, 271–72). Arguing that "his madness illuminates the dark places of normal behaviour" as well as the ideological climate of the interwar period, Huxley observes that the "reasons for holding the doctrines of materialism . . . may be predominantly erotic" as well as—or instead of—being "predominantly political, as they were in the case of Karl Marx" (*EM*, 272). As the proponent of a philosophy of "meaninglessness" based on a denial "of any values, any idealism, any binding moral imperatives whatsoever" (*EM*, 271), de Sade is Huxley's quintessential "reverse" romantic, exemplifying the spiritual aimlessness of the 1920s and 1930s that Huxley traced back to the superficially "liberating" effects of the French Revolution and the intellectual iconoclasm of the romantic period.

Huxley also linked de Sade's taste for violence with the "intense hatred," the "longing to destroy" (*DWW*, 225) that he detected within the frustrated malaise of postwar England. In *The Contrary Experience*, Sir Herbert Read observed of the widespread notion of cultural decline haunting victor and vanquished alike after the First World War that "the death wish that was once an intellectual fiction" had "become a hideous reality."[20] Huxley believed that "the new romanticism . . . [was] headed straight towards death," (*MN*, 220) and his penchant for characters maimed or warped into grotesque shapes as a consequence of sadomasochistic behavior is in large measure traceable to his employment of sadism as representative of the final, most degenerative stage of historicist and romantic values. In short, the reliance on history as the ultimate ground of value leads inevitably to the nihilistic amorality of de Sade or the oppressive ideologies inspired by Hegel. In Huxley's final novel of the thirties, history is categorically rejected in a satire dominated by the figure of de Sade, by erotic violence and a convergence of history and death in the mortuaries and cemeteries surrounding Joseph Stoyte's castle-museum.

Huxley's satirical attack on historicism and romanticism was inseparable from his attempt to comprehend the great social forces at work in his society, to assess the trauma of the Great War of 1914, and to define the historical and ideological lines of cleavage at work in European as well as English society. He did this discretely in recurring satirical types and comprehensively by means of carefully elaborated symbolic motifs. His ambition to write "the novel of social history" was an extension of his effort to comprehend "the course of psychological history" (OT, 32) from the romantic era to the upheavals of postwar England. And like the narrator of "The Bookshop," a short story appearing in Limbo—Huxley's first volume of fiction—he remained a "deteriorationist" (L, 262); like Rampion in Point Counter Point, Huxley consistently viewed the course of modern history in terms of "regression" (EM, 8), "degeneracy," and "inward decay" (PCP, 554). However, his contention that recent European history manifested an empirically discernible pattern of decline involved him in the kind of historical generalizations that ran counter to his Pyrrhonist conservatism. For example, while arguing throughout Ends and Means for circumspection where sweeping summary statements were concerned, he was not deterred from formulating the kind of broad inductions necessary to a "deteriorationist" perspective:

In our own time the long-drawn violence of Tsarist oppression and the acute, catastrophic violence of the World War produced the "iron dictatorship" of the Bolsheviks. The threat of world-wide revolutionary violence begot Fascism; Fascism produced rearmament; rearmament has entailed the progressive deliberalization of the democratic countries. What the further results of Moscow's "iron dictatorship" will be, time alone will show. At the present moment (June 1937) the outlook is, to say the least of it, exceedingly gloomy. (EM, 28)

Similarly, a hypothetical "non-Euclidean" history that postulates an opposing line of European development, equally sweeping although less confidently framed, is characteristic of the deteriorationist's need to generalize:

It would be interesting to construct a historical "Uchronia" (to use Renouvier's useful word), based upon the postulate that Robespierre and the other Jacobin leaders were convinced pacifists. The "non-Euclidean" history deducible from this first principle would be a history, I suspect, innocent of Napoleon, of Bismarck, of British imperialism and the scramble for Africa, of the World War, of militant Communism and Fascism, of Hitler and universal rearmament. (*EM*, 145)

His theory of historical undulations is itself an ideological formulation, although Huxley—for whom variety and diversity are always preferable to uniformity—would argue that he is not positing a larger, long-standing design mysteriously immanent within the course of events but a contingent state of affairs based on a generalization, both flexibly open-ended and free of the nomological claims essential to Marxism or fascism. The non-Euclidian history briefly envisaged in *Ends and Means* is one free of Sadean violence and its fascination with power. What Huxley will later refer to as "the intellectual key to history" is the recognition that the interplay of factors comprising the modern epoch represented the final degenerative stage of romanticism, a development that he believed had issued in a form of cultural decadence too widespread and intrinsically pathological to permit an unqualified faith in history as the sole or principal source of either meaning or value.[21] Drawn to the notion that history could be cross-referenced with psychology, he consistently interpreted contemporary events in terms of an onward drift which dissolved the present into the past and the past into a welter of fragments symbolized by the "lunatic's mind" of Joseph Stoyte's castle-museum. From such a perspective, Wellsian progress was merely an engrossing fantasy and Hegelian nationalism a menacing form of idealism, the momentum for which was provided not by ideal spirit but by Sadean *realpolitik*.

Morse Peckham, whose theory of romanticism bears a close resemblance to Huxley's,[22] has observed that "historicism pervaded all aspects of Romantic culture,"[23] a statement that could serve as an epigraph to novels like *Those Barren Leaves* and *Eyeless in Gaza*. Equally significant, Peckham's contention that "Byronic Hero, Visionary Artist, Bohemian Virtuosa, Dandy, Historian—are the novel roles that mark the emergence of Romanticism"[24] is a strikingly precise and complete catalogue of the repertory of satirical types that populate Huxley's novels. Visionary artists like Casimir Lypiatt, dandies like Mercaptan, Bohemians like Coleman and Spandrell, or historians like Jeremy Pordage and Henry Wimbush are—to use Huxley's term—"paradigmatic types" who figure prominently in his attempt to first assimilate history to individual psychology and then, once that psychology is judged irredeemably romantic, to transcend history entirely.

The earliest traces of Huxley's Pyrrhonist repudiation of history can be found in *Crome Yellow*, the first novel of the interwar period. In this respect, it can be said that the California highway leading to Stoyte's gargantuan castle begins on the country road winding leisurely to the estate of Crome. In his first novel, insightfully described by one reviewer as the product of a "Cubist Peacock," Huxley created a crisply discursive comedy of manners that masks, with its mellow humor, a deeper level of seriousness. *Crome Yellow* is filled with what were to become Huxleyan conventions; its varied but carefully-orchestrated themes would reappear in the satires to follow but there extended, elaborated, and more deeply probed. One of these thematic strands is history, not a principal issue but still remorselessly present, accounting in part for the darker shades encroaching on what one contemporary reviewer described as the "exhilarating glow of summer" that seemed to suffuse the world of Crome and its occupants.

# CHAPTER TWO

# The Green Heart of England

## 1. Huxley's "Happy Rural Seat": *Crome Yellow* and the Problem of History

Huxley's country houses, so prominent a feature of the early novels, were more than simple narrative hubs around which he mechanically wound the various "Peacockian" strands of his discontinuous plots and interpolated fables.[1] Nor is it possible to account for Crome satisfactorily by tracing its origins, as many critics have done, to Lady Ottoline Morrell's Garsington Manor or, as Richard Gill has more recently proposed, to an architectural conflation of Garsington and Beckley Park, another country house near Oxford with which Huxley was probably familiar.[2] It is true that with its uncluttered facade and three austerely imposing towers, Beckley could easily have served as a model for Crome's unusual exterior, while Garsington Manor doubtlessly influenced Huxley's conception of the social rhythms and daily events of a leisure society spending its summer in an aristocratic great house. Admittedly, Crome does draw upon "the country-house ethos"[3] to the extent that—like Jonson's Penshurst, Jane Austen's Pemberley, or Ford Madox Ford's Groby—it suggests the presiding values of a culture rooted in an apparently enduring tradition of humane order and inherited customs. However, Huxley's estates play a symbolic role traceable to an intrinsically Huxleyan context discernible in the crucial organizing ideas of both the early fiction and the major collections of essays published between 1923 and 1937.

*Crome Yellow* is Huxley's first attempt to chart the treacherous elevations and murky depressions of the "pointless landscape" later traversed by Calamy in *Those Barren Leaves* but with respect to a scale of reference only tenuously worked out by 1921. Huxley's letters during this period reveal a novelist impatient with the restraints of "Realismus"[4] and, like Crome's non-existent satirist Knockespotch, dismissive of rigidly mimetic evocations of the "social plenum."[5] In this respect *Crome Yellow* is the first of Huxley's successful incursions into the irrational, the

[ 31 ]

Richard Gill has argued that Beckley Park, with its three very striking angular towers is the model for Crome. While not conforming with Crome in every respect, the precipitously rising towers do correspond to Scogan's description. (Photograph copyright *Country Life*.)

grotesque, and the absurd. Within such a comic world, Crome functions less as a typical country house richly evoked in terms of the social rules, manners, and traditions of a leisure society than as a peculiarly Huxleyan image of enclosure, the details of which correspond to the theoretical dimensions of his psychological and philosophical ideas. Huxley's critics have tended to underestimate the significance of Crome, arguing for example that its role is simply to provide the novel with a "theatrical ambience"[6] or, more reductively, "a transparent excuse for assembling a company of eccentrics."[7] Crome, as I shall show, is an Arcadian retreat promising a pastoral *otium* that has been overtaken by history. Yet in spite of its idyllic setting, it also serves—at least for Scogan—as an emblem of aristocratic civilization and formal order, superior to nature and antithetically opposed to agrarian society. In addition, it functions as a palace of art, whose towers serve as symbols of aesthetic withdrawal and whose *genius loci* is the Shelleyan romantic Priscilla Wimbush. And finally it is a museum of history, inspiring its introverted curator Henry Wimbush with antiquarian nostalgia. As an ambiguously reticular image, Crome contains the seeds of both Cog's court and the Cybo Malaspina as well as the faint outlines of Joseph Stoyte's castle-museum.

Stated simply, ancient Crome is a symbol of a world narrowed to the dimensions of a debased romanticism, of the vagaries and elations of its romantic occupants and the beguilements of a past that offers the present little beyond the servitude of routine. The atmosphere of Huxley's first novel is suffused with a lightness of tone that is gradually displaced by the emergence of a darker farce lit by flashes of Swiftian urgency. Peter Bowering, commenting on the benign skepticism of *Crome Yellow*, has observed of its satirical undercurrents that "it is all rather good fun, but an underlying gravity is never far beneath the surface."[8] This initially covert moral intent is at the outset principally suggested by the prevailing anomie of Crome's occupants, the consequence of their addiction to a broad spectrum of philosophical beliefs rather than the expression of the narrowly socio-economic traditions of a specific social class. Fenced in with their own thoughts of escape, they confirm their self-imposed imprisonment as well as Crome's function as a symbol of enclosure.

Crome is viewed by Scogan as primarily an emblem of intellectual formality, the product of a sixteenth-century aesthetic explicitly contrasted with Shelley's romantic nebulosity: "The great thing about Crome . . . is the fact that it's so unmistakably and aggressively a work of art. It makes no compromise with nature, but affronts it and rebels against it. It has no likeness to Shelley's tower in the *Epipsychidion*," (CY, 68). Scogan is here alluding to Shelley's evocation of a secluded palace of art in a passage that merits close attention:

> But the chief marvel of the wilderness
> Is a lone dwelling, built by whom or how
> None of the rustic island-people know:
> Tis not a tower of strength, though with its height
> It overtops the woods; but, for delight,
> Some wise and tender Ocean-King, ere crime
> Had been invented, in the world's young prime,
> Reared it, a wonder of that simple time,
> An envy of the isles, a pleasure-house
> Made sacred to his sister and his spouse.
> It scarce seems now a wreck of human art,
> But as it were Titanic; in the heart
> Of Earth having assumed its form, then grown
> Out of the mountains, from the living stone,
> Lifting itself in caverns light and high.[9]

Scogan quotes the last five lines of this passage, which in the poem is followed by a luxuriant description of the decayed tower overgrown with vines and parasitic foliage. The chthonic nature of Shelley's tower, with its dramatic emphasis on darkness and light, is for Scogan—and Huxley —another piece of baroque scene painting, a Piranesian miniature of obfuscating shadows and wavering outline. Crome by contrast, although designed in the sixteenth century, appears to emblematize the thoroughly credible values of Sir Christopher Wren; however, the symmetry and clarity of line and mass, while outwardly impressive, prove to mask an inner disruption of spirit. Shelley's tower in the *Epipsychidion* is a Promethean, or "Titanic," edifice inseparable from its setting, blending with the natural world and functioning as a rustic temple of art, filled (like Crome) with "books and music" and finally associated with both a pastoral landscape as well as an Edenic golden age. Huxley's country house, with its golden yellow facade rhythmically ordered by three stately towers rising precipitously from carefully laid-out grounds—unlike the wild profusion of foliage hiding Shelley's tower—is nevertheless essentially deceptive. In *On the Margin*, where Shelley and Wren were carefully compared, Huxley praised one of Wren's masterpieces, the great palace at Hampton Court, as in essence "a country gentleman's house." Crome, another country gentleman's house, appears to be similarly conceived in terms of an austere aesthetic stressing "reason and order" (*OM*, 179). Huxley described Wren as "a wonderful maker of facades" (*OM*, 177), and it is worth remembering at this point that Scogan's admiration for Crome focuses primarily on the formal severity of its imposing facade. But within, Crome is chiefly memorable for its secret rooms, winding staircases, galleries, and *tromp l'oeil* effects like the illusory bookcases in the library. More important, its occupants have transformed it into a place of cloistral introversion and baroque-romantic aspiration.

Scogan claimed that Crome was designed as "the house of an intelligent, civilized, and sophisticated man" (*CY*, 68), while Huxley in "Centenaries" described Wren as "a gentleman, the finished product of an old and ordered civilization" (*OM*, 179). As the architectural embodiment of an aristocratic and civilized culture, Crome is evaluated by Scogan according to the measure of its "remoteness from the cloddish life" (*CY*, 69), a perspective that clashes with its ostensibly pastoral setting, including Henry Wimbush's dreamy reverence and simplified nostalgia for the lost innocence of a "rustic Crome." Where Scogan sees an aristocratic affirmation of a "grand unnatural" isolation, Wimbush idealizes Crome as an Arcadian dwelling intended to nourish a sense of "conscious community" whose "country pleasures" were expressly conceived as a healthier alternative to "the urban pleasures of the . . .

metropolis" (*CY*, 128). Both interpretations are, in Huxley's terms, "extravagant and one-sided (that is to say . . . romantic)." Scogan is an egotist, conscious principally of his own exigent personality, who locates Crome in a mental landscape apart from nature; Wimbush is a sensitive visionary for whom Crome exists only within an idealized past. For Wimbush's wife Priscilla, however, Crome exists only to house her spiritual "Aura," which she hopes will eventually rise as precipitously as Crome's towers.

Within the narrative structure of *Crome Yellow*, the "three towers" of Crome's facade function as symbolic coordinates or reference points for much of the novel's imagistic and conceptual design. For Henry Wimbush they play a pivotal role in each of his historical anecdotes concerning the lives of Sir Ferdinando Lapith, Sir Hercules Lapith, and George Wimbush. As symbols of the privileged sanctuary of the aesthete or the secluded tower of the romantic visionary, they are to varying degrees mirrored in the "secret tower" (*CY*, 14) of Jenny Mullion's deafness, in "Shelley's tower" of the *Epipsychidion* (*CY*, 68), and in the "enigmatic remoteness" of the artist's "ivory tower" (*CY*, 174). The central tower contains the boudoir of Priscilla Wimbush, the novel's most bizarrely conceived visionary, while Gombauld, Crome's resident artist, paints in a disused granary expressly designed to resemble a tower—crowned with a peaked roof, suspended on four pillars and reached by a ladder. More important, the central tower figures prominently in the novel's central narrative line comprising Denis Stone's abortive courtship of Anne Wimbush. Walled in by his own timidities, Stone finally concludes that "one gets bored by oneself on a tower" (*CY*, 145), yet at the final stage of his ostensibly educative journey, he stands alone on the central tower, cut off from the fair on the grounds below and trapped as a hero in his own *Kunstlerroman*.

The tower is a complex symbol, suggesting at once self-stultifying enclosure and self-expansive aspiration, comprehending both because in Huxley's novels the latter leads inevitably to the former. Huxley's romantic egoists either begin as Promethean visionaries only to succumb to the cynicism of the inverse romantic, or are introduced as sardonic materialists at the outset and show little development. In *Crome Yellow* the link between the tower and the burrow, between self-assertive idealism and an equally egocentric regression, is clearly conveyed by Scogan's diatribe against nature. His lengthy confession of his aversion for the natural world is Huxley's earliest formulation of the subterranean burrow as a metaphor for a pathologically regressive state of mind, in this case appearing in the form of the subway, the underground "tube."

Scogan significantly prefaces his discussion of the necessity for creating a private universe with an admission that he had "always taken particular pleasure in Cubismus," a style in which "nature has been completely banished" in favor of "the human mind," a pleasure he pointedly links to his capacity for savoring any "achievement of engineering." He then goes on to elaborate and refine his theory of "spiritual Tubes," beginning with a repudiation of nature: "Nature, or anything that reminds me of nature, disturbs me; it is too large, too complicated, above all too utterly pointless and incomprehensible" (CY, 170). The incomprehensibility of the organic world is a constant theme in Huxley's work, yet as a fact to be acknowledged and made use of and not as an excuse for a narrowly doctrinaire humanism that celebrates its own myopia. Scogan continues:

'That is why I always travel by Tube, never by bus if I can possibly help it. For, travelling by bus, one can't avoid seeing, even in London, a few stray works of God—the sky, for example, an occasional tree, the flowers in the window-boxes. But travel by Tube and you see nothing but the works of man—iron riveted into geometrical forms, straight lines of concrete, patterned expanses of tiles. All is human and the product of friendly and comprehensible minds." (CY, 170)

Scogan's comically fastidious aversion for nature and his preference for a world that systematically testifies to the power of human intellect is a typical instance of the self-imposed ignorance characteristic of the burrower. Not unexpectedly, Scogan expands on this image:

"All philosophies and all religions—what are they but spiritual Tubes bored through the universe! Through these narrow tunnels, where all is recognizably human, one travels comfortable and secure, contriving to forget that all round and below and above them stretches the blind mass of earth, endless and unexplored. Yes, give me the Tube and Cubismus every time; give me ideas, so snug and neat and simple and well made. And preserve me from nature, preserve me from all that's inhumanly large and complicated and obscure. I haven't the courage, and above all, I haven't the time to start wandering in that labyrinth." (CY, 170)

Scogan's metaphorical journey within the rigidly structured subterranean world of the London subway is one of Huxley's central iconic representations of the enclosed burrow. The "snug" security of Scogan's Tube prefigures the womb-like "closed universe of utter cosiness" (AMS, 196) sought by Jeremy Pordage or the "little cushioned world of privacy" (TS, 214) eagerly anticipated by Veronica Thwale. And like Francis Chelifer, who takes up his "position" in Gog's Court "fully aware of the nature of the reality by which he is surrounded," Scogan's choice of the world of geometrical order and hermetic enclosure is deliberate. His addiction to the predictable and the "geometrical" sheds considerable light on his admiration for Crome's facade. Fearful of the "labyrinth" of experience, especially of the natural world, he sees Crome not solely as a symbol of the values of Wren but rather as an inflated burrow, which he defines in terms of a narrowly conceived rationalism as self-affirming in intent as "Priscilla Wimbush's "astral" metaphysics—a parody of the "spiritual Tubes" celebrated by Scogan as snug havens within an ambiguously complex universe. Scogan's intellectual relativism is a standard theme in Huxley's work, chiefly as the latter's perception of the universe's infinite suggestibility, as a nettle to be grasped and used, not evaded by means of regressive burrowing into the narrow tunnels of either inverse or traditional romanticism.

Tower and burrow, then, are superficially opposed but actually complementary evasions of experience, and both are subtly embodied in the physical features of Crome vividly evoked in the opening chapters. Denis Stone's arrival and departure from Crome exemplifies one of the insistent and characteristic designs of Huxley's novels. Stone's journey to and away from Crome forms a circular movement from frustrated inarticulacy to enforced silence, a closed circle beginning and ending with an episode stressing Stone's egocentric isolation. When he arrives, he discovers an empty Crome; when he does manage to engage someone in conversation, his anecdotes are either interrupted or ignored. When Stone leaves, he cannot communicate his true feelings to Anne Wimbush and makes his departure after sending a telegram to himself—a device that underscores his egocentric predicament. As aspiring poet and novelist as well as the novel's central character, his arrival at Crome is skillfully managed by Huxley. A comparison with Francis Chelifer's arrival at the Cybo Malaspina, or Jeremy Pordage's leisurely drive to Stoyte's castle, reveals the extent to which Huxley could repeat but significantly vary what would become a convention of his novels. In *Crome Yellow* Stone approaches the house slowly, in a way that helps to define its nature and role. In Shelley's *Epipsychidion* the tower of art was defined as a secluded pleasure-house in a pastoral setting of innocent simplicity. Stone journeys towards a similarly "remote and rustic Crome" that, standing on the threshold of "the green heart of England" (*CY*, 1), seems to promise the serenity of Arcadian retirement in a lush and pleasant landscape. Drawing on the traditional pastoral arc of withdrawal, transformation, and return, Huxley introduces Stone as the harried urbanite, ill at ease, apprehensive about his vacation, conscious of wasted time—in sum, a promising candidate for the pastoral *otium*. As a delicate aesthete sickened by the dusty cushions of his compartment on the train, he dreams of escaping the mundane world and penetrating into the higher realm of the imagination. Like Lilian Aldwinkle of *Those*

*Barren Leaves*, who searches for the "one apocalyptic thought" (*TBL*, 64), Stone muses on the "perfect poem" or the "one illuminating book" (*CY*, 1) as monastic evasions of the complexities of the sensible world.

On leaving the train, he is discomfited by the station guard, who deflates his pretensions as a "man of action." He reacts by immediately withdrawing snail-like into his own "spiritual Tube," the private world of language. His bicycle journey to Crome is subtly counterpointed by an inner movement through the "echoing corridors of assonance and alliteration" (*CY*, 3). As he substitutes for an intractable reality the more malleable world of words, the external landscape gradually recedes to the extent that the felt quality of the road on which he is riding survives only in his meditation on the word "curves," which is itself finally lost in a mental catalogue of stock phrases from the French novel. I will show that in the novels of the thirties, especially in *After Many a Summer Dies the Swan*, Huxley identified the soul or self with language, arguing that "Madness consists, among other things, in imagining that our 'soul' exists apart from the language our nurses happen to have taught us" (*AMS*, 310). Denis Stone, unlike Anthony Beavis, who in *Eyeless in Gaza* seeks a level of being where there are "no more words" (*EG*, 472), has surrendered to a hollow idiom of related sounds and verbal rhythms. Awakened from this associative process by the sudden intrusion of "the outer world" in the form of a sharp descent in the road, he is confronted by Crome's radiant facade and stops to contemplate it:

this view of Crome was pleasant to linger over. The facade with its three projecting towers rose precipitously from among the dark trees of the garden. The house basked in full sunlight; the old brick rosily glowed. How ripe and rich it was, how superbly mellow! And at the same time, how austere! (*CY*, 4)

What at first appears to be Crome's uncompromising identity of reference is sufficient to awaken Stone from the hermetic consolations of language. However, the facade subtly insinuates a barely perceptible duality of mellowness and austerity, a divisiveness that is confirmed when Stone enters the house, passing through the formally assured facade to discover an inner anarchy of spirit traceable to the antics of Crome's present and past occupants and mirrored in the eclectic jumble of historical objects amassed by the estate's previous generations. Wandering through the empty rooms and corridors like an "excavator" in a "dead, deserted Pompeii" (*CY*, 5), he is gradually overwhelmed by the conflux of art works, antiques, and historical fragments haphazardly assembled. This collection inspires the novel's preeminent question as Stone asks, while contemplating the Chinese carvings, Venetian chairs, rococo tables, Italian primitives, eighteenth-century paintings, English furniture, family portraits, and seventeenth-century folio volumes: "What could one reconstruct from such data?" (*CY*, 5). With its beds like "ancient hereditary pieces" evoking "every date and fashion" and crowded with "flesh-mortifying antiques" (*CY*, 5), Crome has the atmosphere of an abandoned museum. The "long gallery" filled with Henry Wimbush's display of early renaissance paintings foreshadows a series of collections like Mercaptan's in *Antic Hay*, Hugh Ledwidge's in *Eyeless in Gaza*, and Joseph Stoyte's in *After Many a Summer Dies the Swan*. In *Crome Yellow* the gallery of Italian primitives as well as the museum-like atmosphere of the interior reinforces Crome's role as an image of what Henry Wimbush cherishes as the unchanging past, a vast museum whose collective meaning is initially challenged by Denis Stone and finally lost by Wimbush.

In "Accumulations," an essay on historical collections published in *On the Margin*, Huxley observed that "desolated by the carelessness of our ancestors, we are making very sure that our descendants shall lack no documents when they come to write our history. All is systematically kept and catalogued. Old things are carefully patched and propped into continued existence; things now new are hoarded up and protected from decay" (*OM*, 76). Filled with such "patched and propped" accumulations, Crome poses a problem that many of the characters will attempt to solve in their effort to come to grips with what Scogan calls the "melancholy story" (*CY*, 162) of post-Reformation European history.

Crome, then, in Veronica Thwale's terms, is both a house and an "attitude," an outward and concrete extension of "a state of mind" (*TS*, 214). In order to define more precisely this state of mind, Huxley continues his hero's prefatory journey towards the symbolic heart of Crome, the central tower. On his way Stone discovers and opens a volume of his own poems, turning by chance to a passage appropriately evocative of darkness, silence and enclosure:

> . . . But silence and the topless dark
> Vault in the lights of Luna Park
> And Blackpool from the nightly gloom
> Hollows a bright tumultuous tomb. (*CY*, 6)

As a monument to the past yet enlivened by the comic antics of its present occupants, Crome is a kind of "tumultuous tomb" in which Stone encounters mainly silence, despite the endless babble of competing voices. Brooding on the failure of his poems to compensate for his Prufrockian inability to say what he feels or address an issue directly, he enters Priscilla Wimbush's boudoir in the central tower, only to be silenced by his operatic hostess's effusions on horoscopes, the Occult, and horseracing. Priscilla's preoccupation with "the Infinite," including her own "Aura," like Stone's obsession with words, is a form of subjective withdrawal that Huxley comically parodies in her taste for the outlandish metaphysics of Barbecue-Smith. But where faced with the chaos of Crome's interior, Stone acknowledged that he could reconstruct little from such fragmentary "data," Priscilla unhesitatingly proclaims that "all that happens means something; nothing you do is ever insignificant" (CY, 9). A disciple of Barbecue-Smith—who paraphrases Keats's "Ode on a Grecian Urn" and proselytizes for an idealism of "things . . . unseen"—Priscilla is Crome's *genius loci*, crazily celebrating the romantic Barbecue-Smith's sentimental travesty of the *hortus conclusus*, an ideal burrow disguised as "a little dell embowered" with foliage (CY, 11), in the midst of which sings Keats's nightingale. Priscilla vacillates comically between her mentor's vision of the mystical "Lotus Pool" and her own less ideal perception—through a pair of field glasses—of the sexual escapades occurring nightly in Crome's bathing-pool. By the time Stone takes his leave of Priscilla and encounters the rest of the family surrounded by their houseguests on the terrace, Crome's role as a baroque-romantic stage for, in Cardan's words, "incessant amateur theatricals" (TBL, 25) has been firmly established, while its more "menacing" aspects (CY, 68) have been subtly insinuated into the descriptions of both the facade and the interior.

Denis Stone's courtship of Anne Wimbush unfolds leisurely against a background of country house amenities: breakfast on the terrace, an evening stroll through the gardens, a dance to pianola music, a portrait-sitting, and a tour of the estate farm. These events are enlivened by the arrival and departure of eccentric guests like Barbecue-Smith and Ivor Lombard. The intellectual and sexual antics of Anne Wimbush's houseguests, including Mary Bracegirdle's obsession with her virginity, Gombauld's attempt to paint in a style uncontaminated by Cubist influences, Ivor Lombard's seduction of Mary, and Anne's hedonistic reserve, form a backdrop to Stone's own futile posturings and ultimately fill the pages of Jenny Mullion's notebook. The latter is a guest who, from the undistracted vantage-point of her deafness, has deftly recorded in the Cromean present what Henry Wimbush, with less awareness and no satirical intent, has painstakingly unearthed from the Cromean past. "The archaeologist's will to historical truth" (TV, 216), emblematized in Henry Wimbush's recently completed *History of Crome*, adds a further dimension to the narrative in the form of a series of antiquarian tales read by Wimbush to the assembled guests, each historical anecdote turning on the bizarre activities of his ancestors Sir Ferdinando Lapith, Sir Hercules Lapith, and George Wimbush. These chapters from Wimbush's manuscript are carefully designed to clarify the ideas that form the base of Huxley's novel and to shed further light on the incidents that constitute its plot.

To begin with, Wimbush's scholarly shuffling through Crome's "grimy little sixteenth-century account books" (*CY*, 114) is another variation on Scogan's theme of "spiritual Tubes" and private burrows. In *Crome Yellow*, as in all of Huxley's novels, the theme of history, its nature and utility, is a pervasive element within a larger pattern of interlocking topics. For Wimbush history is an obsession, and the past a haven from a present that inspires only "weariness" (*CY*, 203). His historical research is pointedly self-referential, focusing narrowly on his own family and the spectrum of eccentricities apparently passed from generation to generation. The first of the three anecdotes concerns the Elizabethan Sir Ferdinando Lapith, who inheriting the state of Crome from his father, built his "grand new house of brick" by quarrying the old church buildings handed over to the family during the dissolution of the monasteries in the sixteenth century. Moreover, in creating Crome he was obsessively preoccupied by "only one thought—the proper placing of his privies" (*CY*, 69). This curious piece of information is offered by Wimbush immediately following Scogan's comparison of Crome's architectural integrity with the chthonic style of Shelley's tower in the *Epipsychidion*. Scogan's aversion for nature and the earthly origins of Shelley's tower is a neurotic stance shared by Sir Ferdinando Lapith but in a radically Swiftian form. Scogan's more abstractly generalized anxiety in the face of a macrocosmic nature "too large, too complicated . . . and incomprehensible" is reversed in Sir Ferdinando's revulsion for the microcosmic nature of man. In *Certaine Privy Counsels* published in 1573, the latter argued "that the greatest possible distance should separate the privy from the sewage arrangements" and "that the privies were to be placed at the top of the house, being connected by verticle shafts with pits or channels in the ground" (*CY*, 69–70).

Henry Wimbush, after noting that Sir Ferdinando was motivated by more than merely "material" considerations, offers a brief explanation of his ancestor's neurotic obsession with "the waste productions of metabolism and digestion" (*DWW*, 93). Wimbush's description of Sir Ferdinando's architectural solution to the exigencies of "base and brutish" human nature is, at least on the surface, a darker reflection of his belief (impossible for Scogan or, for that matter, Wimbush himself) that man is the "noblest" creature "of the universe." The tower latrine was designed to neutralize the "degrading effects" of human metabolism by its placement in a "room nearest to heaven" and the incorporation of both "windows commanding an extensive and noble prospect" as well as "bookshelves containing all the ripest products of human wisdom . . ." (*CY*,

70). Despite its elevation, Sir Ferdinando's tower is another, more absurdly fanciful version of the burrow, a "home-made universe, hollowed out of the real world by means of [the burrower's] organs of perception and intellectual faculties" (*EM*, 256). Sir Ferdinando's desire to escape what he regards as the damning evidence of human excrement reappears in a significantly altered form in *After Many a Summer Dies the Swan*, where the Earl of Gonnister incarcerates himself in a subterranean prison in order to prolong his life by means of an excrementally related diet of carp intestines. Scogan's "spiritual Tubes" or "narrow tunnels" are variations on the same theme, except the noble prospect envisioned by Sir Ferdinando is replaced by a geometricized perspective of subway tiles. In both cases the vista is a self-imposed delusion, mirroring the fixated ideas and values of the neurotic perceiver.

The second historical episode recorded in Henry Wimbush's "fragmentary notebook" concerns the attempt of Sir Hercules Lapith to remodel his world according to his own contracted dimensions. Born a dwarf, he creates an exclusive realm delicately miniaturized to correspond not merely to his physical size but, more important, to his fastidious distaste for human physiology. The manuscript poem quoted by Henry Wimbush reveals the typically Lapith disgust with the "gross and repulsive" body and the attendant hope that as mankind evolves, the "soul" will eventually free itself from "all superfluous matter" (*CY*, 86). His Lilliputian world demolished by his normally proportioned son, he commits suicide as a final act of rejection and withdrawal. Significantly, Sir Hercules's death occurs immediately after his reading the Roman historian Suetonius. Himself the subject of an historical anecdote in Henry Wimbush's history of Crome, Sir Hercules's reading of Suetonius confirms his own experience, much as his own story is an exemplary historical narrative drawing together the episode of his ancestor Sir Ferdinando and the third and final episode, the story of his descendants the three Lapith daughters. The history of Crome and Suetonius's *History of the Twelve Caesars* share one overriding trait best summarized by Scogan's title for a projected historical work, "The Lives of Queer Men" (*CY*, 72). Taken together, they reinforce one of the presiding themes of *Crome Yellow*, the futile appeal to history for meaning and guidance.

The raw data of history is both available and unavoidable at Crome, and its ubiquity inspires a number of the inhabitants of the estate and its immediate environs to adopt conflicting theories concerning the meaning and mechanism of history. For Mr. Bodiham, the local rector, the "nineteen centuries" of European history have unfolded according to a discernibly providential design. The spectrum of history, he argues, especially "since the Franco-Prussian War" (*CY*, 57) and the resulting tensions of the Dual Alliance and the Entente Cordiale, reveals an increasingly apocalyptic pattern of confrontation between papal and antipapal states. What, for Bodiham, can "be identified in history" (*CY*, 56) is the dimly veiled presence of the apocalyptic forces catalogued in *Revelations*, a synoptic guide to world history and the inspiration for the little pamphlet he has written for the benefit of his congregation. "The Dragon, the Beast, and the False Prophet" are Bodiham's symbols of ideal, general laws operating in history and culminating in the rise of "German world-power" (*CY*, 58).

"Historically speaking" (*CY*, 55), he argues, the nineteen centuries of European history bear the chronic testimony of God's wrath against the "wickedness of mankind" (*CY*, 54). Bodiham's obsession with World War I, the Easter Rebellion, and the rise of German power is inseparable from his view of the people of Crome, who remained as "wicked" and "indifferent as ever" to his philosophy of history (*CY*, 59). Furthermore, his pamphlet was composed four years earlier, in 1915, and nothing has since occurred to revise his ideological expectations. History *is* meaningful, its purpose and design everywhere evident and urgent:

> Four years, he reflected; what were four years, after all? It must inevitably take a long time for Armageddon to ripen, to yeast itself up. The episode of 1914 had been a preliminary skirmish. And as for the war having come to an end—why, that, of course, was illusory. It was still going on, smouldering away in Silesia, in Ireland, in Anatolia; the discontent in Egypt and India was preparing the way, perhaps, for a great extension of the slaughter among the heathen peoples. The Chinese boycott of Japan, and the rivalries of that country and America in the Pacific, might be breeding a great new war in the East. (*CY*, 60)

The ideologically historicist assumptions embedded in Bodiham's turgid, strained, and repetitious prose contrast vividly with the seemingly unprejudiced historicist sympathies of Henry Wimbush and his love for what he regards as "the murdered past" (*CY*, 129). Wimbush's sympathies and methodological procedures qualify him as an historicist to the extent that his chronicle of Crome's inhabitants appears to be the record of a unique series of events rendered as concretely as possible and based on carefully sifted empirical evidence. In its narrowest sense, historicism can be defined as the attempt to portray the unsystematic variety of particular historical facts as they develop in time, but it is an attempt inspired by an empathy with the past and a desire to recreate it on the basis of hard empirical evidence free of a priori meta-historical assumptions. Wimbush's "favourite reading" consists of "grimy little sixteenth-century account books" (*CY*, 114) and "ancient records" (*CY*, 81) unearthed at Crome. Not unexpectedly, he clashes with Bodiham over the issue of a fitting war memorial for the local church. The Great War of 1914, or what Huxley called "the largest war and the stupidest peace known to history" (*OM*, 45), has been shorn of meaning by Wimbush and Bodiham, its significance lost in a quarrel over a suitable commemorative symbol. The apocalyptic historian Bodiham, true to his predilection for religious symbolism, prefers "a stained-glass window" or "a monument of marble" (*CY*, 126), while Wimbush, the indefatigable historicist, "was all for a library—a library of local literature, stocked with county histories, old maps of the district, monographs on the local antiquities, dialect dictionaries, handbooks of the local geology and natural history" (*CY*, 125). But in turning the key in the lock of Lapith-Wimbush history, Wimbush has imprisoned himself in an antiquarian fantasy as false, in Huxley's view, as Bodiham's Draconian prophecy of an endless cycle of violence and war.

Wimbush's "fragmentary notebook" is as much the result of the projection of a subjective bias onto history as Bodiham's "little pamphlet"; the former, despite Wimbush's seemingly objective historicist values, conceives of history as safely static, an intellectual alternative to a troubling present: "give me the past. It doesn't change; it's all there in black and white, and you can get to know about it comfortably and decorously and, above all, privately—by reading" (*CY*, 204). Wimbush's empirically grounded "black and white," like Bodiham's supernaturally inspired papal and anti-papal, is a cynical evasion of the historian's complex task, best expressed by Denis Stone, who confronted by Crome's jumble of historical objects of "every date and fashion," asks, "What could one reconstruct from such data?" Wimbush's *History of Crome* is only one possible answer, more reasonable in terms of its historicist methodology than Bodiham's pamphlet but corrupted by a fear of the present as intense as Sir Hercules Lapith's, whose reading of Suetonius's history provides the final impetus for suicide.

Scogan also adopts a specific stance towards the historical implications of Suetonius's chronicle of the early Caesars. His own particular assumptions concerning history are wider than Wimbush's yet less rigidly confined than Bodiham's. Henry Wimbush's historicist approach has resulted in a history shorn of moral purpose. While Scogan's view of history robs it of historicist particularity and diversity in favor of broadly moral-psychological categories, it contains a moral emphasis increasingly favored by Huxley himself. The substance of Wimbush's readings from his *History* contradict both his professed admiration for the past as well as his historicist values. Indeed, the central irony of the three chapters selected by Wimbush to be read aloud to his houseguests lies with their resemblance to Voltairean satiric parables. In his essay on Voltaire published in *On the Margin* shortly after the appearance of *Crome Yellow*, Huxley described Voltaire's *Candide* as "a record of the facts and opinions of 1922" (*OM*, 13); that is, of a society shaped by "the Great War, the Russian Famine, The Black and Tans, the Fascisti, and all the other horrors" (*OM*, 14). It is not surprising that Huxley, a satirist with a keen interest in modern history, should find the work of the satirist who first employed the term "philosophy of history"[10] both brilliant and topical—a parable to be read as a "record" of the political and economic disarray of 1922, in which the bitter "wisdom" of its characters "has become the everyday wisdom of all the world since 1914." For Huxley "the happy Victorian and Edwardian past" (*OM*, 14) had been buried at Ypres and the Somme, and the one intellectual stance he stated as possible in the essay on Candide was associated with another historian-satirist, Edward Gibbon. Huxley's preference for what he called the polite gentility of a "Gibbonish environment" (*OM*, 16) sheds additional light on the role of Wimbush's *History of Crome*, as well as upon the connection between Suetonius's *History of the Twelve Caesars* cited there and Scogan's theory of the "Caesarean environment" (*CY*, 111), including the latter's dismissal of the nineteenth-century belief in historical progress.

In both his *Philosophy of History* and the later *Essay*, Voltaire had no sympathy with or comprehension of historicism. The past was at best a source of useful truths, but to view it "en philosophe" was to recognize its intrinsic inutility as an authority for judging present institutions or beliefs. This radical dismissal of history is present in *Crome Yellow* and becomes progressively more central to Huxley's thinking about European culture in his essays and novels of the thirties. In *Crome Yellow* it is obliquely hinted at in Wimbush's exemplary narratives designed by Huxley to reveal a record of recurrent mental aberration—not a vivid historicist reconstruction of a past culture conforming to its own unique characteristics, despite Wimbush's respect for historical documents.

What Wimbush cannot or will not comprehend, the "Gibbonish" satirist Scogan understands and dismisses. For him the single verifiable principle of uniformity in history is human appetite, always verging on the edge of madness and best dramatized by the Roman Caesars of Suetonius and Gibbon, whom he claims form an index to recurring human types in which the more radically aberrant tend to predominate. The Caesarean environment is one of complete freedom, including the opportunity to gratify without restraint all of one's appetites and desires. In a manner reminiscent of the situation of Kurtz in Conrad's *Heart of Darkness*, the

Caesarean freedom offers those men "the chance to develop, untrammelled, the full horror of their potentialities" (CY, 110), and according to Scogan "the twentieth century" has provided such a setting. Citing the British intervention in Ireland, the Polish oppression of the Silesians, and the rise of Italian fascism, Scogan argues that the Europe of the Versailles settlement had become a breeding ground of Caesarian dictators. In Scogan's philosophy of history, the Great War is "reality," and the "melancholy story" (CY, 162) of post-Reformation European history a depressing chronicle of the irrational quest for power:

"Consider, for example, the case of Luther and Erasmus. . . . There was Erasmus, a man of reason if ever there was one. People listened to him at first—a new virtuoso performing on that elegant and resourceful instrument, the intellect; they even admired and venerated him. . . . And then Luther appears, violent, passionate, a madman insanely convinced about matters in which there can be no conviction. He shouted, and men rushed to follow him. Erasmus was no longer listened to; he was reviled for his reasonableness. Luther was serious, Luther was reality—like the Great War. Erasmus was only reason and decency; he lacked the power, being a sage, to move men to action. Europe followed Luther and embarked on a century and a half of war and bloody persecution. It's a melancholy story." (CY, 162)

Scogan resembles Bodiham and Wimbush to the extent that he too employs a binary schema in his selection and ordering of historical events. In Scogan's interpretation of modern history, Bodiham's papal and anti-papal and Wimbush's nostalgic pastoral past and urban present are replaced by the wider psychological-moral categories of maniac and rationalist, a position gradually adopted by Huxley himself. History, then, becomes an etiology of racial or national neurosis and its accompanying delusions. However, like Bodiham, Scogan refers to himself as a "prophet" (CY, 164) of a new social order, and like Bodiham and Wimbush, he feels a profound aversion for the twentieth century. Indeed, all three are united in their repudiation of modern history as well as notions of historical advancement.

Such a categorical denial of human progress is subtly underscored by Huxley's manipulation of the historicist Wimbush, whose Cromean History is represented by three moral-psychological parables, each of which involves an emphasis on subjective withdrawal and neurotic disgust with the human body. Stylistically, each parable takes a quasi-allegorical form whose gnomic meaning undercuts Wimbush's idealization of the past and accords with Scogan's aversion for what Huxley will later call "the descending road of modern history." Looking back with a certain wistfulness on a rustic Crome, the restorative normality of which is denied by his three historical narratives, Wimbush acknowledges his revulsion for the present and his preference for "primitives" or "seventeenth-century books" (*CY*, 203), or for safely distant historical figures like Caesar Borgia or St. Francis:

"No, give me the past. It doesn't change; it's all there in black and white, and you can get to know about it comfortably and decorously and, above all, privately—by reading. By reading I know a great deal of Caesar Borgia, of St. Francis, of Dr. Johnson; a few weeks have made me thoroughly acquainted with these interesting characters, and I have been spared the tedious and revolting process of getting to know them by personal contact, which I should have to do if they were living now." (*CY*, 204)

Denying the possibility of progress and human perfectibility, he listlessly hopes for a different kind of perfection, ironically comparing himself to "Godwin and Shelley" but substituting for their romantic philosophy of history, with its endorsement of human progress, a degenerate preference for "the perfectibility of machinery" that will permit an anti-social seclusion entirely "secure from any human intrusion" (*CY*, 204). Wimbush's final historical revelation, the counterpart of Scogan's "spiritual Tubes" and a parody of Bodiham's apocalyptic history, occurs when he takes Denis Stone out into the grounds of Crome at night and suddenly illuminates the darkness with an electric torch, revealing the excavated drain-pipes of ancient Crome:

"Here we are," he said, and taking an electric torch out of his pocket, he cast a dim beam over two or three blackened sections of tree trunk, scooped out into the semblance of pipes, which were lying forlornly in a little depression in the ground. (*CY*, 202)

Gazing down on his recently unearthed "oaken drain-pipes," Wimbush himself takes his place in the history of Crome, his historicist values overturned by the Voltairean satire informing his own *History*, while his characteristically neurotic Lapith-Wimbush urge to shrink from human contact (the essential but covert subject of his *History* but of which he remains unaware) confirms Scogan's dismissal of history as a record of madness.

In *The Devils of Loudun* Huxley demonstrated not only his awareness of the nature of historicism but also his interest in a related problem that complicated his approach to European cultural history in a manner reflecting Scogan's role in *Crome Yellow* as an ironic sociologist. Huxley's historical study of Father Grandier is premised on firm historicist principles, including the recognition that seventeenth-century men could not "think about their experiences except within the frame of reference which, *at that particular time and place*, has come to seem self-evident. Interpretation is in terms of the *prevailing thought-pattern*, and this thought-pattern conditions to some extent the expression of urges and emotions, but can never completely inhibit them" (*DL*, 172—italics mine). Huxley's approach to history would seem to be free of extra-historical considerations and preconceptions of a metaphysical or theological kind, yet he does insist on a principle of uniformity: "The charm of history and its enigmatic lesson consist in the fact that from age to age, nothing changes and yet everything is completely different. In the personages of other times and alien cultures we recognize our all too human selves and yet are aware, as we do so, that the frame of reference . . . has changed . . . out of all recognition." He then adds: "But however great, however important for thought and technology, for social organization and behavior, *the differences between then and now are always peripheral* (*DL*, 284—italics mine). What suddenly emerges at this point is a distinctly Voltairean philosophy of history but—as I shall clarify later—modified to assimilate a more Spenglerian outlook. And between the two, historicism simply ceases to count. What does count is the perennial oscillation "between unregeneracy and enlightment" (*DL*, 285), a constant factor in Huxley's interpretation of modern history first hinted at in Scogan's diatribes.

The meta-historical implications of Scogan's doleful polemics, the three chapters of Wimbush's *History of Crome*, and Bodiham's apocalyptic essay on modern history (itself an *actual* historical document inserted into the text) are further developed by the lyric meditations on the meaning of history composed by Sir Hercules and Denis Stone. Taken together, all of these documents and theories provide the basis for a satire of speculative philosophy of history. The answer to Denis Stone's initial question borders on a simple negative; very little can be reconstructed from the haphazardly arranged collections of Crome because history as memorialized there is intrinsically meaningless. The only design it exhibits is a regressive pattern of neurotic withdrawal, a tendency that when linked to Scogan's theory of history as pathology, anticipates Huxley's later judgement that the "intellectual key to history" can best be provided by the "psychologist" (*AMS*, 324).

If Crome, the "ghostly-peopled necropole" (*CY*, 149), is the novel's prime symbol of the collected detritus of history, the annual Charity Fair on its grounds is an emblem of the confusing flux of contemporary society. Henry Wimbush views it as both vestigial obligation and unwelcome invasion at best, a hollow parody of his cherished ideal of earlier, more ideally rustic rituals, especially the "old, earthly, Panic rite" (*CY*, 128) of moonlight dances ended in the seventeenth century by Puritan intervention. For Bodiham the fair is simply "disgusting" (*CY*, 198), while for Scogan it is an opportunity for sexual seduction, in which the "prophet" of the rational state is satirically reduced to an absurdly costumed libid-inous "oracle" (*CY*, 190). Denis Stone, a timid solipsist recently trau-matized by his discovery of Jenny Mullion's "red notebook" crowded with satirical sketches of Crome's occupants, regards the fair as an epi-stemological challenge. Like Wimbush's "fragmentary notebook" filled with unintentionally satiric studies of Crome's past owners, Jenny's derisive sketches bring Wimbush's chronicle up-to-date and awaken Denis Stone to "all the vast conscious world of men outside himself" (*CY*, 174). Like Sir Hercules Lapith, Denis's rude awakening to the real-ity of that world is associated with suicide. Indeed, Denis Stone's at-tempted suicide reinforces his resemblance to Sir Hercules. While the lat-ter had more justification for his deliberate withdrawal from the world, both are inward-turning subjectivists, both are poets, and both are physically humiliated by women—Sir Hercules picked up and shaken by a young lady to whom he proposed marriage and Denis physically humiliated by Anne when he is unable to carry her after her accident. And while Sir Hercules was a dwarf, Denis Stone is emotionally stunted, as grotesque in his emotional inhibitions as Sir Hercules in his Procrus-tean amibitions "to create . . . at Crome a private world of his own, in which all should be proportionable to himself" (*CY*, 87).

This resemblance extends to their poems. Sir Hercules's poem is a meditation on evolutionary history, beginning with the "ancient days" of Hebraic history and surveying human progress from the discovery of various arts, including writing and painting, to a "prophetic" vision of increasingly spiritual refinement culminating in a "perfected" state of human culture:

> In ancient days, while yet the world was young,
> . . . . . . . . . . . . . . . . . .
> Flesh grown corrupt brought forth a monstrous birth
> And obscene giants trod the shrinking earth,
> . . . . . . . . . . . . . . . . . .
> Long ages pass'd and Man grown more refined,
> Slighter in muscle but of vaster Mind.
> . . . . . . . . . . . . . . . . . .
> Thus man's long progress step by step we trace;
> The Giant dies, the hero takes his place;
> . . . . . . . . . . . . . . . . . .
> But can we think that Providence will stay
> Men's footsteps here upon the upward way?
> Mankind in understanding and in grace
> Advanc'd so far beyond the Giant's race?
> Hence impious thought! Still led by God's own hand,
> Mankind proceeds towards the Promised Land.

> A time will come (prophetic, I descry
> Remoter dawns along the gloomy sky),
> When happy mortals of a Golden Age
> Will backward turn the dark historic page,
> And in our vaunted race of Men behold
> A form as gross, a Mind as dead and cold,
> As we in Giants see, in warriors of old.
> A time will come, where in the soul shall be
> From all superfluous matter wholly free:
> When the light body, agile as a fawn's,
> Shall sport with grace along the velvet lawns.
> Nature's most delicate and final birth,
> Mankind perfected shall possess the earth.
>
> (CY, 86–87)

Sir Hercules's philosophy of history is premised on human perfectibility, a belief in spiritual-biological progress, and an assertion of an immanent force within history—a "Providence" associated with the realization of a hidden plan of "Nature." The motive force of history propels man along an "upward way," where "led by God's own hand" he ascends towards a "Promised Land" of a perfected "nobler breed." Sir Hercules's revulsion for "the dark historic page," however, is the opposite of Wimbush's nostalgic grief over "the murdered past." Born in 1740, Sir Hercules's belief in human progress bears a vague resemblance to Enlightenment speculative philosophy of history, but it is important to note that as the central tragicomic figure in Wimbush's *History of Crome*, his views are rejected by Scogan and Wimbush and undermined by his own predicament, including his self-serving subjectivity. Even the apocalyptic history espoused by the equally "prophetic" Bodiham, with its emphasis on an approaching Armegeddon, contains no hint of Sir Hercules's perfectibilist idealism.

Denis Stone's ode is, at least in part, an answer to Sir Hercules's perfectibilist prophecy. Influenced by Scogan's mordant ruminations on the fixed nature of man and "the frightful limitation of . . . human faculties" (CY, 183), Denis's meditative lyric affirms Scogan's belief that "complete and absolute change" is "the thing we can never have" (CY, 182). Like Sir Hercules, Denis raises the possibility of historical change and freedom, but after brooding on the violence of Roman culture, he shifts abruptly but logically to the Russian Revolution:

> You do not know
> How to be free. The Russian snow
> Flowered with bright blood whose roses spread
> Petals of fading, fading red

That died into the snow again,
Into the virgin snow; and men
From all the ancient bonds were freed
Old law, old custom, and old creed,
Old right and wrong there bled to death:
The frozen air received their breath,
A little smoke that died away;
And round about them where they lay
The snow bloomed roses. Blood was there
A red gay flower and only fair.
                                                    (CY, *194*)

As the most recent effort to effect a radical transformation of European society, the upheaval in Russia was an appropriate, even inevitable subject for Stone's ode. But while he initially acknowledges the success of the revolution in freeing Russian Society from "all the ancient bonds" of "old law" and "old custom," the poem ends inconclusively with a pessimistic emphasis on "blood" and death. The ironic "laughter" that greets the human boast of attained freedom is a twentieth-century revision of Sir Hercules's perfectibilist hypothesis as well as an early anticipation of what Eustace Barnack in *Time Must Have a Stop* will call the "Historical Jokes" of modern history.

Beguiled by his neatly tailored sentiments, ensnared in the web of words, and frustrated by sexual longings for which he can find no outlet, Stone—like Sir Hercules—chooses suicide. The actual attempt is prefaced by a self-destructive surrender to his own smothering inhibitions: "Denis did not want to talk, could not have talked. His soul was a tenuous, tremulous pale membrane. He would keep its sensibility intact and virgin as long as he could" (CY, 188). In this respect, Denis Stone is the first of Huxley's self-absorbed romantics meandering through all of the early novels, while as the potential "excavator" of Crome's cluttered past, he stands haplessly at the crossroads for many diverging interpretations of human history. In his resemblance to Sir Hercules, he is, like Henry Wimbush, drawn into the history of Crome; his near escape from self-inflicted death on Crome's western tower being in essence another chapter in Crome's ongoing chronicle of irrationality and self-immolation. His poem, strategically placed at the novel's conclusion, is an inadequate response to Bodiham's apocalyptic history, Wimbush's illusory historicism, Sir Hercules's providential progressivism, or Scogan's Voltairean repudiation of the past. Its hesitant ambiguity, characteristic of Stone, completes Huxley's comic analysis of meta-history in *Crome Yellow.*

In the novels and essays that follow, Huxley will develop and refine his approach to the philosophy of history through ideas derived from art history and psychology, drawing especially on romanticism and baroque aesthetics, in an effort to create a psychological typology of recurring historical sensibilities. His primary focus will be cultural history, but Scogan's Voltairean anti-historicism, including the effort to gauge the past by extra-historical moral judgements, informs all of Huxley's writing on modern history. Sir Hercules's terror of "the dark historic page" leads inevitably to Henry Ford's dogmatic assertion that "History is bunk," one of the intellectual cornerstones of *Brave New World*. Huxley clearly rejects the rigidly mechanistic vision of Scogan's "rational state," a society of programmed illusion and solemn efficiency, but he is in 1921 tentatively swayed by Scogan's Spenglerian pessimism regarding European history—an undercurrent of skepticism that will gradually surface in *Antic Hay* and, with greater emphasis, in *Those Barren Leaves*.

The various historical texts, anecdotes, and poems—as well as the arguments and discussions focusing on history—that fill the pages of *Crome Yellow* are reinforced by the symbolic setting of Crome itself, a Tudor mansion filled with the detritus of the past. This complex pattern of references to history is not merely a unifying thematic thread but, more important, can be seen as Huxley's first experiment with contrapuntal form, each poem or text taking on meaning only when juxtaposed with a preceding story or discussion. The resulting interplay involves, to use Philip Quarles' words, a theme stated, "then developed, pushed out of shape, imperceptibly deformed" by means of "sets of variations" (*PCP*, 408). An example is Denis Stone's question concerning reconstruction of the historical "data" in chapter two—variations of which are provided by the opposing assumptions regarding the meaning of history formulated by Wimbush, Bodiham, Scogan, Sir Hercules, and Denis Stone himself. Crome, then, is indeed, on one level "a dead, deserted Pompeii" (*CY*, 5), a "ghostly-peopled necropole" (*CY*, 149), and a "tumultuous tomb" (*CY*, 6), although it must not be forgotten that it is also a charming Tudor great house. In his *Life in the English Country House*, Mark Girouard observed that "the country houses portrayed by Buchan, Wodehouse and others are mellow, dignified, creeper-clad, lawn encompassed, and bathed in perpetual sunshine."[11] Huxley's Crome takes its place in this company by exhibiting a seasoned mellowness and ripened serenity of atmosphere that appears to hold out the promise of civilized tradition and pastoral regeneration. In fact, its starkly aggressive facade and the baroque illusionism of its interior are counterpointed by the romantic delusions of its owners and guests, past and present, while its history is bound up with neurotic fantasy, suicide, and intellectual futility on a grotesque scale.

In *The Olive Tree* Huxley commented on a motif that pervades the early novels, the attempt of so many of his romantic egoists to encompass either the future or the past by means of prophecy: "And the ideals of an earnest and very intelligent Englishman of the early twentieth century may be studied, in all their process of development, in the long series of Mr. Wells' prophetic books. Our notions of the future have something of that significance which Freud attributes to our dreams." Prophetic texts reveal not only the prevailing ideals or intellectual conventions of a specific period but also the more irrationally covert intentions Huxley briefly associates with Freudian analysis and dream experience. He then adds:

And not our notions of the future only: our notions of the past as well. For if prophecy is an expression of our contemporary fears and wishes, so too, to a very great extent, is history—or at least what passes for history among the mass of ordinary unprofessional folk. Utopias, earthly paradises and earthly hells are flowers of the imagination which contrive to blossom and luxuriate even in the midst of the stoniest dates and documents, even within the fixed and narrow boundaries of established fact. (*OT*, 135)

The "glimpses into the Cromean past" provided by Wimbush's *History* do not suggest, as Peter Firchow has argued, "that a meaningful relation between the ideal and the real once existed, even if it exists no longer."[12] Most of Crome's occupants, past and present, are neurotic dreamers whose "prophetic" interpretations of past and future history are symptomatic of the predicament in which they find themselves bereft of direction and any possibility of fulfillment. The poetic prophecy of Sir Hercules Lapith is as irrational and escapist as Priscilla Wimbush's astral projections or the Reverend Bodiham's apocalyptic history, and if Henry Wimbush's Cromean research demonstrates anything, it is the continuity of Crome's ludicrous past with its comically absurd present.

In the concluding episode of *Crome Yellow*, Denis Stone, in a fit of romantic posturing, narrowly avoids hurling himself from one of Crome's towers. After discovering Anne Wimbush in the embraces of Gombauld, he climbs to the top of the western tower and in a moment of "exaltation" (*CY*, 210), prepares to leap to the terrace below, only to be suddenly awakened from his suicidal trance by Mary Bracegirdle. Together, they effect his release from an intolerable situation by concocting the ruse of the false telegram, a ploy that permits him to leave the following day. But in departing from Crome, he abandons an Arcadian "necropole" (*CY*, 149) for an urban "Necropolis" (*CY*, 216), the setting of Huxley's second novel *Antic Hay*, in which Stone's virtual avatar, Theodore

Gumbril, will move about the streets of London much the same as Denis Stone wandered from room to room in Crome—yet in a world where the consequences of romantic fantasy and subjective idealism exact a greater price.

In a letter written after the publication of *Antic Hay*, Huxley defended his second novel as "a book written by a member of what I may call the war generation for others of his kind," adding "that it is intended to reflect—fantastically, of course, but none the less faithfully—the life and opinions of an age which has seen the violent disruption of almost all the standards, conventions, and values current in the previous epoch."[13] Such a statement of intent can be applied to all of Huxley's work during the interwar period, where the problematical relationship between generations, between the individual and history, and between old and new romantics are subsumed under Huxley's awareness of radically new forces operative in contemporary history. *Antic Hay* is his first attempt to define such forces and to dramatize them in satirically emblematic figures.

## 2. History and the Urban Labyrinth in *Antic Hay*

In *Antic Hay*, Huxley expanded the rural setting of *Crome Yellow* to embrace the architectural chaos of London, substituting for the comparatively serene activities of an English country house the fitful peregrinations of a collection of restive urbanites. The pastoral arc of withdrawal, transformation, and return that shaped the structure of *Crome Yellow* reappears briefly in Theodore Gumbril's journey to Robertsbridge and the idyllic imagery associated with Emily. But as in *Crome Yellow*, the promise of Arcadian metamorphosis remains unfulfilled, the pastoral arc itself a time-worn convention that in the aftermath of the Great War can provide only an occasion for irony. Both *Antic Hay* and *Those Barren Leaves* are comprehensive studies of the "baroque-romantic" impulse as the hub around which the wheel of historicist progress spins aimlessly, an erratic motion that becomes the dominant motif of Huxley's second novel.

The plot of *Antic Hay* is, on the level of narrative action, less statically episodic than *Crome Yellow*, the flow of events twisting and eddying about Theodore Gumbril's efforts to enter the mainstream of urban London, an activity that he sees primarily in terms of immersing himself in two activities—the accumulation of capital and the seduction of women. He resigns as a teacher of history, turning instead to a business career in hopes of, first, marketing his own design for a pair of pants equipped with an inflatable cushion and, second, effecting a radical alteration in what he has come to regard as his hopelessly introverted personality. The narrative structure of *Antic Hay* is constructed around a series of brief social journeys taken by Gumbril as he progressively and unwittingly loses himself in the architectural "jumble" of London, a chaos that his father is attempting to order by constructing an elaborate table-top model of the renovated city refashioned according to the ideas of Sir Christopher Wren.

Walking or riding through parks or down streets, dropping in on friends, visiting art galleries, restaurants, studios, or nightclubs—alone or accompanied by groups of acquaintances—Gumbril becomes increasingly, if inadvertently, enmeshed in the exfoliations of his own aimless movements. He traverses a social circuit permitting him a short-lived pastoral excursion with Emily that is swiftly overtaken by the urban exigencies of Myra Viveash. Unlike his father, Gumbril is not a proponent of any coherent set of ideas beyond a preoccupation with his own personality. The principal narrative complication of *Antic Hay* is Gumbril's random encounter with Emily and his equally random betrayal of her. The social and architectural maze in which he finds himself entrapped is the symbolic axis of the novel, in which the related motifs of wasteland, labyrinth, and random motion combine to create a world given over to historicist assumptions and values. However much Gumbril hopes to change and however rapidly he moves, his world—like Myra Viveash's—remains fixed and unchanging. Neither the science of Shearwater, the aesthetics of Lypiatt, the capitalist projects of Boldero, nor the urban planning of Gumbril Senior offer a practicable avenue of escape. His father's historical reconstruction of London based on his interpretation of Sir Christopher Wren's architectural principles and Mr. Porteous's dedication to historical scholarship (the study of late Roman poetry) are civilized activities associated with order and discipline. Both men refuse to abandon moral principle, and their work seems to stand as a warning to Gumbril that if history is abandoned, it must be replaced by something equally meaningful. Yet the two older men are ineffectual, at least to the extent that Gumbril Senior is prevented from putting his ideas into practice and ultimately is forced to surrender his model of an architecturally rejuvenated London, while Porteous is required to sacrifice most of his research library. Focusing on the intellectually ordered past, they are unprepared for the surprising exigencies of the present, although they are with Emily the only characters who possess, albeit in highly vulnerable form, an alternative vision to that of Myra Viveash, Huxley's exemplar of the "new consciousness" of the 1920s.

Theodore Gumbril, the central figure in this deliberately kinetic panorama of "the war generation," is a teacher of history who repudiates his profession on chiefly analytic grounds. Early in chapter one he is deluged by sixty-three student papers on "the Italian Risorgimento," a subject he mournfully labels a caprice on the part of a headmaster who regards it as "the most important event in modern European history" (*AH*, 10). Anticipating Sidney Quarles of *Point Counter Point*, Gumbril's rejection of history is based less on a penetrating assessment of the course of modern history and more on his egocentric involvement in his own personal history. Setting aside the student essays on the character and career of Pope Pius IX, he wanly reconstructs his own personality and life in an autobiographical fragment replete "with dates" (*AH*, 11). The resulting sense of failure, coupled with his despair over the historical exercises of his students, culminates in his resignation and a vague determination to do "something about life" (*AH*, 16). He defends his refusal to continue encouraging students to choose the study of history as a profession by defining historical inquiry as an unscientific subject. He complains that the absence of a "hard and definite" (*AH*, 22) nomological structure, or an empiricist methodology on which to base the study of history, has resulted in a "soft vagueness" that inspires "generalizations about subjects on which only our ignorance allows us to generalize" (*AH*, 22).

> "Well, in any case," said Gumbril Junior, "you didn't try to feed them on history. That's the real unforgivable sin. And that's what I've been doing, up till this evening—encouraging boys of fifteen and sixteen to specialise in history, hours and hours a week, making them read bad writers' generalisations about subjects on which only our ignorance allows us to generalize; teaching them to reproduce these generalisations in horrid little "Essays" of their own; rotting their minds, in fact, with a diet of soft vagueness, scandalous it was." (*AH*, 22)

Gumbril's indictment of history, however, is not serious inasmuch as he himself lives exclusively on a mental diet of nebulous dreams. His decision to resign as a teacher is reached after a lengthy mental fantasy of Byronic pilgrimage through "empty plains" on the way to Mantua, Rome, Athens, and Seville. This sudden introduction of the journey motif (with Myra Viveash as its goal) reveals the erratic bent of Gumbril's ambition, a preoccupation with romantic posturing and aimless self-assertion shared by most of the members of his circle.

The significance of history returns almost immediately with Mr. Bojanus, the class-conscious "admirer of Lenin" (*AH*, 36), who instructs Gumbril to "look at [h]istory" (*AH*, 38)—only as reflected in Bojanus's distorting mirror. An early version of Marxists like Illidge in *Point Counter Point* and Mark Staithes in *Eyeless in Gaza*, Bojanus's theories are shot through with political contradictions. Despite his approval of

Lenin, he regards ideologically inspired revolutions as inherently futile, a skepticism derived from a rejection of fundamental historicist goals of achieving freedom and meaning within the historical process itself. His version of modern economic and political history is informed by a dour futilitarianism that overrides any notion of historical progressiveness. Suddenly dropping his h's to establish his connection with "the Proletariat" and the "Red Guards" (*AH*, 37), he launches into an historical inventory of modern political revolutions and reform movements. Despite Gumbril's aversion for generalizations, he listens passively as Bojanus traces the increasing tempo of democratic reform, beginning with the French Revolution, then moving on to the revolutions of 1848, the British Reform Bill of 1832, and concluding with the final extension of the franchise during the period of the Great War: Bojanus dismisses history as a "[h]oax" because he cannot discover any evidence of regular pattern and design in human affairs, only Scogan's "melancholy story" of aberrant behavior. Instead of a chronicle of progressively widening liberty, he sees only "fundamental slavery":

"Look at 'istory, Mr. Gumbril, look at 'istory. First it's the French Revolution. They ask for political liberty. And they gets it. Then comes the Reform Bill, then Forty-Eight, then all the Franchise Acts and Votes for Women—always more and more political liberty. And what's the result, Mr. Gumbril? Nothing at all. Who's free for political liberty? Not a soul." (*AH*, 38)

Bojanus's insistence on the "uselessness" of revolutions is rooted in a systematic denial of historicist progress; yet he eagerly anticipates a revolutionary upheaval in England for the shallowest of historicist reasons, a delight in change as an end in itself: "It would be a nice change. I was always one for change and a little excitement." He adds that a "scientific interest" exists as well, conceiving of a revolution as a social "experiment" (*AH*, 40), the conclusions of which cannot be predicted despite his earlier confidence in the foreseeable consequences of revolutionary change.

Bojanus discards the possibility of achieving either liberty or an enriching degree of leisure within any social system, regarding such illusory goals as simply the millenarian dreams of romantic poets "like Shelley" (*AH*, 38), reinforced by a misplaced belief in the ability of the "ordinary man" to exercise independent political judgement or to endure for long "indefinite leisure" (*AH*, 40). He concludes that the imputed advances of modern economic and political history constitute a great "swindle" as a result of intrinsically unrealizable historicist aims. Bojanus's conviction that modern history, to use Eliot's phrases in "Gerontion," "guides us by vanities" and "deceives with whispering ambitions"—like Theodore Gumbril's belief that it lacks a comprehensive framework of demonstrable laws—is at best a groping toward what Huxley would regard as the basis for a comprehensive indictment of historicist assumptions. But in *Antic Hay* history and historicism are neither successfully probed nor transcended, despite Bojanus's attack on history or Gumbril's resignation as a teacher of it. All the characters are either immersed in the swirl of events, lending their faint notes to the swelling discords of a society emblematized in the roaring traffic and flashing "sky-lights" of Piccadilly Circus, or their partial insights are betrayed by an inability to conceive of a viable substitute for historicist values. Bojanus, for example, substitutes for a history informed by an immanent logic a violent welter of events provoking interest only as a result of their momentum. For Bojanus motion and change—that is, process itself—are all that remain; cheated by history, he sees it only in terms of a cynical immersion in events, a mindless anomie intended both to thwart interpretation and deny the most rudimentary trace of political or economic advancement. Nevertheless, Bojanus's ambivalent approval of Lenin and disdain for Shelley as apologists for two distinct approaches to cultural and political revolution can be traced to a similar juxtaposition in Huxley's essay "The New Romanticism":

The exclusive idealism of Shelley denies the obvious facts of human biology and economics. The exclusive materialism of Lenin denies the no less obvious and primary facts of men's immediate spiritual experiences. The revolutionary liberals were romantic in their refusal to admit that man was a social animal as well as an individual soul. The Bolsheviks are romantic in denying that man is anything more than a social animal, susceptible of being transformed by proper training into a perfect machine. Both are extravagant and one-sided. (*MN*, 215)

In *Antic Hay* the spatial labyrinth of London finds its temporal counterpart in the maze of history, the various "burrows" and retreats of characters like Lypiatt, Mercaptan, or Coleman exhibiting an historical dimension as well. The anarchic and sadomasochistic Coleman, for instance, yearns for another "third Empire" and "another comic Napoleon" (*AH*, 67). Lypiatt is dismissed by Mercaptan as a survivor from "the age of Rostand" (*AH*, 57), and Lypiatt in turn accuses Mercaptan of having withdrawn into a "sham eighteenth century" world (*AH*, 56). The capitalist Boldero manipulates history to mystify his customers, relying on "Egyptology" to create an obfuscatory context for his discovery of secrets known only "in the past" (*AH*, 154). Rosie Shearwater, who clearly subscribes to Boldero's dictum that "newness is an intoxication" (*AH*, 157), prefers the twentieth century and "the New Season's Models" (*AH*, 123)—the opposite of Emily, who appears to Theodore Gumbril as an anachronism unaccountably "born within the twentieth century" (*AH*, 181). Myra Viveash hopes "to recapture, to re-evoke, to revivify" the past in a series of "desperate experiments" (*AH*, 211) as meaningless as Bojanus's eagerly awaited revolutionary experiment. Gumbril, opposing Myra's addiction to the past, attempts to transcend history by announcing that "the past is abolished" and warning Myra Viveash, mentally entrapped within the year of her fiance's death (1917), that "One should . . . never think of the past . . ." (*AH*, 209). But Gumbril cannot escape so easily; he is accompanied on his journey to Robertsbridge to find Emily by a *memento mori* of the Great War, an old gentleman with the face of "the Emperor Francis Joseph" of Austria-Hungary (*AH*, 243) who entertains him with a lengthy denunciation of European culture and its approaching collapse—a vision compounded equally of anti-Semitism and fears of overpopulation, as cynical as Bojanus's philosophy of history and as confusedly anarchic. The most ambiguous insight into temporal process, and by implication history as well, is attained by Theodore Gumbril when he briefly enters the trans-historical world of Emily, a curious psychological study in sexual frigidity whose quasi-mystical pastoralism represents a fragile accommodation to history and time. Emily's function within the narrative structure of *Antic Hay* is important because she is the only character who appears to hold the key to the labyrinth in which Gumbril wanders aimlessly.

*Antic Hay* is structured around a sequence of five stages in Theodore Gumbril's vaguely conceived project of "doing something about life," in which his encounter with Emily is the principal challenge. It is important to note that at the outset Gumbril's rejection of history is not accompanied by a rejection of historicism. In the initial stage, his adoption of a disguise designed to transform his personality, his pursuit of capitalist profit, and his slavish subordination to Myra Viveash suggest the strength of his allegiances to essentially ephemeral values. In the second stage, he becomes involved with two women, the promiscuous Rosie Shearwater, loyal to the values of the twentieth century, and Emily, an anachronistic and frigid neurotic, who in spite of her psychological condition is linked to a fundamental purity that stands outside of history—an "innocence" that survived the Great War up to "the time of the Armistice, November 11, 1918" (*AH*, 181). Gumbril successfully seduces the former and then, in the third stage, tentatively submits to the spiritual ministrations of the latter. Returning to Myra Viveash, he betrays Emily—the fourth stage—and in the final section of the novel joins Myra on a series of peripatetic journeys around London, desperately trying to populate the "interminable desert of sand" (*AH*, 240), the result of his apostasy, by seeking out his friends and visiting nightclubs. The trackless wilderness in which he finds himself at the novel's conclusion was foreshadowed in the "empty plains" (*AH*, 15) through which he mentally journeyed during his Byronic fantasy in the opening chapters. Intervening between these two wastelands is the green world of Emily's pastoral *otium*, a Marvellian landscape of spiritual repose that Huxley describes as *in* time but not wholly *of* it.

Gumbril's pursuit of the tense and obsessed Rosie Shearwater is a prelude to his eventual surrender to the more deeply corrupt Myra Viveash. Rosie's anxious striving to realize her imaginative fantasies of social and sexual success is, within the wider thematic context of *Antic Hay*, a form of time-bound promiscuity deliberately juxtaposed with the apparently more durable and self-contained world of Emily, a more serene level of experience best dramatized in chapter thirteen. When Gumbril and Emily return to his rooms after listening to the Sclopis Quartet, they enter a world purged of the anarchy of the city and the frantic pace of the various members of Gumbril's circle. Perpetually conscious of time, Gumbril cannot completely imitate Emily's surrender to the "now" that, while it "vanishes and changes" (*AH*, 194), remains poised on the threshold of a world of serene intimacy where "for them there were no more minutes" (*AH*, 195).

Huxley's use of pastoral conventions in *Crome Yellow* and *Antic Hay* is traditional to the extent that his Arcadian landscapes pose a moral and spiritual challenge to the mechanistic complexities of urban life. Gumbril, for example, conceives of Emily "in her native quiet among the flowers" as an emblem of "integrity" and "perfection" (*AH*, 204), while her adversary, Myra Viveash, is repeatedly associated with fragmentation and disorder. The Marvellian "greenness of the garden" in which Emily and Gumbril slowly pace, with its "symmetrical pine trees" and "crystal quiet," is a typical pastoral landscape in which the "outward quiet of grass and trees" inspires a correspondingly "inward quiet" (*AH*, 187) of psychological and spiritual repose. But the precarious balance of pastoral illusion, a self-consciousness integral to the Renaissance pastorals of Spenser, Marvell, and Milton, takes on the more troubled exigencies of the romantic pastorals of Blake, Wordsworth, Shelley, and Keats. Neither time nor the gears and cams of technological "progress" can be banished from Huxley's landscapes. And just as the monstrous chaos of London dwarfs Gumbril Senior's table-top model of an ideal London inspired by Sir Christopher Wren, the fragile equipoise of change and stasis promised by Emily is subtly transformed by Gumbril into a more sinister apprehensiveness: "But time passed, time passed flowing in a dark stream, staunchlessly, as though from some profound mysterious wound in the world's side, bleeding, bleeding for ever" (*AH*, 195). It is only a short step from this organic trope of a cosmic lesion hemorrhaging time to Myra Viveash's conviction that "time kills everything"—"kills desire, kills sorrow, kills in the end the mind that feels them; wrinkles and softens the body while it still lives, rots it like a medlar, kills it too at last" (*AH*, 200).

Gumbril, the denouncer of history, must choose between the partisan of contemporary fashion Rosie Shearwater, whose peripatetic sexual escapades, as she passes from Gumbril to Mercaptan and then on to Coleman, exemplify the "antic" motions of a "degenerate" culture (*AH*, 254); and the anachronistic Emily, whose calmer perspective constitutes a threshold that once crossed would finally release him, if only in a qualified way, from the exigencies of time, history, and the "unceasing St. Vitus's dance" (*AH*, 297) of modern London. Gumbril characteristically does not reach a decision but instead acquiesces in Rosie's seduction by Coleman and, swayed by Myra Viveash, his old mistress whom he no longer loves, postpones his trip to join Emily in Sussex. His careless submission to the sheer randomness of events is finally emblematized in his taxi journey with Myra Viveash, who displaces Rosie Shearwater as Emily's true adversary. Despite his rejection of history, Gumbril is continually at the mercy of past events, incapable of taking control of his life or even freeing himself from a past that ought at the very least to render him impervious to the languid charms of Myra Viveash. In denying Emily and remaining in London with Mrs. Viveash, he has chosen merely to go through the motions of loyalty to a dead past: "In this white dress patterned with flowing arabesques of black she looked, he thought, more than ever enchanting. There had been times in the past. . . . The past leads on to the present. . . . No; but in any case she was excellent company" (*AH*, 204). Having rejected history, he resembles Bojanus to the extent that he has nothing to replace it with, while his advice to Myra Viveash—not to dwell on the past and his insistence that "the past is abolished" (*AH*, 209)—is doubly ironic coming after his capitulation on the basis of a past attraction to a woman epitomizing the limbo of modern historicism.

The seemingly endless taxi drive that dominates the closing chapters of *Antic Hay* is a culminating variation on the ubiquitous metaphor of random motion, an incrementally developed motif that includes the labyrinthine street plan of London as well as the aimless but frenetic peregrinations undertaken by so many of the characters. Early in the novel Myra Viveash complains, "Why was it that people always got involved in one's life? If only one could manage things on the principle of the railways! Parallel tracks—that was the thing" (*AH*, 100). Her desire for the rigid geometry of predetermined movement is a naive and self-stultifying version of Gumbril Senior's more sophisticated aspiration to redesign the street plan of London in order to harmonize its "senseless discords and . . . horrible disorder" according to the aesthetics of Wren (*AH*, 168). Like Emily, Gumbril's father is an anachronism, outside the flow of contemporary history and hearkening back to the ideal vision of an earlier age. Myra Viveash, on the other hand, is the embodiment of accident, chance, and the purposeless dynamism of modern London.

Myra Viveash's centrality within the narrative structure of *Antic Hay* is a function of her symbolic role. In "Time and the Machine," published in *The Olive Tree* thirteen years after the appearance of *Antic Hay*, Huxley, analyzing "the modern time-sense" (*OT*, 124), argued that a "new consciousness" had emerged in the course of modern history—one "purchased at the expense of the old consciousness" and associated with "urbanism," specifically with the anarchic energy of the "neon tubes" of "Piccadilly" (*OT*, 124). Just as Spandrell in *Point Counter Point* will identify himself with the Great War, claiming that it "was exactly like me" (*PCP*, 393), so Myra Viveash, confronted with the flickering neon lights of Piccadilly Circus, exclaims, "They're me. . . . Those things are me" (*AH*, 298). Like Spandrell, Myra Viveash is one of Huxley's exemplary figures, a distillation of the values, manners, and presiding conventions that inform and characterize a specific period. Thus Gumbril unwittingly identifies Myra Viveash's emblematic role when he responds to the pulsating "sky signs" of Piccadilly by defining them as "the epileptic symbol" of the prevailing unrest of "contemporary life" (*AH*, 297). Mrs. Viveash's empathy with the spasmodic kineticism of "their unceasing St. Vitus's dance" contradicts her earlier professed desire for the regularity of parallel tracks. Like her literary descendents, Lucy Tantamount of *Point Counter Point* and Mary Amberley of *Eyeless in Gaza*, she is essentially anarchic. Moving through *Antic Hay* like the carrier of some terrible disease, she accidentally, if no less decisively for that, intervenes in the lives of Gumbril Junior, Shearwater, and Lypiatt. Indeed, her structural role in each of these three related but distinct narrative lines is disruptive, crossing the path of each man as a present or former lover and associated with their failure to achieve order and "proportion" within both their emotional lives and professional careers. Shearwater, for example, sees her as a feral creature, avid and insatiable, pursuing him and reducing his life and work to a welter of fragments. At the novel's conclusion, his dilemma is vividly dramatized as he sits in the sanctuary of his laboratory astride a stationary bicycle, pedalling furiously in a physiology experiment but chiefly conscious of the spectre of Myra Viveash pursuing him through a wasteland. As part of the journey-motion motif, his bicycle excursion down "the nightmare road" (*AH*, 324) is an attempt to avoid the "horrible confusion" that he associates with Myra. Just as Gumbril will sacrifice the pastoral serenity of Emily to Myra's restless dynamism, Shearwater's "calm clarity" of scientific detachment is "shaken . . . to pieces" by Myra's violent intrusion into his placidly ordered existence (*AH*, 167). Huxley links Shearwater's farcical paralysis at the novel's conclusion with Gumbril's romantic obtuseness at its outset by means of the journey motif. As the experiment progresses, Shearwater traverses a mental landscape composed of "a lot of dirty rocks" (an echo of the empty plains crossed by Gumbril during his fantasy of Byronic pilgrimage in chapter one), advancing towards a goal symbolized by the dome of St. Paul's cathedral on a journey compounded equally of flight and pilgrimage. Acknowledging his need to "cage himself" from Myra, he pedals fiercely toward Wren's dome, only to be suddenly confronted by "the face of Myra Viveash" (*AH*, 325), who has arrived by taxi accompanied by Gumbril. Similarly, Casimir Lypiatt, equally the slave of Myra, mortified by her insulting characterization of his painting as reminiscent of "'Italian vermouth advertisements'" and deeply depressed by her rejection of him as a lover, commits suicide in his studio shortly after her arrival by taxi. The last thing he hears in the hall beyond his apartment is Myra's voice, an event corresponding to Shearwater's startled glimpse of her face in his laboratory. Theodore Gumbril's submission to Myra is equally devastating in that it sets him on a course of moral drift and spiritual paralysis far from his ostensible goal of "doing something about life" and at an even greater distance from the pastoral *otium* associated with Emily.

The elder Gumbril's room, harboring the immense architectural model of London, is an imaginative creation testifying to his intellectual vigor and social concern as well as the power of the past to inform the present. But the room is also a retreat, an ineffectual gesture that offers him an escape from the turbulence of London and a form of aesthetic relief from his customary projects as an architect. In this respect, the Wren-inspired model resembles Gumbril Junior's pastoral retreat with Emily, an experience that also seems to stand outside of time, delicately fabricated and equally vulnerable to the grosser pressures of "contemporary life." The failure of Gumbril Junior to sustain his relationships with Emily, like his father's decision to sell the model, suggests Huxley's unwillingness to introduce any beyond the most ephemeral solutions to the maze of urban London. Admittedly, Gumbril Senior's self-renunciatory act is inspired by his concern for Mr. Porteous's suffering, a disciplined moral decision that contrasts with his son's languid surrender to Myra Viveash. But in a wider sense both events are capitulations to the exigencies of modern history and "the new consciousness" emblematized in the anarchic restlessness of Myra Viveash and Rosie Shearwater.

The latter's role in the final chapters of *Antic Hay* anticipates, albeit in somewhat sketchy form, Huxley's later and more elaborate employment of sadomasochistic behavior as a symptom of social decadence. In this regard, Rosie Shearwater's erotic escapades constitute something more than a randomly inspired series of farcical encounters—a satirical progress in which her sexual life becomes increasingly reckless and violent. Early in the novel she is introduced as a frustrated and neglected wife, bored with her self-absorbed husband and swiftly seduced by Gumbril in his new disguise as the complete Rabelaisian man. Her second affair begins in an equally haphazard way, but it also registers a further decline as she surrenders to the blandishments of the more corrupt Mercaptan. Arriving at the latter's rooms on the mistaken assumption that they belonged to Gumbril, she discovers Mercaptan, who has just completed an essay on the history of the supposed medieval custom of the "Jus Primae Noctis, or Droit de Seigneur" (*AH*, 250). Mercaptan's "historical" exercise, like those of Gumbril's students in the opening chapter, is another minor variation on the theme of history; his essay with its erudite references to the "Council of Carthage" or the "baroque imagination of the seventeenth century" is little more than a frivolous debasement of history in the service of Mercaptan's vision of a "golden age" of universal sexual license (*AH*, 251). His rooms are filled with a collection of objects that define his attitude toward the "late, degenerate days" of postwar England (*AH*, 254), his white satin sofa playing host in his fancy to an historical ghost, the French novelist and satirist Crebillon the Younger. Mercaptan's "sacred boudoir" (*AH*, 252) is another Huxleyan burrow, a subjectively conceived response to the pressing realities of modern London filled with various aesthetic and historical items, including African masks, Chinese carvings, a medieval French Madonna, Italian medals, and a painting by Marie Laurencin. His collection is a tiny museum, and Mercaptan explicitly adopts the role of curator upon Rosie Shearwater's arrival:

> After tea Mr. Mercaptan played cicerone in a tour of inspection round the room. They visited the papier mache writing desk, the Condor fans, the Marie Laurencin, the 1914 edition of "Du Cote de chez Swann," the Madonna that was probably a fake, the Negro mask, the Chelsea figures, the Chinese object of art in sculptured crystal, the scale model of Queen Victoria in wax under a glass bell. (*AH*, 263–64)

History, particularly the "late, degenerate days" of the past decade, has been banished by Mercaptan and replaced by a "sympathetic" world where 1914 means Proust instead of the Great War, and the Victorian age has been safely reduced to a comic wax figurine. For Rosie Shearwater such an aesthetically sophisticated array is "the definitive revelation" (*AH*, 264).

Her surrender to the hedonistic Mercaptan is a prelude to Rosie's final submission, in chapter twenty, to the cynical masochist Coleman. Her brief sexual progress from Gumbril to Mercaptan and then to Coleman parallels Gumbril's equally erratic movement from his initial affair with Rosie to Emily and, finally, to Myra Viveash. *Antic Hay* is structured around these two degenerate plot-lines, and in both cases the final stage is the most hopelessly sterile. Arriving at Coleman's Rosie is confronted with a bloody spectacle that simultaneously shocks and intrigues her. Having been stabbed in the arm with a penknife by the prostitute Zoe and unable to staunch the wound, Coleman greets Rosie smeared with blood, melodramatically discoursing on the close relationship between physical disgust and erotic stimulation, drawing her attention to his blood-dabbed beard and threatening to embrace her. Fascinated by his professed sexual enjoyment of physical pain yet frightened by his violence, she attempts to escape, only to be seized and raped by Coleman—who is sadistically aroused by her uncontrollable weeping: "And she had cried, she had struggled, she had tried to turn away; and in the end she had been overcome by a pleasure more piercing and agonizing than anything she had ever felt before" (*AH*, 309). Coleman's parody of "Gladstone" (*AH*, 288) as he sadistically threatens to bite Rosie, Mercaptan's wax statue of Queen Victoria, and Myra Viveash's reference to Browning's "Last Ride Together" as she and Gumbril drive aimlessly through the streets of London, collectively register a sense of radical discontinuity with the past and perception of a present that can only be approached ironically. The "march of civilization" (*AH*, 312), according to both Myra and Gumbril, has transformed the inevitability of a new generation—that is, the bearing and rearing of children—into a tenuous hypothesis in which history and process have become "the most desperate experiment of all" (*AH*, 312).

Gumbril links Myra to ideas of darkness and anxiety-ridden walks through London at night. Early in *Antic Hay* he tells Shearwater of his affair with Myra, connecting the fact that he had "totally lost" his "head about her" with "walking up this dismal street one night, in the pitch darkness, writhing with jealousy" (*AH*, 85). His consciousness of "the darkness of the park" where he has just encountered Myra and its "vast" and "melancholy" perspective created by a string of "receding lights" (*AH*, 83) anticipates the later night journey through Piccadilly Circus and reinforces the reader's sense of Myra's representative role. Indeed, she herself is perceived for an instant—appropriately enough by a "taxi-man"—in what I would argue is a central iconic depiction of the novel's theme: "He watched her as she crossed the dirty street, placing her feet with a meticulous precision one after the other in the same straight line, as though she were treading a knife edge between goodness only knew what invisible gulfs" (*AH*, 88). Casimir Lypiatt, like Myra an emblematic figure—only more intricately explored—is equally isolated: "like a man who walks along a sinister road at night and sings to keep up his own spirits, to emphasise and magnify his own existence" (*AH*, 94). Huxley's characters cannot *progress;* their lonely night journeys circle endlessly within the "labyrinth" of modern London, at the center of which stands Myra Viveash immobilized by the trauma of the Great War and casting a similar spell over everyone with whom she comes into contact. Shearwater not only remains in place on his stationary bicycle but, in his final encounter with her, sees Myra as the moral antithesis of the values embedded in the architecture of Sir Christopher Wren. Lypiatt, who had hoped among other things to become a "Wren" (*AH*, 46), simply ends his life. Theodore Gumbril, whose father is an impassioned disciple of Wren, joins Myra on a "last ride" that passes Wren's cathedral on its way to no discernible destination within a world of increasing stasis and darkness.

Never comfortable with his repudiation of the historical past, Gumbril swings erratically between his own personal history in the form of a preoccupation with his "memoirs" or his projected "autobiography" (*AH*, 295) and the opposite extreme of his "cosmic history" (*AH*, 293)—an epic inventory of chaotically unrelated historicist facts and anecdotes he creates for the entertainment of Myra Viveash (who sleeps throughout his ruminations). The final juxtaposition of the "human symbol" of Wren's dome (*AH*, 327) and "the epileptic symbol" of Myra Viveash's neurotic milieu is an implied judgement on the course of modern history that can only be fully comprehended when placed in the context of Huxley's "historical philosophy"—in particular, his analysis of baroque-romantic values. Myra Viveash is a typical Huxleyan "inverse" romantic, closely related to an opposed but related figure, the traditional Shelleyan romantic represented in *Antic Hay* by Casimir Lypiatt. In Huxley's unfavorable diagnosis of contemporary life, the abandonment of moral principle is counterpointed by the sacrifice of aesthetic standards; the two are portrayed as psychologically linked. The strident romanticism and vitalism of Lypiatt is the counterpart of the moral and spiritual chaos emblematized in Myra Viveash, and it is no accident that the former will paint her portrait in a style that expresses their fundamental complicity. In the essays of this period, Huxley argued that apocalyptic vision or prophecy "is mainly interesting for the light it throws on the age in which it is uttered" because "prophecy is an expression of our contemporary fears and wishes." He adds: "so too, to a very great extent, is history—or at least what passes for history" (*ENO*, 108).

The connection between history, prophecy, and romanticism is the subject of both *Antic Hay* and, to a greater extent, *Those Barren Leaves*. In *Antic Hay* Bojanus is a prophet intent on denying even a muted apocalyptic end to history, while Casimir Lypiatt has identified prophecy with the prophet's mantle, confusing the professed role with the substance of attained vision. Gumbril Senior has achieved the vision but lacks the capacity to proclaim it, hiding it in a darkened room and eventually forced to surrender it to save his friend Mr. Porteous. Nevertheless, his icon of the prophetic artist "walking in peril among the still smouldering ruins" (*AH*, 171) of a London reduced to a wasteland is an ideal he never betrays; in terms of the journey motif, it is the sole image of rational advancement in the novel. Casimir Lypiatt, Huxley's archetypal romantic, is the exponent of an aesthetic diametrically opposed to Sir Christopher Wren's. This aesthetic merits our close attention as a result of its connection with Huxley's speculative interpretation of modern history and its continuing presence, in the form of an extensive pattern of references to apocalyptic vision in Huxley's third novel, *Those Barren Leaves*.

### 3. Prophecy and Piranesi in *Antic Hay*

The connection between baroque spectacle and romantic subjectivity forms a continuous thread in Huxley's early work, its first significant dramatization occurring in *Antic Hay*. In *Along the Road* Huxley maintained that "almost all baroque art and almost all the kindred romantic art of a later epoch are grotesque because the artists (not of the first order) are trying to express something tragic in terms of a style essentially comic" (*AH*, 174). Abjuring the disciplined restraint of Wren's art and laboring for illusory effects, the baroque-romantic style is always associated in Huxley's mind with both violently comic deformation and histrionic emotions. Casimir Lypiatt is a "grotesque" distillation of such a confused conflation of comic and tragic idioms. He is not, as Milton Birnbaum would have him, an endorsement of the "need for suffering" on the part of the artist[14]—a need that would be incomprehensible to Huxley's Wren. Lypiatt conceived of himself as a medium for the trumpeting imagination. Like Shelley (particularly in *Adonais*), he is fond of identifying himself with prophets and martyrs, including Cain, Christ, Prometheus, and—surprisingly—Wren as well. The reader is first introduced to Lypiatt as an artist dwelling at the end of "a long *cul de sac*" that, significantly, resembles the "entrance of one of Piranesi's prisons" (*AH*, 87).

In *On the Margin* Huxley cited Piranesi as a typical baroque artist, unrestrained and theatrical, while in "Variations on the Prisons," he saw in Piranesi's work an apt expression of modern *acedia* and anxiety.[15] Accordingly, the "Piranesian arch" (*AH*, 87) that spans the entrance to Lypiatt's studio is not a gratuitous architectural detail but rather the fitting emblem of a cultural dead end, an aesthetic impasse that Lypiatt, despite his consciousness of having a "mission" (*AH*, 45), will fail to recognize. Indeed, he eventually commits suicide in his studio. As a crusading Promethean he is associated with Veronese, a baroque master of *trompe l'oeil*, and is busily engaged in the creation of a "great Crucifixion . . . as big and headlong as a Veronese" (*AH*, 48). Referring to Shelley's *Adonais*,[16] Lypiatt insists that the man of genius "bears upon his brow a kind of mark of Cain" (*AH*, 48), and before his suicide in the final chapters, he refers to himself as a "dead Christ" (*AH*, 273), lacking only the evidence of the stigmata. His baroque "Crucifixion" is in essence a self-portrait of the guilt-cursed romantic visionary filled with self-pity and self-exultation. He "sees himself as a misunderstood and embittered Prometheus" (*AH*, 88), and as a self-proclaimed "prophet" (*AH*, 119) speaking with "the voice of Prometheus" (*AH*, 91), he chose as his text Shelley's "Ode to the West Wind"—a poem he repeatedly invokes as a romantic manifesto. Lypiatt's endorsement of "passion and feeling" (*AH*, 96), the "inenarrable emotions" that Huxley repudiated in Wordsworth, lead to his exuberant identifications with Shelley as he casts himself in the role of the poet's voice in the ode, rhapsodizing about the "great wind that is in me," and "the wild west wind" that he conflates with "life itself, its God" (*AH*, 94). For Lypiatt the wind is the divine afflatus, the Promethean spirit of the artist who "rushes on the world, conquers it, gives it beauty, imposes a moral significance" (*AH*, 95). And while he claims to be, "like Wren," an opponent of "abject specialisation" (*AH*, 46), he nevertheless repudiates the basis of the latter's art.

*Antic Hay* is Huxley's celebration of Wren's bicentenary, and in accordance with his definition of what a centenary should accomplish, the novel is a reappraisal "that we may see precisely where, in relation to [his] achievement, we stand at the present time." Throughout the novel Gumbril Senior is systematically associated with Wren's architecture and is explicitly placed in opposition to the baroque style represented by Piranesi. In chapter eleven Theodore Gumbril listens to his father expounding on his plans for the architectural renovation of London in which Wren's dome of St. Paul would be employed as the hub of a rationally ordered community: "Looking at him, Gumbril Junior could imagine that he saw before him the passionate and gesticulating silhouette of one of those old shepherds who stand at the base of Piranesi's ruins demonstrating obscurely the prodigious grandeur and the abjection of the human race" (*AH*, 177). In Gumbril Junior's mental picture, Piranesi's ruins are the charred remnants of old London after the great fire, a "disgusting chaos" (*AH*, 158) that his father, as a disciple of Wren, will reorder by means of an "intellectually ripened" aesthetic. However, Lypiatt, entrapped within one of "Piranesi's prisons" (*AH*, 87), prefers the baroque illusions of Veronese and eventually dies in his *cul de sac*.

In a letter to Mrs. Flora Strousse written on 9 May 1929, six years after the publication of *Antic Hay*, Huxley criticized one of her short stories dealing with an insane artist, insisting that "it wd [sic] have been more interesting, because more cruel, if it had been about a less extreme case— not a madman but somebody like B. R. Haydon, sane but with an infinite faith in himself completely unjustified by forty years of passionate and industrious self-expression. The fact that faith *can't* move mountains is one of the corner-stones of tragedy—also of comedy."[17] Huxley's portrait of Casimir Lypiatt is based in part on the life of the romantic painter Benjamin Haydon, an artist whose huge canvases and ambitiously conceived historical subjects failed to assure him the renown he so passionately sought. Haydon's suicide, like Lypiatt's, was a grotesquely nihilistic gesture that Huxley regarded as entirely characteristic of the romantic's inflation of both the artist's powers and, as an inescapable corollary, his expectations as well. What he was to remark in his essay "B. R. Hayden" published in *The Olive Tree* is equally true of Lypiatt: "Hayden was at all times . . . his own favourite hero of fiction" (*OT*, 248).

Lypiatt, then, is Huxley's satirical portrait of "romantic bardism" (*MN*, 282). Living under a Piranesian arch that "threw vivid lights and enormous architectural shadows" (*AH*, 87) exemplifying the baroque obsession with dramatic contrasts of light and dark, Lypiatt is a self-dramatizing illusionist who alternately adopts the highly emotional roles of outcast (Cain), savior (Christ), and visionary martyr (Prometheus). His "fantastic egoism" (*AH*, 46) leads him to believe he lives more intensely, feels more deeply, than the average man and that consequently his creations are somehow consecrated by a spirit of prophecy. But in *Jesting Pilate* Huxley rejected "prophetic visions" or the "New Jerusalems of prophecy" (*JP*, 141) that could only thrive on a romantic aesthetic conceiving of art as "something sacred" (*JP*, 264) and the artist as a "priest" (*JP*, 265) or "prophet of heroic grandeurs" (*AH*, 119).

In *Music at Night* Huxley condemned what he saw as the "new romanticism," a style that, like the suicidal Lypiatt, was "headed straight towards death" (*MN*, 220). The new or "reversed romanticism," as a counterpart of the "old romanticism," betrayed a self-destructive impulse because "its subject-matter [was] arbitrarily simplified by the exclusion of all the great eternal obviousness of human nature" (*MN*, 30). Fundamentally egocentric, the old romanticism involved an "exaggeration of the significance of the soul and the individual" (*MN*, 220), while the new was founded upon a profoundly inhumane "disparagement of spiritual and individual values" (*MN*, 216). Lypiatt embodies both tendencies, but his painting of Myra Viveash is a crucial and instructive example of the growing predominance of the latter. As a conventionally romantic artist who believed in "the aristocratic individual" (*AH*, 90) and based his work on "passion and feeling," he characteristically selected Promethean subjects—"Crucifixions, martyrs, and triumphs of great men" (*AH*, 96). But his portrait of Mrs. Viveash demonstrates his affinity with the "new romanticism" as well: "It was a stormy vision of her, it was Myra seen, so to speak, through a tornado. He had distorted her in the portrait, had made her longer and thinner than she really was, had turned her arms into sleek tubes and put a bright metallic polish on the curve of her cheek" (*AH*, 93). Lypiatt's deformative style is symptomatic of what Huxley refers to in the essays as "the Cubist dehumanization of art," a style marked by "a romantic . . . admiration for machines" (*MN*, 217). The term "romantic" had, by the time Huxley wrote "The New Romanticism," come to mean any style that, like the baroque, is "extravagant and one-sided (that is to say . . . romantic)," and "modern romanticism" was simply an inversion of the "romanticism of Shelley"; that is, romantic Prometheanism "turned inside out" (*MN*, 212). Thinking probably of Ferdinand Leger, or as Marovitz has suggested, of Modigliani, Huxley depicts Lypiatt's "stormy" portrait as the misguided attempt of a modern romantic "to reproduce the forms invented by engineers" (*MN*, 217). The "sleek tubes" and "bright metallic polish" represent a turning away from "reason and order" (*MN*, 219)—the same phrase Huxley used earlier to characterize the art of Sir Christopher Wren in *On the Margin*—while the "tornado" that shaped the portrait is the modern counterpart of Shelley's west wind.

Similarly, Lypiatt's poem "Look down, Conquistador" (*AH*, 95) is a parody of Keats's sonnet "On First Looking into Chapman's Homer," both celebrations of the artist's visionary power to discover new worlds metaphorically structured around the Spanish exploration and conquest of Central America. Lypiatt's "coming man" is the romantic Promethean whose "golden dream," like Keats's "Realms of gold," is a long-awaited apocalyptic revelation. Looking down from the Promethean heights, the artist as conquistador—like Keats's Cortez—experiences a sweeping vision, but significantly the poem ends abruptly in a manner that foreshadows Lypiatt's failure to realize his ambition and as a consequence his eventual suicide. Moreover, his obsession with the prophetic disclosure of a "reality more than human" (*AH*, 64) extends to the other characters but in an increasingly debased form. Rosie Shearwater, fascinated by "fortune-teller's prophecies" (*AH*, 249), views the egocentric aesthete Mercaptan as "the definitive revelation" (*AH*, 264). The old anti-Semite whom Gumbril Junior encounters on the train rants "like the prophet Jonah" (*AH*, 224), and Gumbril Junior feels like a "prophet in Nineveh" (*AH*, 80), where the only "revelation" (*AH*, 213) is the cacophony of jazz.

The basic components of Huxley's interpretation of romanticism, which his early novels were intended to expand and develop, involve two separate but related strands of thought that I wish to briefly summarize at this point. The first, Huxley's concept of the older Shelleyan romanticism, is often inextricable from the second, his view of modern or inverse romanticism. The former is rooted in a quest for a realm of nebulous transcendence inspired by the dreamy idealism and self-assurance of the romantic Promethean, which he sees as symptomatic of a monistic evasion of life and its essentially pluralistic diversity that gains strength from the promptings of some latent but frustrated desire. Its explanation, then, is fundamentally psychological. The major proponents of this form of romanticism are typically both emotionally and sexually thwarted; like Marjorie Carling and Maurice Spandrell of *The Point Counter Point* or Lilian Aldwinkle of *Those Barren Leaves*, they form a compensatory but extra-ordinarily energizing bias in favor of supernatural idealism and essentially fugitive Platonic "revelations." Like Maurice Spandrell, the "romantic, Piranesian" (*AR*, 93) Casimir Lypiatt commits suicide as a consequence of the circumstances in which he becomes entangled, circumstances involving a complicated matrix of sexual rejection and an admiration for Shelleyan subjective idealism. The baroque-romantic, then, is a divided man for Huxley, dominated by the "accursed antitheses" of mind and body and, like Maurice Spandrell or Lilian Aldwinkle, pursuing one (usually spirit or soul) to the vertiginous heights of Shelley's skylark or Wordsworth's Snowdon.

The second component, inverse romanticism, is the mirror image of the first but one in which the variegated, hallucinatory colors of, for example, Jeremy Pordage's Brighton Pavilion in *After Many a Summer Dies the Swan* are replaced by the monochromatic vacancy of Francis Chelifer's Gog's Court. Of the two forms of romanticism, Huxley wrote: "Personally, I have no great liking for either of the romanticisms. If it were absolutely necessary for me to choose between them, I think I would choose the older one. An exaggeration of the significance of the soul and the individual at the expense of matter, society, machinery, and organization, seems to me an exaggeration in the right direction" (*MN*, 220). In Huxley's view, what distinguishes inverse romanticism is its deliberate design of robbing man of his individuality, its collectivist outlook, and its alliance with modern technology. Where the Shelleyan romantics were "democrats and individualists," their modern counterparts, like Illidge in *Point Counter Point* or Mark Staithes in *Eyeless in Gaza*, champion "the great 'Collective Man'—that single mechanical monster who, in the Bolshevik millennium" (*MN*, 213), will supplant the conventional romantic's "individual with a soul" (*MN*, 219). To the dogmatic "materialism" of an Illidge or the admiration for machinery of a Lucy Tantamount, who, obsessed with aircraft, insists there is no room for the soul in the airplane and who falls in love with an engineer, Huxley adds what he regards as the arbitrarily oversimplified subject matter of the modern painter—particularly the cubist substituting "the machine, the crowd, the merely muscular body" for the "great eternal obviousness of human nature" (*MN*, 29–30). The road from Chaucer to Bernini and the baroque-romantic now stretches to Georges Braque and "the Cubist dehumanization of art" or Ferdinand Leger's "romantic . . . admiration for machines" (*MN*, 217), an aesthetic adopted by Casimir Lypiatt in his cubist-inspired painting of Myra Viveash in *Antic Hay*.

Huxley's interpretation of modern history aligns itself to a surprising degree with his ethical classification of styles in art. Rejecting Virginia Woolf's well-known observation that the mind of Europe had changed decisively around December 1910, he wrote in "Art and the Obvious" that "those who proclaim that human nature has changed since August 4th, 1914, are merely rationalizing their terrors and disgusts" (*MN*, 31). In "Accidie," however, he admitted the undeniable impact of "the appalling catastrophe of the War of 1914" and lamented that "in no century have the disillusionments followed on one another's heels with such unintermitted rapidity as in the Twentieth" (*OM*, 25). But Huxley claimed that modern history, like modern art, does not represent a shift so radical that it must be viewed as absolutely unique. Rather, he insisted on the centrality of the romantic period, arguing "that something has happened is surely simply history since 1789" (*OM*, 23). In his opinion, the War of 1914 had merely provided additional momentum for tendencies that had already come into play as a consequence of the revolution of 1789. The unfulfilled aspirations of the "Romantic Revival," particularly as they took the form of a quest for a fundamentally evasive apocalypse—

whether aesthetic, religious, or political—were responsible for the destructive cleavages of postwar society. The early twentieth century was for Huxley a period of cultural drift, in which modern values and ideals remained historically enmeshed with the obsolescent conventions of both a traditional romanticism and a significant variation in the form of a new "reversed" romanticism. The result was a malaise first defined in "Accidie" and more carefully analyzed in "The New Romanticism." This preoccupation with the baroque-romantic mode extends throughout the Huxley canon; it is founded on a perception of a society constantly jeopardized by its confused allegiances to worn-out conventions: "The activities of our age are uncertain and multifarious. No single literary, artistic, or philosophic tendency predominates. There is a babel of notions and conflicting theories. But in the midst of this general confusion, it is possible to recognize one curious and significant melody. . . . the tune of our modern romanticism" (*MN*, 212). In *Antic Hay* this tune is played with a vengeance by the histrionic Lypiatt, the "ridiculous actor of heroic parts" (*AH*, 274). In *Those Barren Leaves* its final exhaustion is embodied in both Francis Chelifer, who will climb the sacred mountain of English romanticism, Wordsworth's Snowdon; and in Lilian Aldwinkle, who will attempt to inspire Chelifer by introducing him to the mysteries of her baroque palace of art, the Cybo Malaspina.

## 4. Lilian Aldwinkle's Palace of Art: Historicism and the Baroque in *Those Barren Leaves*

In *Crome Yellow* Huxley confined his attack on both historicism and romantic subjectivity to the narrow dimensions of George Wimbush's country estate, while the novel was structured according to the conventional pastoral arc of withdrawal, transformation, and return. In *Antic Hay* the stage was further expanded to embrace the more inclusive setting of London, while the pastoral arc shrank to Theodore Gumbril's brief and fruitless trip in search of Emily. In Huxley's third novel *Those Barren Leaves*, the scene is again significantly enlarged, in this case to comprehend both modern European as well as ancient history, the pastoral arc being entirely displaced by a feverish linear journey through the Italian countryside towards the beckoning silhouette of St. Peter's cathedral (as opposed to St. Paul's in *Antic Hay*) and a deliberately open-ended conclusion. The structural echoes of the earlier novels help define the degree to which Huxley has pushed the boundaries of Wimbush's family history of Crome to accommodate a second and more universally representative family, "the lords of Massa Carrara" (*TBL*, 23) and their modern counterparts, the fascists of twentieth-century Europe. The increase in scope involved in such a movement from Crome to London and then to continental Europe is reflected in Huxley's preoccupation throughout the novel with medieval, Renaissance, and ancient history. Denis Stone's question in *Crome Yellow* concerning the challenge of reconstructing the jumbled "data" of Crome's history is transformed in *Those Barren Leaves* to Francis Chelifer's more urgent desire to find the means "to escape in 1924" (*TBL*, 93), a flight inspired by his growing apprehension of the essential decadence of "modern civilization" (*TBL*, 372).

In *Those Barren Leaves* Huxley's archetypal historicist is Lilian Aldwinkle, a woman who has literally purchased "history" and who looks to the past to provide a means of interpreting the present. In her quest for a durable source of value and a distinctly secular form of "apocalypse," she has eagerly embraced a past far more comprehensive and unstable than anything to be found in the pages of Wimbush's chronicle: "With the palace Mrs. Aldwinkle had purchased vast domains unmentioned in the contract. She had bought to begin with, the Cybo Malaspina and their history." Huxley adds that in doing so, she has "acquired a sister soul" in "Napoleon's sister, Elisa Bacciochi," who had once occupied the Cybo, as well as a family she believes comparable to "the Gonzaga, the Esti, the Medici, or the Visconti" (*TBL*, 18). Furthermore, she has acquired an artist-hero, the Renaissance painter "Pasquale da Montecatini," whose frescoes decorate the walls of the Cybo. Art history is a major motif in *Those Barren Leaves*, and vivid, often elaborate descriptions of Renaissance frescoes, Etruscan sculpture, and Roman mosaics alternate with references to—and detailed evocations of —both modern and baroque painting and architecture. This motif is designed as a commentary on the course of European history, but it also, at least at the Cybo itself, serves to define Lilian Aldwinkle's romantic sensibility, suggestively adumbrating her second role in the novel. In this request, she is more than simply a wealthy hostess such as Priscilla Wimbush of *Crome Yellow*. Like Casimir Lypiatt, she is a restless promoter of the imaginative life, particularly as it endeavors to realize unpossessable ranges of experience. As a woman of "romantic yearnings" (*TBL*, 185), she radically distorts her world "through the dense refractive medium of her imagination" and feverishly endorses Lypiatt's romantic Prometheanism. Leading the "higher life" (*TBL*, 60) on the heights of the Cybo, she is the inhabitant—or more precisely the prisoner—of an ivory tower. Like the poet Denis in *Crome Yellow*, who at the novel's conclusion is helplessly isolated in Crome's tower, gazing down at life in the form of the charity bazaar, Lilian clings to her belief in the artist as a superior being, insisting that "through art man comes nearest to being a god" (*TBL*, 60). In saving Chelifer, she believes that she has "rescued a poet from death" (*TBL*, 184), and in restoring him to the Cybo Malaspina, itself a baroque projection of her histrionic imagination, believes she will place him in the one setting where "he should gather . . . new inspiration" (*TBL*, 180). Like Lypiatt, she dramatizes her role, conceiving her relationship with her new guest in terms of a baroquely theatrical painting by Augustus John: "She saw herself standing there on the beach between sea and sky, and with mountains in the middle distance, looking like one of those wonderfully romantic figures who, in the paintings of Augustus John, stand poised in the meditative and passionate ecstasy against a cosmic background," while Chelifer lies "at her feet, like Shelley" (*TBL*, 180).

This ostentatious inflation of the imaginary painting is reflected in the Cybo itself, a world wholly defined by idealized history and romantic aesthetics. But Lilian, who searches forlornly for the "one supremely important, revealing, apocalyptic thing" (*TBL*, 63), is discouragingly inarticulate, having been endowed "with no power of self-expression," even in ordinary conversation unable "to give utterance to what she wanted to say." Her language is a muddle of "fragments of sentences" (*TBL*, 58), yet she searches untiringly for the means to "utter the significant word or think the one apocalyptic thought" (*TBL*, 64). Her quest for the one significant word, or what Wordsworth saw as the "Characters of the great Apocalypse" (the vision in the Vale of Gondo Huxley criticized in *Do What You Will*),[18] is also a pursuit of "the one word" that Byron despaired of achieving in *Childe Harold's Pilgrimage*.[19] The sardonic empiricist Cardan, in pursuit of a baroque sculpture, later discovers a statue of Byron, or "what in the imagination of a monumental mason of 1830 figured as a poet." But this "slenderer Byron" holds out a "square tablet" that, significantly, is "a blank" (*TBL*, 251), while later in the novel, "the house" of Byron is associated with "self-inflicted boredom" (*TBL*, 275). Mrs. Aldwinkle is a victim of romantic accidie, "a mixture of boredom, sorrow and despair" (*OM*, 22) that according to Huxley manifests itself in a desire to be "anywhere, anywhere out of the world" (*OM*, 22–23). Romantic accidie lies at the root of Huxley's treatment of romantic Prometheanism and its complementary baroque beguilement with the new and the marvellous. Lilian Aldwinkle's drifting peripatetic behavior is governed by a generalized anxiety that she has been "kept . . . away from the places where the exciting things were happening" (*TBL*, 16), a fear that reinforces her search for some kind of apocalyptic revelation.

The problem of narrative structure in *Those Barren Leaves* has occupied a number of Huxley's critics, most of whom appear to be united in their condemnation of the novel's thematic complexity. Most recently Keith May has described the book as comprised of "heterogeneous elements" that yield a fictive structure "less unified" than *Antic Hay* or *Crome Yellow*.[20] Laurence Brander finds it "strangely lengthened," padded out with digressive subplots and "much irrelevant material,"[21] while George Woodcock simply asserts that the novel "has several themes."[22] However, Peter Firchow argues that while the novel has "virtually no plot," it does exhibit "tight thematic unity,"[23] and Jerome Meckier discovers the organizing principle in the various love stories that display both "similarity in situation and simultaneity in action."[24] As both Firchow and Meckier have noted, Huxley has a more cogent and holistic grasp of his materials than has often been admitted, although I would argue that the unity of *Those Barren Leaves* also proceeds from a further but related source first defined in *Antic Hay* and the essays of *On the Margin*.

The plot of *Those Barren Leaves* centers initially on a social gathering of apparently heterogenous characters, including Miss Thriplow, a novelist; Lord Hovendon, a Guild Socialist; Mr. Falx, a labor leader; Irene Aldwinkle, Lilian Aldwinkle's niece; Cardan, an elderly social parasite; Calamy, a young eligible bachelor; and Francis Chelifer, an uninvited guest rescued from a boating accident by Mrs. Aldwinkle's party. Chelifer is an erstwhile poet who has cynically turned to minor journalism. The novel exhibits an intricately elaborate structure, divided into five parts yet essentially binary in form—the first three parts taking place at the Cybo Malaspina and its surrounding landscape, and the fourth and fifth section in the plains and hills of Umbria and Latium as the party journeys to Rome. Both sections constitute a structural pattern developing in consistent direction (from the Cybo, a Renaissance palace, to St. Peter's cathedral—two architectural symbols that symbolically bracket the narrative line of the novel), while all five parts are firmly yoked by means of a subtle manipulation of correspondences. Even the apparent asymmetry of part three, Chelifer's autobiographical text, is carefully integrated into the presiding imagistic configuration of the novel. The ascent of the Cybo to its crowning "temple," the climbing of Mt. Snowdon, the journey to St. Peter's—a third towering edifice—and finally the description of the mountains contemplated by Calamy at the novel's conclusion are parts of an incrementally developed pattern of correspondences. Similarly, the panoramic fresco of Cardinal Malaspina's apotheosis, the elaborately detailed Etruscan tomb murals, and the Roman mosaic carefully described by Chelifer also function to bind together the superficially diverse episodes of the novel. The structure is further reinforced by four ironically conceived "revelations":

Part I: An Evening at Mrs. Aldwinkle's

A. Principal works of art:
1. The Cybo Malaspina as a baroque edifice
2. Montecatini's fresco of Cardinal Malaspina's Apotheosis

B. Principal revelation: The ascent of the Cybo to the crowning "temple"

Part II: Fragments from the *Autobiography of Francis Chelifer*

A. Principal works of art:
1. Chelifer's autobiographical text
2. Wordsworth's *Prelude*
3. Chelifer's Caesarean lyrics

B. Principal revelation: The Ascent of Snowdon and the vision of Barbara Waters

Part III: The Loves of the Parallels

A. Principal work of art: The "marble effigy" of the Byronic poet of 1830 (*TBL*, 251)

B. Principal revelations:
1. Cardan's "visions of disease, decrepitude, death" (*TBL*, 218)
2. The unveiling of the Byronic sculpture

Part IV: The Journey

A. Principal works of art:
1. The Etruscan tomb murals
2. The Roman Mosaic

B. Principal revelations:
1. The illumination in the Etruscan tomb
2. The revelation of the futility of history
3. The various revelations of the significance of St. Peter's Cathedral

Part V: Conclusions

A. Principal work of art: Replacement of baroque-romantic art by the growing recognition of the intractable nature of reality

B. Principal revelations:
1. Calamy's meditation on molecular structure
2. Calamy's contemplation of the "shining peak" (*TBL*, 380)

The symbolic structure of *Those Barren Leaves* involves a gradual dilation of meaning through repeated motifs in which meaning tends to expand and reverberate throughout the superficially aberrant adventures, social gatherings, and retrospective meditations that interrupt the narrative sequence with increasing regularity. It is also evident that the novel is structured around a height-depression pattern, descending movements like Cardan's descent into the marshy plain of Marmora or into the Etruscan tumuli, or ascents to presumably sacred temples and the illuminating perspectives of mountain peaks. Keith May has shrewdly characterized the structure of *Those Barren Leaves* as evincing "something akin to a symphony, with breaks and changes of mood, rhythms, and melody," although he also argues that each of the episodes could easily stand independently of the others. As I shall show, while episodic on the surface, Huxley's third novel is organized with remarkable dexterity and poetic finesse; its nomadic characters and seemingly straying chapters arranged in accordance with a solidly conceived design.

The various characters and subplots of *Those Barren Leaves* are drawn together by means of skillfully interrelated motifs dealing with journeys, acting, and the possibility of reaching the threshold of some kind of final prophetic disclosure. All three of these motifs are elaborated within the more general context of Huxley's criticism of historicist illusions and baroque-romantic art. Indeed, they are symptomatic of a culture that has not freed itself of "the cult of the emotions" that "began in the nineteenth century" and its attendant quest for prophetic vision. Lilian Aldwinkle waits patiently for the one supremely important, revealing, "apolcalyptic thing" (*TBL*, 63), and like the youthful Francis Chelifer, she hopes for a "revelation" (*TBL*, 122) as a consequence of her ambition to "think the one apocalyptic thought" (*TBL*, 64). Mrs. Aldwinkle will fail to impose her "mythopoeic faculties" (*TBL*, 300) on a recalcitrant world, much as Chelifer's Shelleyan idealism "revealed . . . apocalyptically" (*TBL*, 130) what was in fact merely a self-imposed delusion. Mary Thriplow searches for "emotional revelations" (*TBL*, 266), while the "eloquently prophetical" Mr. Falx (*TBL*, 61), an embittered socialist, also confesses his willingness to play the "prophetic part" (*TBL*, 189). Even the idiot Grace Elver is busy "conjuring up fairy palaces" (*TBL*, 242), and her brother Philip boasts of his own sinister ability to "prophesy" (*TBL*, 235). Mrs. Aldwinkle's niece Irene looks "prophetically forward" (*TBL*, 335) to a new life apart from her aunt, who in turn provides Chelifer with an architecturally contrived "moment of revelation" (*TBL*, 170) at the Cybo, the counterpart of Chelifer's earlier and equally disappointing "divine revelation" (*TBL*, 122) on the summit of Wordsworth's Snowdon.

The symbolic setting for much of the action in the early chapters of *Those Barren Leaves* is the Cybo Malaspina. If as Huxley repeatedly argues, romanticism (old or new) is a matter of roles, posturings, and histrionics, then Mrs. Aldwinkle's villa is the most suitable stage for the enactment of such a "farce." Indeed, for Huxley it is the "comic," as opposed to the cosmic, lengths to which the romantic artists and poets were willing to go that most impressed him, and the Cybo is the concrete embodiment of "the grand theatrical flourish" so deeply and persistently admired by his romantics. The Cybo is a vast ensemble of gardens, stairways, and buildings surrounded by allegorical and mythological sculpture and designed to impress the visitor with its arcades that dramatically open onto complex architectural compositions. In concept and ambition, the Cybo evokes both "Versailles and Caserta," although on a much-reduced scale. Describing the characteristic effect of baroque architecture, Cardan is in fact sketching the murkily dramatic features of the Cybo: "Look how all the architecture of the period is conditioned by the need for display. The architect was there to make backgrounds for the incessant amateur theatricals of his employers. Huge vistas of communicating saloons to march down, avenues for processions, vast flights to do the Grand Monarch descent from the skies" (*TBL*, 26). Huxley took great care in his description of the villa, introducing it through the eyes of Chelifer in a series of fragmented glimpses through the trees as he approaches by car. The most prominent feature of the Cybo is one that Huxley repeatedly stresses and Chelifer perceives immediately. As the car approaches, he spies a bewildering accumulation of features that suddenly arrange themselves into a dramatic spatial sequence (characteristic of the baroque) in the form of "a great flight of steps, set between cypresses, mounting up past a series of terraced landings to a carved doorway in the centre of the long facade" (*TBL*, 168). At the center of the Cybo's complex web of corridors, arcades, and immense grounds crowded with statues is a symbolic pattern of ascent towards a sacred temple, a symbol of Promethean aspiration and baroque spectacle that will find its counterpart in Chelifer's autobiographical fragments.

The villa is composed of the gradual accretion of centuries of architectural ideas, but its most marked feature is the striving for dramatic effect by means of complex interwoven spaces. Mrs. Aldwinkle, who regards it as a "very fine specimen of early baroque" (*TBL*, 19), accompanies the unwilling Chelifer on a tour of the estate, where after walking through the house, they arrive at a "great quadrangle formed by an inner court surrounded on three sides by the villa and on the fourth by an arcade." Obsessed with the Cybo as a patrician dwelling, a museum of history, and a palace of art, Mrs. Aldwinkle leads Chelifer to the statue of one of the princes of Massa Carrara. "With the expression of one who is about to reveal a delightful secret," she excitedly ushers Chelifer into position at the foot of the statue and produces her "moment of revelation": "From the central arch of the arcade, a flight of marble steps climbed up to where, set against a semi-circle of cypresses, at the crest of the hill, a little round temple played gracefully at paganism . . . (*TBL*, 170). The architectural ensemble of statue, arcade, stairs, hill, and crowning temple is a baroque tableau that Chelifer repudiates as little more than one of the "pretty peep-shows" (*TBL*, 170) that were the hallmark of the baroque *trompe l'oeil* style. The Cybo, "infected by a touch of the baroque folie de grandeur," typifies the "stage houses" (*OM*, 181) that Huxley saw as a betrayal of Wren's aesthetic. Mrs. Aldwinkle's momentary apocalypse is a Piranesian vista, a complex of arches and flights of stairs, of "vaulted corridor" and tunnel that recur endlessly in Piranesi's engravings, where they typically arrange themselves in spatial sequences that conduct the eye towards dramatic culminations. It is a dynamic perspective that like Casimir Lypiatt's taste for Veronese, a master of *trompe l'oeil*, is rooted in what Huxley viewed as a radically debased style.

The theatrical character of the architecture, overwhelmingly evident to Chelifer, extends to the interior of the house as well. Mrs. Aldwinkle's own *trompe l'oeil* tendencies have transformed the "Saloon of the Ancestors," with its ceiling painting of "the rape of Europa" and a sculptured "group of marine deities" (*TBL*, 20) writhing furiously in its niche, into an artist's mecca; that is, into "what it had never been except in Mrs. Aldwinkle's fancy" (*TBL*, 23). Similarly, her niece Irene, whom Mrs. Aldwinkle is attempting to win over to her religion of art, is given a bedroom which had once been occupied by Cardinal Alderano Malaspina. The room is a setting for an elaborate historical fresco in the style of Veronese of the cardinal's "apotheosis" (*TBL*, 25)—a deification of the cardinal who sits as an allegorical symbol of the spirit of art surrounded by the "Nine Muses and three Graces" (*TBL*, 259). For Mrs. Aldwinkle, who believed that "through art man comes nearest to being a god," the *trompe l'oeil* apotheosis of the Cardinal is a suitably murky conflation of history, art, and religion embodying her belief that aesthetic creation is a lower form of mystical ecstasy.

If as Cardan would have it, the Cybo is a baroque stage for "incessant amateur theatricals" (*TBL*, 26), its occupants have clearly imbibed that spirit of the place. Mary Thriplow observes that "life tends to become a bit operatic" in Italy and throughout the novel eagerly plays the "part assigned to her" (*TBL*, 52). She regards her affair with her dead cousin as a "comedy" (*TBL*, 82) and cultivates a role more suitable to a "comic opera by Offenbach" (*TBL*, 169). Mr. Cardan describes his confrontation with Mr. Elver as a "queer pantomime" (*TBL*, 231) leading first to a "tragedy" that in turn eventually reveals itself as a "farce . . . in the worst of bad taste" (*TBL*, 334). Miss Thriplow maintains that "those in real life perform as much for an inward as an outward gallery" (*TBL*, 264), a judgement corresponding to Cardan's cynical observation that in life it is "only the acting that matters" (*TBL*, 337). Similarly, Mrs. Aldwinkle falls in love with her idea of Chelifer and consequently plays "the part assigned to her" (*TBL*, 326), shocking Chelifer by her assumption of a role that is "not in the programme" (*TBL*, 327). In short, the Cybo is a stage-setting designed to symbolize the universal "love of a show" (*TBL*, 29), in which Huxley skillfully manages to integrate the themes of baroque-romantic aspiration and its fundamental insincerity, its propensity for self-dramatization and artifice.

The model for the Cybo was probably the baroque monastery of Montesenario visited by Huxley in 1923 and carefully described in *Along the Road*. Perched on a hill like a "little New Jerusalem" and harboring a statue of a saint in the throes of visionary ecstasy, it is evoked in a manner that foreshadows the architectural composition of Lilian Aldwinkle's palace of art:

"We climbed on. . . . And now at last we were at the gates of the heavenly city. A little paved and parapeted platform served as a landing to the flight of steps that led up into the heart of the convent. In the middle of the platform stood a more than life-sized statue of some unheard-of saint. It was a comically admirable piece of eighteenth-century baroque. Carved with coarse brilliance, the creature gesticulated ecstatically, rolling its eyes to heaven. . . . the heavenly city was a handsome early baroque affair with settecento trimmings and additions." (*AR*, 76–77)

The dramatically elaborate features of the Cybo's exterior extend to the interior of the house as well, concentrating with special intensity in the fresco that covers the walls of the room in which Mrs. Aldwinkle has installed her niece:

Round her, on the walls of the enormous room which had once been the bedchamber of the Cardinal Alderano Malaspina, fluttered an army of gesticulating shapes. Over the door sat God the Father, dressed in a blue crepe de Chine tunic and enveloped in a mantle of red velvet, which fluttered in the divine afflatus as though it had been so much bunting. His right hand was extended; and in obedience to the gesture a squadron of angels went flying down one of the side walls towards the window. At a prie-Dieu in the far corner knelt Cardinal Malaspina, middle-aged, stout . . . The Archangel Michael, at the head of his troop of Principalities and Powers, was hovering in the air above him, and with an expression on his face of mingled condescension and respect—condescension, inasmuch as he was the plenipotentiary of the *Padre Eterno*, and respect, in view of the fact that His Eminence was a brother of the Prince of Massa Carrara—was poising above the prelate's head the red symbolic hat that was to make him a Prince of the Church. On the opposite wall the Cardinal was represented doing battle with the powers of darkness. Dressed in scarlet robes he stood undaunted on the brink of the bottomless pit. (*TBL*, 258)

This detailed evocation of a Renaissance fresco serves a number of purposes in the novel. As an elaborate historical exhibit, it is part of the substance of history in which Mrs. Aldwinkle has immersed herself, reinforcing the atmosphere of the Cybo as a memorial to a superficially alluring past. The fresco appears to define the line of cleavage between past and present in that the celebration of Cardinal Malaspina's apotheosis was only possible within a sacramentally conceived universe, a world both hierarchically ordered and informed by a divine power. But the ostentatious display of the Cardinal's elevation is a pointedly satirical panorama that finds its contemporary reflection in Mrs. Aldwinkle's search for the crowning revelation. A fresco is, as Huxley was to observe in *The Devils of Loudun*, a product of "the prevailing thought-pattern" of its age. More important, it serves to dramatize a second feature of Huxley's philosophy of history, his belief that in the midst of a cultural "frame of reference" that in the course of history has "changed . . . out of all recognition," it is possible to perceive in "the personages of other times and alien cultures" an enduring human nature—"our all too human selves" (*DL*, 274). Accordingly, the Cardinal's floridly recorded aspirations are a constant factor at work in human history, emblematizing a deeper baroque-romantic continuity linking past to present and the Cardinal's apocalyptic elevation to Lilian Aldwinkle's romantic ambitions.

The fresco also includes "a carefully painted view of the Malaspina palace" as well as a further elaboration of the Cardinal's role: "In the wall space over the windows the Cardinal's cultured leisures were allegorically celebrated. Nine Muses and three Graces, attended by a troop of Hours, reclined or stood, or danced in studied postures; while the Cardinal himself, enthroned in the midst, listened to their conversation and proffered his own opinions without appearing to notice the fact that all the ladies were stark naked" (*TBL*, 259). Mrs. Aldwinkle aspires to such a role of patron of the arts and, like the Cardinal, remains oblivious to the nakedness of the muses, the aesthetic sterility of her Shelleyan poet Francis Chelifer, or more crucially the dangers inseparable from too naive a faith in the proffered gifts of Clio, the muse of history. The final satiric touch is provided by Mrs. Aldwinkle's niece Irene, who "in the midst of the Cardinal's apotheosis and entirely oblivious to it," sits on her bed, "half undressed," sewing "her underclothes" (*TBL*, 259).

The accommodating mutuality of self and history exists only in Mrs. Aldwinkle's hectic imagination. As she envisions a Renaissance banquet served in the historical "Saloon of the Ancestors" (*TBL*, 22), her "enthusiastic imagination" transforms it into a symposium of medieval and Renaissance figures including a chronological mélange of Acquinas, Dante, Peter of Picardy, Boccaccio, Pico della Mirandola, Michelangelo, and Galileo. Her endeavor "to revive" a world of "ancient glories" (*TBL*, 22) is satirically undercut by Huxley, who weighs the balance against Mrs. Aldwinkle by permitting the illustrious guests to converse only about absurdities, an inventory of bizarre notions including hermaphroditic Hyaenas, Platonic mistresses, discarded astronomical concepts, the genealogy of the gods, the kabbala on the doctrine of the Trinity, and the possibility of predicting the future. Equally significant, Huxley not only cocks a knowing snook at the "great man" theory of history[25] but also places immediately after Mrs. Aldwinkle's historical fantasy a detailed description of the Malaspina family busts chronologically arranged in niches high in the walls of the Saloon of the Ancestors. Collectively, the busts record the increasing degeneration of the family: "And as marquess succeeded marquess and prince, prince, an expression of ever profounder imbecility made itself apparent on the faces of the Ancestors. The vulture's nose, the formidable jaw of the first robber marquess transformed themselves by gradual degrees into the vague proboscides of ant-eaters, into criminally prognathous deformities. The foreheads grew lower with every generation, the marble eyes stared ever blanklier and the look of conscious pride became more and more strongly marked on every countenance" (*TBL*, 23). This lapidary chronicle of the Malaspina family is designed to dramatize the distance between historical reality and historicist illusion. Mrs. Aldwinkle's version is, in Cardan's words, "history by some master of fiction" (*TBL*, 304). It resembles Wimbush's Cromean chronicle in that it records a process of psychological aberration and looks forward to the history of the Tantamount family in *Point Counter Point*, where the theme of psychological decadence assumes greater prominence and detail.

In *Those Barren Leaves* the concept of historical progress, contemporary history, and Huxley's notion of historical undulations come together in the various conversations of Cardan, Chelifer, and Calamy. Despite his conscious recognition of the subtle affinity between "history" and "fiction" (*TBL*, 304), Cardan shares Aldwinkle's tendency both to simplify and idealize the past. Like Lilian, who worships art, he hopes to discover "a chunk of a bas-relief designed by Giotto" that he can "fall down and worship," and when he turns to history, especially "the one kingdom one would like to live in—the kingdom of ancient Greece," he can only envision it "purged of every historical Greek that ever existed" and "colonized out of the imaginations of modern artists, scholars and philosophers" (*TBL*, 205). Cardan's assessment of the past is a consequence of his fear of the present, yet he differs from Mrs. Aldwinkle, who in spite of the graphic evidence surrounding her, remains oblivious of the historical reality of the Malaspina family. Cardan, however, consciously embraces an historical fiction, arguing that "in such a world one might live positively, so to speak—live with the stream, in the direction of the main current—not negatively, as one has to now, in reaction against the general trend of existence" (*TBL*, 206). Cardan, then, is obviously conscious of the intellectual motivation underlying his historicist values. Furthermore, while he is the chief critic of the baroque-romantic aesthetic in *Those Barren Leaves*, he also confesses his admiration for the baroque style and is the first character in Huxley's novels to invoke, however faintly, Huxley's metaphor of historical undulations or trends. However, his active opposition to "the general trend" of contemporary history and his sardonic dismissal of "romanticism" and "the seventeenth-century baroque style" (*TBL*, 207) does not vindicate his misplaced dedication to an historicist fabrication, a "main current" of historical development that he conceives of as somehow dammed up in the imaginary Greek past.

Calamy's response to history contrasts sharply with Cardan's. Indeed, it marks an advance on the latter's calculated misrepresentation of Greek history, just as Cardan's conscious acknowledgement of his historicist bias is a step beyond Lilian Aldwinkle's unwitting allegiance to the annals of the Malaspina past. Calamy welcomes the contingency of the present, neither tempted by historicist nostalgia nor interested in ideological hypotheses: "I don't see that it would be possible to live in a more exciting age. . . . The sense that everything's perfectly provisional and temporary—everything from social institutions to what we've hitherto regarded as the most sacred scientific truths—the feeling that nothing, from the Treaty of Versailles to the rationally explicable universe is really safe, the intimate conviction that anything may happen, anything may be discovered—another war, the artificial creation of life, the proof of continued existence after death—why, it's all infinitely exhilarating" (*TBL*, 34). Cardan, however, remains apprehensive to the "insecure and unprosperous peace" of the early years of the Versailles Settlement and looks regretfully back to his youthful faith in "Mr. Gladstone" and Victorian notions of "progress" (*TBL*, 35). History offers him little solace or security, while he shares with Chelifer a number of misgivings concerning the present—in particular, the dangers of twentieth-century nationalism and the threat of universal intellectual mediocrity encouraged by the "modern educated democratic state" (*TBL*, 372).

Chelifer's philosophy of history superficially resembles that of Mr. Bojanus in *Antic Hay*. Conscious of the disparity between the "later age" of the 1920s and "Shelley's days" (*TBL*, 92)—a period when the Viareggio was uncluttered, free of tourists and "the Grand Hotel"—he observes: "In Shelley's days, when the coast was all but uninhabited, a man might have had some excuse for forgetting the real nature of things"; but as "a man of the present generation, brought up in typical contemporary surroundings" (*TBL*, 92), the unhampered idealism of the romantic poet is necessarily displaced by the cynicism of the modern reverse romantic, in this case a sterile Pyrrhonist wholly dominated by his desire to discover a way "to escape in 1924" (*TBL*, 93). I shall turn to Chelifer's anti-Wordsworthian autobiography momentarily. For the present it is sufficient to note that Cardan, Chelifer, and Calamy each exemplify a specific attitude towards history and historicism. Both Cardan and Chelifer are, like Mrs. Aldwinkle, either tempted by the past or, even when they recognize the futility of the attempt in Chelifer's words "to escape in time" (*TBL*, 94), are unable to imitate Calamy in adjusting to the world of the post-Versailles Settlement. Calamy will eventually discover a different kind of "historical fact" (*TBL*, 370), but Chelifer remains enmired in his own personal past and (like Bojanus in *Antic Hay*) critical of Godwinian and Shelleyan meliorism. He argues that history engenders only panic; in essence, it is simply a chronicle of gradually diminishing hopes: "To escape, whether in space or time, you must run a great deal further now than there was any need to do a hundred years ago when Shelley boated on the Tyrrhenian and conjured up millennial visions. . . . And the millennium which seemed in the days of Godwin not so very remote has receded further and further from us, as each Reform Bill, each victory over entrenched capitalism dashed yet another illusion to the ground" (*TBL*, 93). Indeed, Chelifer goes even further, denying not only the coherency of the past but also the existence of any "reason to suppose that there is going to be a future at all" (*TBL*, 94). Chelifer's intellectual paralysis, Cardan's controlled but sardonic skepticism, and Lilian Aldwinkle's romantic historicism are contrapuntal variations on the theme of history—a discordant music that finds its most comic cacophony in the conversations at Chelifer's boarding house, Gog's Court. There the idealized Renaissance symposium envisioned by Mrs. Aldwinkle finds its modern counterpart, a vulgar babble of lower middle-class nationalism, racism, and political cliches directed against the "Huns," the "Yanks," the Indians, the Irish, and the "working class" (*TBL*, 112–13). For Chelifer the world bequeathed by Godwin and Shelley offers no social consensus rising above either historicist illusion or political irrationality. His longing to escape what he sees as an onward drift universally mistaken for social and moral "progress" (*TBL*, 107) finds no outlet in 1924 beyond a cynical surrender to what Huxley calls an "enclave" of "non-historicity" (*CE*, 232), the "void" of "nothingness" (*TBL*, 106–7) emblematized by Gog's Court itself.

In *Those Barren Leaves* the symbolic significance of the Cybo Malaspina is carefully developed in relation to a countervailing architectural setting, Gog's Court—a lower-class boarding house that in the *Fragments from the Autobiography of Francis Chelifer* is celebrated as "the navel of reality" (*TBL*, 98). The *Fragments* is a loosely structured *Bildungsroman*, or more accurately a parodic version of a romantic *Kunstlerroman*,[26] based on Wordsworth's *Prelude* but designed to move in an opposite direction in keeping with Chelifer's role as a "reversed sentimentalist" (*TBL*, 371). It closely parallels *The Prelude* in its choice of subjects. Like Wordsworth, Chelifer records his childhood, his university years, his ascent of Mount Snowdon, his experiences of war in France, his flirtation with political violence as an "ardent revolutionary" (*TBL*, 132) and a "democrat" (*TBL*, 86), his crisis as lover and artist, and finally his revelation of "the heart of reality" at Gog's Court (*TBL*, 108). Consequently, and contrary to what Keith May has argued, the *Fragments* is not a pointless digression that raises "the technical problem of how to attach the beliefs and life-story of Chelifer to a comedy set in Italy."[27] Identified with both Wordsworth and Shelley, Chelifer is the romantic Lilian Aldwinkle's accomplice. Their accidie proceeds from similar sources, and as Lilian falls in love with Chelifer, who as a result is forced to hide from her, they become their own nemeses, punishing one another for their mutual sterility. Mrs. Aldwinkle loves not Chelifer but an idea, a product of her baroque-romantic imagination, while Chelifer, "lacking a native enthusiasm for Love" (*TBL*, 323), avoids human relationships, preferring to passively "slide" through life. As romantic and "inverse romantic," they are in Huxley's eyes superficially opposed but intrinsically identical, much as the Cybo Malaspina is the obverse of Gog's Court.

Rather than repudiating the blankness of life as it is conceived at Gog's Court, Chelifer actively embraces it as the only avenue to truth—as far removed from the exclusive idealism of the Cybo Malaspina as he can make it. Located in "Fetter Lane" as an inhabitant of Gog's Court, Chelifer is a reversed Prometheus who has deliberately sought out his place of bondage. Obsessed with the idea of Shelley, he nevertheless repudiates the latter's "millennial visions" (*TBL*, 93) as well as Calamy's belief in a "realm of Absolute Art" (*TBL*, 99). The recovery of life's meaning is for Chelifer somehow connected with a surrender to the "void" (*TBL*, 106), to the "one unceasing slide through nothing" (*TBL*, 108), the origins of which are traced in the autobiographical fragments.

Like Mrs. Aldwinkle, Chelifer suffers from "extravagant spiritual cravings," yet he remains a cynical dilettante, reading "a page of Wittgenstein" and playing "a little Bach" in the midst of a "monotonous and tedious" existence (*TBL*, 85). The autobiographical *Fragments* records the two formative experiences that have contributed to his nihilistic passivity, satirizing along the way Wordsworth's doctrines of the spots of time, of nature, and of the poet as prophet. The *trompe l'oeil* "moment of revelation" engineered by Mrs. Aldwinkle, the romantic muse of the Cybo, finds its earlier and more decisive counterpart in the *Fragments* when the youthful Chelifer ascends Mount Snowdon with his "Wordsworthian" father who "knew most of the *Prelude* by heart." Climbing to the top of Snowdon, "gazing at the astonishing landscape" (*TBL*, 121), and listening with wonder to his father's quotations from "Tinturn Abbey," Chelifer rapturously surrenders to what "seemed an oracle, a divine revelation" (*TBL*, 122). But like his ascent into the baroque spatial sequences of the Cybo, his experience remains vague and elusive. All he remembers is the animal appetite of his father, who descending the mountain and sniffing the air, cries out, "Onions" (*TBL*, 122). This is an ironic version of Mrs. Aldwinkle's "significant word," the one apocalyptic utterance that the Cybo is designed to inspire and enshrine. Chelifer cannot shake off this memory, and just as Wordsworth's *Prelude* was intended to affirm the renovative power of memory, the imagination, and the abiding reality of love, Chelifer's autobiography founders on precisely these same concepts.

The longer fragment dealing with the Barbara Waters affair is dextrously handled by Huxley as a further development of Chelifer's dreamy romanticism. He is hardly conscious of Barbara as a human being but instead, like Mrs. Aldwinkle, pursues an elusively nebulous phantom of his own creation, always associating Barbara with fire (the romantic emblem of the imagination) and Promethean vision, as a consequence of having first encountered her where "fire-bearing hands" moved round "a pyre" and "a new small universe" was "suddenly created" (*TBL*, 129). In *On the Margin* Huxley had criticized Wordsworth for erecting "a whole cosmogony" on the basis of an obsession with "inenarrable emotions." Now Chelifer proceeds to do the same thing as "the leaping flame" reveals "apocalyptically" what he insists is "the embodiment of life itself," an image of "an intense and secret and unutterable happiness" (*TBL*, 130–31). He sees Barbara as an enigmatic symbol in the midst of alternating light and darkness, a typically baroque image, "flushed, bright and with an air of being almost supernaturally alive in the quivering, changing light of the flames" (*TBL*, 130). She is also transformed by Chelifer's hectic fancy into an emblem of the superiority of intuition to mere intellect: "I felt that I ought to have known that she wouldn't like reading. After all, what need was there for her to read? When one is life, one has no use for mere books" (*TBL*, 132). Chelifer's idealization of Barbara Waters explains the title of the novel, taken from 'The Tables Turned" where Wordsworth renounced books as mere "barren leaves." Thus Chelifer, in spite of his experience on Snowdon, is still dealing in "Wordsworthian formulas" (*TBL*, 122) and ruefully confesses that he had loved Barbara only "as a symbol" (*TBL*, 190). Like the inarticulate Mrs. Aldwinkle's inability "to give expression to what she wanted to say" or the statue of Byron holding a blank tablet, Barbara Waters' imputed superiority to "mere books" is another strand in an interlacing pattern of references to Huxley's view of the romantic belief in the supremacy of emotion or intuition over reason and intellect. However, for Huxley it is not books that are barren but rather the Sybilline leaves of romantic prophecy. The title, then, is intentionally ironic, turning back on Wordsworth rather than endorsing the glib generalizations of 'The Tables Turned."

With her mysterious expression of secret joy, Barbara becomes consolidated in Chelifer's mind as a Wordsworthian spot of time, "a memory of a kind of symbolic loveliness" (*TBL*, 135) that he retained for years. This radiantly aureoled vision of "profound and lovely mysteries" somehow "incarnate in one face" (*TBL*, 140), like Wordsworth's revelation of the "one face" in the valley of the Gondo, is a projection of Chelifer's "spiritual cravings": "I had not yet learned to reconcile myself to the fact that Barbara's higher nature was an invention of my own, a figment of my proper imagination" (*TBL*, 142). Chelifer's faith in Barbara's "higher nature" (like Mrs. Aldwinkle's "higher life" at the Cybo) is his last illusion. When it shatters, he becomes—like Lypiatt of *Antic Hay* and Maurice Spandrell of *Point Counter Point* (both repeatedly associated with Shelley)—intensely suicidal, cherishing a "little-hand grenade" (*TBL*, 146) in a hat box and fantasizing about mass-murder. Huxley underscores Chelifer's irrational submission to Barbara as a kind of romantic muse by means of Hans Baldung Grien's "Aristotle and Phyllis," an engraving also cited by James Joyce in *Ulysses:*[28] "There is a German engraving of the sixteenth century . . . which represents a naked Teutonic beauty riding on the back of a bald and bearded man, who she directs with a bridle and urges on with a switch. The old man is labelled Aristotle" (*TBL*, 147). His idealization of Barbara has reduced him "to a state of abjection at her feet" (*TBL*, 148), just as later in Mrs. Aldwinkle's imagination he will lie "at her feet, like Shelley" (*TBL*, 180). But after his disillusionment with Barbara Waters, Chelifer will reject Mrs. Aldwinkle and the "old romanticism" embodied in the Cybo Malaspina and embrace instead the "abyss" (*TBL*, 108) of Gog's Court. Shelley, the Cybo, and the possibility of a Promethean vision of Shelley's "Platonic eternity" are contemptuously dismissed as an escape "into the ideal" (*TBL*, 94). Indeed, he encounters Mrs. Aldwinkle at precisely the point at which he admits "I had no right to Shelley" (*TBL*, 153). Mrs. Aldwinkle, "living inside of one of Shelley's poems" (*TBL*, 92), retreats into the Cybo and takes Chelifer with her. Both fear "the pointless landscape" of a world that resists their naively ideal formulations, and as a consequence they express themselves in acts of regression or withdrawal, seeking out sharply demarcated sanctuaries like the Cybo Malaspina or Gog's Court that are really outward extensions of their inner fears, metaphors for the "state of mind" (*OM*, 25) that Huxley defined as romantic accidie. In Calamy's words, "the bad principle is the same in both cases—an excessive preoccupation with what is illusory" (*TBL*, 371).

Chelifer's poems are obliquely symptomatic of his intellectual and aesthetic dilemma. At first glance, a sequence of poems on the Roman Caesars would appear to be at a far remove from the sordid "reality" of Gog's Court, where after his final disillusionment at the hands of Barbara Waters, Chelifer eagerly embraced "the difficult art of exclusive concentration on the relevant." Yet even at this stage in his life, he is busy casting his resentments and perversely subjective inclinations into erudite molds aimed in part at defining his own baroque-romantic impulse as well as his view of classical history—a theme further elaborated later in the novel in his analysis of the historical meaning implicit in the Roman mosaic in the Lateran Museum. The first lyric in the unfinished sequence appropriately inspired by a baroque painting is entitled "Caligula crossing the bridge of boats between Baiae and Puteoli. By Peter Paul Rubens (b. 1577; d. 1640)" (*TBL*, 123). The poem evokes a vast canvas, a composition whose historical drama and allegorical complexity would have appealed to Casimir Lypiatt of *Antic Hay*. The Caligula lyric is the first in a series of meditations on Promethean figures whose energies and aspirations have in "romantic" fashion imposed themselves on their surrounding worlds:

> And they have filled the vacant skies
> With waltzing Gods and Virtues, set
> The Sea Winds singing with their shout.
>
> (*TBL*, 123)

Bearing in mind that the Caligula poem created by Chelifer celebrates a painting created by another artist, Rubens, whose allegorical meaning in Chelifer's eyes proclaims the inspired power of "Caesar's lifted fist," it thus becomes a series of reflecting mirrors in praise of Promethean power, in particular the power of "Beauty, like conscious lightning" to transform Caligula into a "God." The Nero lyrics continue to develop and augment this theme. Chelifer celebrates Nero as a type of the artist, declaring his superiority to Christ and identifying his art with divinity:

> Christ died, but living Nero turns
> Your mute remorse to song; he gives
> To idiot fate eyes like a lover's,
> And while his music plays, God lives.
>
> (*TBL*, 127)

In retrospect, Chelifer regards his incomplete sequence as a failure, the lyrics fundamentally spurious, governed by "romantic and noble sentiments" (*TBL*, 127) and, with the sole exception of the Tiberius poem, devoid of the epistemological reductiveness the older Chelifer has come to value.

Chelifer's romantic pilgrimage is a spiritual journey that illuminates the structure of *Those Barren Leaves* by drawing the reader's attention to the centrality of the journey motif. All of the characters are seeking some form of "revelation," and all are drawn into a final hectic car race for Rome. Miss Thriplow pursues Calamy, hoping to achieve an authentic emotional relationship; Lilian Aldwinkle chases Chelifer in her desire to possess poet and lover in one; Cardan hopes to marry the idiot Grace Elver and finally realize his goal of financial security; Mr. Falx journeys to his socialist convention; Hovenden pursues Irene; and Calamy hopes to escape his increasing sense of intellectual and spiritual despair.

Huxley achieves closure in *Those Barren Leaves* mainly by stressing the theme of apocalyptic revelation but also by placing this quest firmly in the context of history. The journey to Rome finds all of the characters "dizzily switchbacking up and down the periods of history" (*TBL*, 286), moving rapidly through a landscape that at every turn raises new perspectives on either the irrelevancy of the past or, more important, evidence of a sinister continuity between past and present. The journey through "Umbria and Latium" (*TBL*, 286) is a museum tour, where "Poussin's ideal of the world revealed itself," a classical and Renaissance past composed of Hadrian's villa and Coliseum, the forum of Trajan, the frescoes of Filippo Lippi at Spoleto, and the Sistine Chapel. The resemblance between the Cybo Malaspina and the tour of "historical periods" is suggestively adumbrated as they drive past "a little city of colonnades and cupolas and triumphal arches" (*TBL*, 290), an architectural composition reminiscent of the Malaspina villa itself. Mrs. Aldwinkle and her guests are travelers in a territory of irony and complexity—irony at the Etruscan tombs and complexity at St. Peter's Cathedral. The brief visit to "the sacred city, the Tarquinii of the Etruscans," involves an archaeological exploration of a "necropolis" (*TBL*, 308) whose tumuli they enter prior to their arrival in Rome. As a significant stage in their pilgrimage, it is described in terms of a movement through "geological time" as well as "the Middle Ages" (*TBL*, 309) while they descend through layers of archaeological excavation in order to confront an historical apocalypse. When the guide raises his lamp, a vision of color and form suddenly shimmers before them:

Called magically into existence by the bright white light, a crowd of gaily coloured forms appeared on the walls of the vault in which they were standing. Set in front of conventionalized trees, a pair of red-brown wrestlers with Egyptian eyes and the profile of the Greeks who disport themselves round the flanks of the earliest vases were feeling for a hold. On either side of them, beyond the trees, stood two couples of long-legged black horses. Above them, in the segment of a circle between the upper line of this band of paintings and the vaulted roof, a great leopard lay couchant, white-skinned, with a pattern of black spots arranged like those on the china dogs and cats of a later age. On the wall to the left they were feasting; red-brown Etruscans reclined on couches; porcelain white women, contrasting as voluptuously with their tanned companions as the pale, plump nymphs of Boucher with their brown pastoral lovers, sat by their sides. With hieratic gestures of mutual love they pledged one another in bowls of wine. On the opposite wall the fowlers were busy—here with slings, there with nets. The sky was alive with birds. In the blue sea below they were spearing fish. . . . The vaulted roof was painted with chequers, red, black and white. (*TBL*, 305–6)

The Etruscan fresco is a detailed Huxleyan set piece intended to be contrasted with the similarly amplified Renaissance fresco painted by Pasquale da Montecatini for the Cybo Malaspina. As elaborately particularized as the Cardinal's apotheosis, it celebrates a pagan, natural world, as opposed to the sacramental ritual of the Cybo fresco. The Etruscan tomb painting also hints at the continuity of human nature, an inventory of mundane activities that while contrasting with the spiritual minutiae of the Renaissance work, reaffirms the same human appetite—only in this case an appetite that refuses to overstep the limits by which life is normally bounded. In this sense, the Etruscan painting is an emblem of normality, memorializing human pleasures even in death and refusing to surrender its earthly serenity to the self-aggrandizement of a Cardinal Malaspina. The natural detail, including leopards, horses, birds, and fish, reinforces the predominant theme of mundane pleasures and links this evocation of Etruscan tomb-painting with the Etruscan sculpture, the terra-cotta "Apollo of Veii" described in *After the Fireworks* as "a lovely symbol of the small, the local, the kindly." But the fresco reveals nothing new beyond an affirmation of simpler desires lost upon its observers. Cardan, raising the problem of the utility of history, remarks that "archaeologists" deciphering the mysterious inscription running across the wall of the tomb would be wasting their time: "For after all, what would they discover? Nothing that we don't already know. They would discover that before the Romans conquered Italy men ate and drank, made love, piled up wealth, oppressed their weaker neighbours, diverted themselves with sports, made laws and so on. One could have divined that walking down Piccadilly any day of the week" (*TBL*, 305). Cardan's assessment of history is remarkably close to Huxley's, but he underestimates the sanely normative values implicit in the fresco. Mrs. Aldwinkle, the admirer of Montecatini's floridly agitated painting of egocentric ambition as well as the "virility of [Italy's] Fascists" (*TBL*, 18), gazes despondently at the serenely depicted Etruscan lovers and laments characteristically that it can "throw no new light on love, if lovers they are" (*TBL*, 306).

The tour of the excavated barrows culminates in a second tomb filled with paintings of men and women reclining on couches, feasting, listening to musicians playing on Etruscan double-flutes, and watching female dancers. After Cardan comments on their "simple tastes," Chelifer injects a more sinister note, observing that "they fall a long way behind the later Romans" and then introduces the third significant work of art in *Those Barren Leaves*, a Roman mosaic: "Do you know that huge mosaic in the Lateran museum? It comes from one of the Imperial baths, I forget which, and consists of portraits of the principal sporting heroes of the epoch—boxers and wrestlers—with their trainers and backers." He adds that the mosaic, a monumental image like the Cardinal's apotheosis, forty feet long by thirty wide, is constructed of "the most durable materials ever devised by the ingenuity of man" and serves as a testimonial to human brutality, to "monied interests," and to the metamorphosis of men into "gorillas." It exists principally for the profit of its "backers," who are portrayed "in the noblest attitudes," and secondarily for the sadistic entertainment of "the Roman mob," the ancient counterpart, he adds, of "the mobs of our modern capitals" (*TBL*, 311). Chelifer then concludes that "the future historians of Rome" must set aside historicist "fiction" for historical reality, or at least what can be known of it: "For no man can claim that he had really understood the Roman empire till he has studied that mosaic. That pavement is the quintessence of Roman reality. A drop of that reality is enough to shrivel up all retrospective Utopias that historians have ever made or ever can make out of the chronicles of ancient Rome" (*TBL*, 312). Lilian Aldwinkle's Cybo Malaspina is such a retrospective Utopia, an historicist simplification of the Renaissance founded on the annals of a brutally degenerative family. Chelifer, however, dissatisfied with his indictment of Roman history, turns suddenly on the frescoes of the Etruscan vaults and, after conceding their "archaic charm" and "freshness," insists "that the impression is entirely fallacious" and that "the artists were probably quite as sophisticated and quite as repulsive as their Roman successors" (*TBL*, 312).

It is thematically significant that Calamy makes no response to the Etruscan paintings nor to Chelifer's description of the Roman mosaic. Conscious of a contrasting class of "historical fact" (*TBL*, 370), he accuses Chelifer of being a "reversed sentimentalist" who "gloats" over the "horrors" of history, ancient and contemporary (*TBL*, 371). But the transformation of men into primitive gorillas—that is, to a lower animal level of existence—like the elevation of the Cardinal in the Cybo fresco to a higher more ideal sphere, is part of the undulations of history recorded in works of art, while the Etruscan murals appear to emblematize a human norm, however precarious and unsatisfactory.

All of these aesthetic compositions are illustrations of Sir Hercules Lapith's "dark, historic page" and as such suggest both the continuity as well as the limitations of history as a source of human value and significance. But Calamy, who is the first example of Huxley's "non-attached man" (with the possible exception of Gumbril Senior in *Antic Hay*), comes closest to evolving a coherent and morally informed philosophy of history, a perspective on time and historical process free of Cardan's anxiety and Chelifer's cynicism, and engendered principally by Calamy's acceptance of reality as "perfectly provisional and temporary" (*TBL*, 34). He maintains that "human beings have selected three-dimensional space and time as their axes" (*TBL*, 377), a judgement that indicts the epistemological limitations of both the Cybo Malaspina, as the most elaborately intricate spatial symbol in the novel, and the pilgrimage "up and down the periods of history" of Mrs. Aldwinkle's party on their journey to Rome. Calamy defines history itself as a shifting axis dependent on the values of the observer. Arguing that "some observers are clear-sighted and in some way more advantageously placed than others," he concludes that the study of history as conventionally practiced is invariably pernicious: "The incessantly changing social conventions and moral codes of history represent the shifting axes of reference chosen by the least curious, most myopic and worst-placed observers" (*TBL*, 377). Through Calamy, Huxley is not merely drawing attention to the historicist illusions of a Lilian Aldwinkle. Rather, he is attacking the purported objectivity of historicism and its concern with art history, political and diplomatic history, the history of science and technology, and indeed all forms of historical inquiry. Calamy substitutes for historicist research what he regards as the solitary "historical fact," the mysticism and morality of "Buddha, Jesus, Lao-tsze," and "Newton, who practically abandoned mathematics for mysticism" (*TBL*, 370).

For Calamy it would appear that history reveals either a continuity with the present, so firm and obvious it has nothing beyond that continuity to reveal, or is subject to being manipulated and reshaped to accord with the observer's values. In either case, its "social conventions and moral codes" are never fully revealed because the perspective of the historicist is always contaminated by his particular values and customary expectations. The sole significant recommendation emerging from Calamy's attack is that history itself is a broad continuum of error, in which if truth constantly eludes the historian, it is at least possible to recognize the historicist fabrications of the "most myopic and worst-placed observers." Huxley, however, by means of his evocation of the baroque Cybo, the Renaissance frescoes of Pasquale da Montecatini, and the Roman mosaic, manages to insinuate his own satirical perspective into the problem of historical continuity. The Etruscan tomb-paintings symbolize a brief moment of civilized equipoise in a longer chronicle of egocentric aspiration and unremitting violence—an abiding irrationality characteristic of life lived on the level of spatio-temporal experience.

The central symbol at the end of the journey, gathering up the various threads of aspiration and disillusion that dominate the novel's final chapters, is "the silhouette of St. Peter's" (*TBL*, 294). Its dome reflects thematically back to "the top of Snowdon" and the "round temple" of the

Cybo Malaspina and forward to the "shining peak" (*TBL*, 380) of Calamy's mountain. The symbolic meaning of St. Peter's exceeds in range and depth that of Wren's dome of St. Paul's in *Antic Hay* because it is not merely a "human symbol" celebrating proportion and reason (*AH*, 327). Rather, each of the pilgrims reacts differently to the dome, also described by Huxley in *Two or Three Graces* published the year after *Those Barren Leaves*, as "the great symbolic dome of the world (*TG*, 176). The "silhouette of St. Peter's" stands at the end of the journey to Rome as the culminating symbol of human diversity and at the same time of a final mystery that is inherently unknowable. Huxley accomplishes this by having his pilgrims react to St. Peter's in diverse but individually circumscribed ways. Mrs. Aldwinkle, the book's representative romantic monist searching for her one "apocalyptic thing," is disappointed and lamely remarks, "St. Peter's isn't much of a work of art" (*TBL*, 292). Chelifer, loyal to Gog's Court, disavows St. Peter's by exclaiming, "what has it or he to do with us" (*TBL*, 294). The socialist Mr. Falx bristles angrily, denouncing the dome as a symbol of "the secular oppression of millions of human beings" and of "their degraded lives in order that St. Peter's might be what it is" (*TBL*, 291). The cynical hedonist Cardan opposes Mr. Falx, seeing the dome as primarily an opportunity for aesthetic pleasure: "Allow us to amuse ourselves with Michaelangelo if we want to" (*TBL*, 294), while in the background "the Pilgrim's Chorus out of Tannhauser" is drowned out by a jazz band (*TBL*, 295). The mingled political, aesthetic, and philosophical responses of the pilgrims are not resolved by Huxley because he intends the dome to symbolize the intractability of what he will celebrate in *Do What You Will* as a world of "distinctions and relations" (*DWW*, 63), in which the soul's "principal food is the direct . . . physical experience of diversity" (*DWW*, 93), and "Shelley's . . . prophetic escape" (*DWW*, 99–100) is displaced by a belief that "knowledge is mostly a knowledge of diversity" (*DWW*, 91).

In the essay "One and Many," Huxley closely equated human experience with the experience of diversity, but he also insisted that reality is inherently "unknowable." He rejected monism, declaring that "the One is the equivalent of the Nothing" (*DWW*, 12), but at the same time in another essay in the same collection "Spinoza's Worm," he held out the possibility of "apocalypses" revealing an "all-comprehending unity" (*DWW*, 63). In *Antic Hay* and *Those Barren Leaves*, Huxley vigorously denied such a mode of perception, particularly as it was often associated with art or history. But his attack on baroque self-aggrandizement and romantic Prometheanism did not extend to mysticism or preclude a mystical apprehension that transcends both language and plastic form. The

Cybo's "round temple" and the *Fragments'* Mount Snowdon are discredited as inflated symbols celebrating art as a sacred enterprise and the artist as prophet. But the "shining peak" that Calamy gazes at in the final chapter is not a consequence of an aesthetic experience or a romantic imposition of the imagination upon the external world.

In that chapter Calamy rejects the cynicism of Cardan, who nostalgically looks back to "the Romantic Revival" (*TBL*, 37) as the "good old days" when there was "no seen reality; only imagination" (*TBL*, 36). Cardan admits that he "really and sincerely like[d] the baroque only," despite his awareness that its "essence is exaggeration" (*TBL*, 207). His quest for "extravagant, romantic, grotesqueness" (*TBL*, 209) ends when he carries off a living grotesque, the retarded Grace Elver, whom he hopes to marry. Cardan's allegiances, however, are easily overturned. His cynicism is in part the product of fear and confusion, and just as Chelifer seeks the security of Gog's Court and Mrs. Aldwinkle hides herself in the Cybo, Cardan idealizes the past, "the simple faith of nineteenth-century materialism" (*TBL*, 35). He opposes Calamy's patient openness to the world around him, particularly the latter's "sense that everything's perfectly provisional and temporary" (*TBL*, 34). Cardan is not Huxley's spokesman in *Those Barren Leaves*; rather, he represents "the babble of notions and conflicting theories" (*MN*, 212) that Huxley saw as characteristic of modern culture. It is no accident that Cardan, who loved the baroque, achieves the final insight into the theatrical absurdity of life as it is led at the Cybo. He loses Grace Elver when she dies of food poisoning and is confronted with the same revelation of human vulnerability that he had encountered earlier on the plain of Maremma, "visions of disease, decreptitude, death" (*TBL*, 218), in which life becomes a "farce" of mere "struttings and posturings" where "it is only the acting that matters" (*TBL*, 337).

In *Antic Hay* "the monster" in the night club drama insists that "Brunelleschi's dome" (*AH*, 230) contains a spiritual meaning that validates his endeavor to "reach aloft" (*AH*, 231). In that parable of romanticism, the monster struggles to ascend, only to fall head first to the floor, just as Chelifer collapses when confronted with the two hundred and thirty-two steps of Mrs. Aldwinkle's tower at the Cybo. The attempt to transcend the inescapable diversity of human experience by means of an ascent towards a monistic ideal is for Huxley an evasion of life lived on a human, rather than a baroque, level. The dome of St. Paul's is a symbol of human achievement, revealing only human truths, as opposed to Casimir Lypiatt's "reality more than human." In the trilogy of Huxley's early novels, it stands in the shadows of the "silhouette of St. Peter's" as a symbol of order in a world of overwhelming darkness and diversity and in opposition to "the top of Snowdon" as an emblematic repudiation of romantic Prometheanism. Yet the "shining peak" that Calamy confronts in the final chapter of *Those Barren Leaves* would seem to only resurrect the already discredited "exclusive idealism" of baroque-romantic art. Shimmering beneath the surface of the "great pinnacle" is the promise of apocalypse, of the divulgence of an "enormous secret" (*TBL*, 363) similar to Mrs. Aldwinkle's Cybo or Barbara Waters' mysterious smile. However, Calamy is neither a Casimir Lypiatt nor a Francis Chelifer.

In *Crome Yellow* the poet Denis Stone ascends the ivory tower of art that isolates him from the vitality of the charity bazaar on the grounds below Crome's tower. In *Antic Hay* the Promethean Lypiatt commits suicide in a Piranesian *cul de sac*, and in *Those Barren Leaves* the cynical Chelifer, equally self-destructive after the failure of his idealization of Snowdon and Barbara Waters, buries himself in what he thinks is the reality of Gog's Court. In these three early novels, Huxley has radically and uncompromisingly evoked the isolation, self-destructiveness, and misguided cynicism that inevitably follow once an artist surrenders to the baroque-romantic mode and its hollow Prometheanism. Yet Calamy is *not* an artist and refuses to endorse either the posturing self-consciousness of a Lypiatt or the superficial despair of a Chelifer. In keeping with Wren's aesthetic, he calmly observes, "If one desires salvation, it's salvation here and now. The kingdom of God is within you . . ." (*TBL*, 366). Turning his back on conventional history, conventional religion, and the religion of art, he adopts a position of sensitive alertness to the landscape around him, open to its influence and "somehow reassured" (*TBL*, 380). Meanwhile, Cardan continues his life of dependency and aimless wandering with the restless Lilian Aldwinkle, who has decided "to move on to Monte Carlo," and Chelifer anticipates his return to the "familiar horrors of reality" at Gog's Court (*TBL*, 379). Calamy has at least recognized the sterility of their lives and made the difficult decision to stop, to step outside the confinement of the illusory Cybos and Gog's Courts and look into his own soul. In doing so he has made a step, albeit an inconclusive one, towards establishing "the human reality in the centre of a pointless landscape" (*TBL*, 127). Lilian Aldwinkle, however, is unable to free herself of her romantic historicism, and as the novel moves towards closure, she is left in the midst of a "pointless landscape," a Piranesian setting where "seated on a fallen column in the ruins of Hadrian's Villa," she re-creates her biography "with various modifications of the facts, modifications in which she herself had long ago come implicitly to believe" (*TBL*, 299). The past, whether personal or broadly social, remains a vexing issue for Huxley, one that he will repeatedly return to in the novels of the 1930s. In *Point Counter Point*, published two years after the appearance of *Those Barren Leaves*, he turned again to the problem of historicism but within a richer, more varied social context. *Point Counter Point* is Huxley's most ambitious attempt to define and dramatize the nature of the history "by which individuals are surrounded and within which each of them does at least some of his living" (*CE*, 221).

# CHAPTER THREE

# The Descending Road of Modern History

### 1. History and Decadence in *Point Counter Point*

With the notable exception of *Eyeless in Gaza, Point Counter Point* is Huxley's most ambitious attempt to diagnose the matrix of symptoms comprising "the disease of modern man" (*PCP*, 161), consolidating and extending the presiding ideas of the previous novels and essays in what can be viewed as a satirical *summa* of historicist values and assumptions. His masterpiece also marks the increasing ascendency of the Marquis de Sade in Huxley's thinking on the related subjects of history and ideology, an emphasis that finds its proper context in Huxley's analysis of the baroque-romantic impulse that in turn plays a major role in his endeavor to define and trace the historical genesis of a culture progressively undermined by rampant individuality and anarchy. In "History and the Past" Huxley described historical explanation as a temporary consensus in which the basic premises determining the selection of facts will always be arguable and mutable: "The past and the future are functions of the present. Each generation has its private history, its own peculiar brand of prophecy. What it shall think about past and future is determined by its own immediate problems. It will go to the past for instruction, for sympathy, for justification, for flattery. It will look into the future for compensation for the present—into the past, too. For even the past can become a compensatory Utopia, indistinguishable from the earthly paradises of the future, except by the fact that the heroes have historical names and flourished between known dates. From age to age the past is recreated. A new set of Waverley Novels is founded on a new selection of the facts" (*MN*, 139). For Huxley the historicist ideal of an objective reconstruction of the past, wholly accurate in detail and faithful as well to the spirit of the age, is an elusive *ignis fatuus* dancing before the eyes of the historian and leading him further into such depths as Joseph Stoyte's castle-museum in *After Many a Summer Dies the Swan* (where the Waverley novels will be again involved as an emblem of historicist illusion). In this respect, *Point Counter Point* continues Huxley's exploration of history, especially the attempt to discover meaning and value in the historical process itself.

To vary slightly W. H. Auden's famous metaphor, *Point Counter Point* is a novel in which one can discern, if not all the dogs of Europe barking, certainly the earliest snarls heralding the advent of the "low, dishonest decade" of the 1930s. In *The Auden Generation*, Samuel Hynes has carefully catalogued the collective idiom central to what he calls "the thirties myth," a homogeneous matrix of ideas that converge with particular force and clarity in the work of Auden, Christopher Isherwood, Stephen Spender, and Louis MacNeice.[1] This complex interweaving of mood and symbol includes the motific repetition of certain themes and images, especially those that combine to form the emblematic topography of what has been termed "Auden country." This overarching typology involves both a set of affiliated images such as the frontier, the journey, the healing hero or new leader, maps, and sinister land-scapes—as well as recurrent themes like the malevolent import of history, the rise of fascism, the sickness of the past, the impact of the Great War, and the divergence of the older and younger generations. The result is the carefully calculated atmosphere of public crisis and private betrayal that pervades, for example, the early lyrics of Auden or the *Berlin Stories* of Isherwood. Within Huxley's canon its completest expression can be found in his 1936 novel *Eyeless in Gaza*. There Huxley employs the Audenesque idiom of frontier, journey, and the appearance of the healing hero with an intensity that testifies to his interest in the work of his contemporaries and his responsiveness to the political exigencies of the thirties. However, in *Point Counter Point* one of the principal stylistic links between Huxley's masterpiece of the late twenties and "the thirties myth" is the subject of history, including the contending ideologies of fascism and Marxism.

In *The Orators*, composed in 1931 approximately three years after the appearance of *Point Counter Point*, Auden described England as "this country of ours where nobody is well," a leitmotif of the thirties that finds its counterpart in Huxley's attempt to anatomize "the disease of modern man." Samuel Hynes has argued that throughout the thirties "history provided the new greatness; and writers, it seemed, had only to draw upon that new source."[2] In *Reading the Thirties* Bernard Bergonzi has also stressed the importance of history to Auden and his contemporaries both as a word that recurs repeatedly in Auden's poetry and as a concept that forms the principal context for much of the other writing throughout this period. By the end of the decade, references to "history," Bergonzi observes, "were as frequent as ever, but that entity was no longer a god-like force inexorably directing the course of human development; it seemed, now, the very embodiment of the irrational and the destructive."[3] The association of history with anarchic violence and irrationality is the subject of Huxley's final novel of the thirties, *After Many a Summer Dies the Swan*. In *Point Counter Point*, however, it makes its first appearance as a principal motif, associated with the surroundings or professions of many of the characters and dramatized primarily in the lives of Maurice Spandrell and to a lesser extent Lucy Tantamount. Huxley consistently argued that the large-scale phenomenon of public history was a collective projection of the private acts and beliefs of individual men and women. This meta-historical postulate, formulated and stressed throughout Huxley's work in the 1930s, is the fundamental principle underlying his aim of writing the "social novel" with its socially paradigmatic character. It can be traced as far back as *Crome Yellow* and *Antic Hay* but emerges with greatest force and clarity in *Point Counter Point*, where Huxley focused on a carefully evolved paradigmatic protagonist in order to give shape and coherency to his sense of the direction gradually being taken by contemporary history. In the following pages I shall argue that Maurice Spandrell is such an emblematic figure, endowing the novel's historical theme with a more determinant symmetry and unity than has been commonly acknowledged. His centrality within the numerous subplots and motific patternings of *Point Counter Point* can be accounted for principally in terms of Huxley's concern with history, in particular with the idea of a cultural ebbing that could be traced back to the Great War. There are of course other characters as pivotal as Spandrell within the contrapuntal intricacy of *Point Counter Point*, for example Philip Quarles or Walter Bidlake; but Spandrell, I believe, conforms more precisely to Huxley's concept of an historical paradigm of "the whole life of the community." Huxley also insisted that history was not only the public projection of individual behavior but that the essence of history lay in the psychology of the individual, a judgement that accounts for the clinically detailed psychological cast to his portrait of Spandrell as the presiding spirit of the age.

Samuel Hynes maintains that the combination of intellectual skepticism and mordant wit that comprises the essential style of the 1920s is to be found most clearly in "the sensibility of *Point Counter Point* and *Gold Coast Customs*, of *The Green Hat* and *Decline and Fall* and *Private Lives*."[4] It must be conceded that *Point Counter Point*, appearing in 1928 as the decade was drawing to its close, gathered up many of the principal themes, situations, and images of a generation conditioned by the forbidding terrain of T. S. Eliot's *The Waste Land*. It is not surprising that the atomistic world of Prufrock, Burbank, Fresca, Tiresias, and Gerontion should find its appropriate reflection in the anarchic society of Burlap, Spandrell, Rampion, and Lucy Tantamount. But Huxley's most sustained attempt to capture the quirks and quiddities of the postwar generation is also a comprehensive expression of his increasingly "deteriorationist" perspective on contemporary British history. In this respect, *Point Counter Point* is the work of a social historian sufficiently prescient to anticipate the shift in political and aesthetic emphasis that marks the emergence of the Auden generation.

*Point Counter Point*, I would argue, is as much a generation-shaping novel as Evelyn Waugh's *Vile Bodies*, a satire published in 1930 two years after the appearance of Huxley's novel. Samuel Hynes praises *Vile Bodies* in terms peculiarly suitable for *Point Counter Point*, citing Waugh's novel as "a precursor of later writing of the decade: in its prophecy of war, in its consciousness of the separateness of the younger generation, in its contemptuous hostility to the politics of the establishment, in its irony, in its bitter, farcical wit," adding that in the attention paid to the younger generation, particularly its emphasis on "weak, inactive" characters, it foreshadows the work of Auden and Isherwood. Such an assessment would be an apt evaluation of Huxley's novels of the twenties, and it is no accident that in concluding his analysis of the tone and direction of Waugh's satire, Hynes observes, "*The Waste Land* itself, *Point Counter Point*, *Vile Bodies*—acknowledged the need for a reintroduction of meaning. But as the 'twenties became the 'thirties, it was only a need; the ferocious theologies were still to come."[5] Nevertheless, it is in *Point Counter Point*, not *Vile Bodies*, that a nihilist and a communist conspire together to murder a fascist, while what Hynes has termed "the Myth of the War" had been a staple convention of Huxley's novels throughout the 1920s. Accordingly, *Point Counter Point* can be regarded as a "transitional novel," in which the trackless wilderness of Eliot's waste land begins to merge with the topographical features of Auden country. The bridge connecting the two is that of history, especially the murderous interpretation of history characteristic of the modern ideologue.

In *Point Counter Point* Huxley endeavored to unify the novel's apparently disparate themes, particularly the political and historical motifs, by representing them as illustrative of a general social condition —the contending antithetical tensions that collectively comprise "the disease of modern man." This pervasive emphasis on conflicting values and beliefs extends to all of the characters and embraces a broad range of subjects, including religion, aesthetics, science, psychology, history, and politics. Keith May has observed that Huxley's novel "is probably best regarded as a rounded presentation of metaphysical inconclusiveness,"[6] a judgment I would endorse in describing Huxley's most exhaustively detailed satire as a satirical anatomy whose governing idea can be defined as the painful dualities of human experience. Maurice Spandrell stands at the nub of this proposition, particularly where it touches upon the subject of history, politics, ideology, and social decadence. If Everard Webley and Illidge dramatize the current political antitheses of fascism and communism, Spandrell has no definable position within the accepted political spectrum. The explanation for this lies with Huxley's concept of "the nihilist revolution," a complete transformation of existing values that he associated with the Marquis de Sade. As a result, with the notable exceptions of Mark Staithes in *Eyeless in Gaza* and the Earl of Gonister in *After Many a Summer Dies the Swan*, Spandrell is Huxley's most detailed portrait of a sadomasochist. More important, however, Spandrell the violent nihilist overshadows both Webley and Illidge, murdering the fascist and psychologically dominating the communist.

In his notebook Philip Quarles observes that "the political and industrial history of the last four centuries" (*PCP*, 443) demonstrates the futility of notions about intellectual progress, while Rampion, equally dismissive of the concept of linear "progress," substitutes a "less optimistic" vision of history as an erratic cycle of alternating "peaks and declines" (*PCP*, 291). The various and contending interpretations of history in *Point Counter Point* range from naive endorsements of H. G. Wells to self-indulgent antiquarianism or highly subjective appropriations of history in the service of violent ideologies. For example, Sidney Quarles only masquerades as a political historian, using his research on "the history of democracy" (*PCP*, 364) and his trips to the British Museum as a screen for his amorous trysts, a frivolous debasement of historical inquiry that accounts for his introduction as the creator of "humorous parodies of Herodotus" (*PCP*, 348). In this regard, it is apt that Quarles's ambitious history of democracy is displaced by another history, a collection of romantic "fragments" constituting a record of his own personal experiences entitled "Memories and Reflections of Fifty [Years]" (*PCP*, 525). However, his egocentric reduction of history to the dimensions of his own personality is a trivially innocuous version of Everard Webley's more sinister preemption of European history in favor of his own political ideology.

Webley's version of the historical process is emblematized in his coin collection, a numismatic simplification of what has been called "the bad King John" theory of history.[7] Eager to create his own "Caesarian environment," to borrow Scogan's term from *Crome Yellow*, Webley's coin collection defines an elementary and even guileless interpretation of history as a succession of military autocrats: "There was the Macedonian tetradrachm, with the head of Alexander the Great in the guise of Hercules; the sestertius of 44 B.C. with the formidable profile of Caesar, and next to it Edward III's rose noble, stamped with the ship that symbolized the beginning of England's power at sea. And there on Pisanello's medal was Sigismondo Malatesta, most beautiful of ruffians; and there was Queen Elizabeth in her ruff and Napoleon with laurels in his hair, and the Duke of Wellington" (*PCP*, 379). His adherence to "economic nationalism" and "individualism" masks a deeper will to power, a desire to control and dominate through a hierarchical and essentially static social structure. His view of European history from the Greco-Roman period to the rise of Napoleon is a version of the "great man" theory of historical development as well as a naively transparent expression of what Huxley regards as romantic self-assertion—only in this case intensified to the point of oligarchic fascism with its worship of charismatic leaders. The presence of Sigismondo Malatesta in the collection is particularly appropriate inasmuch as Huxley associated him with "Nietzschean" values. Webley's fascist predilection for charismatic autocrats and his reduction of history to little more than episodic chapters in the lives of military heroes is reflected in his own bearing "as a great historical character" (*PCP*, 56) as well as his ineluctable movement towards his own assassination. Much later in the novel, as he drives to meet Elinor, he is conscious of an approaching consummation, "as though the future were already history" (*PCP*, 513). Despite his association with powerful automobiles, movement, energy, and erotic potency, Webley is a lifeless figure, defeated by his own peculiar form of historicist illusion. His death is inseparable from his violent interpretation of historical process, and it overtakes him with an inevitability that ironically reinforces Spandrell's theory of the correspondence between character and fate.

If Sidney Quarles is a sham Herodotus, his son Philip represents a more serious challenge, stringently repudiating the entire course of modern history, while the facility with which he produces "the most fantastic and grotesque pieces of historical information" (*PCP*, 276) testifies to his unremitting sense of the past as merely a chronicle of aberrant behavior. His brief excursion into social history, an evocation of life at the country house Gattenden entitled "The Kitchen in the Old House" (*PCP*, 341), typically degenerates into panicky musings on the possibility of losing his freedom in a tangle of historical "roots" (*PCP*, 343). Rachel Bidlake, on the other hand, has deliberately chosen to dwell mentally in the "Tuscan Middle Ages" (*PCP*, 253) on an estate "looking more medieval than anything that the real chronological Middle Ages had ever dreamt of" (*PCP*, 344). The motif of history permeates *Point Counter Point*, extending to minor characters like Peter Slipe, a professional "Assyriologist employed at the British Museum" (*PCP*, 169), and Mrs. Goffer and Miss Hignett, who write "historical plays" (*PCP*, 322) under the pen name of Romola Saville. As I shall show, some characters are regarded by others as representative symbols of discernible stages of historical evolution, while others like Spandrell consciously identify themselves with major historical events. Philip Quarles notes that "the historian" whose perspective is confined to a single "aspect of the event" can, like the physicist or the chemist, at least lay claim to a portion of "reality" (*PCP*, 266). Yet throughout *Point Counter Point*, the single aspect becomes for the romantic historicist the exclusive avenue to a subjectively conceived goal. Moreover, the "reality" perceived by the historian, when uncontaminated by personal bias, reveals a world fundamentally irrational in its own right in that it exhibits no fixed and stable qualities, no immanent spiritual purposiveness, and no grounds for a belief in human progress. Rampion's insistence that contemporary history and "industrial progress," as well as the corresponding decline in social cohesiveness, can be traced to a "psychological impasse" reflects Huxley's emphasis on psychological explanation in history, particularly in *Eyeless in Gaza* and *Ends and Means*. For Rampion "social collapse . . . results from psychological collapse" (*PCP*, 415), an assimilation of broad historical process to individual behavior that became a staple of Huxley's philosophy of history and that, I will show, underlies the historical-psychological centrality of Spandrell in *Point Counter Point*.

Rampion argues that "the root of the evil's in the individual psychology" (*PCP*, 417), and his "two Outlines of History" (*PCP*, 290) are designed to dramatize this principle by contrasting the ascending line of Wellsian progress with the cultural ebb and flow of what Huxley describes as "psychological undulations." Rampion's visual allegory of European history measures the degree of civilization attained in particular historical periods by means of a series of figures increasing or decreasing in stature. The painting includes two full cycles or "undulations," the peaks differing in size. In *Do What You Will* Huxley had objected to the "ridiculous idealization of the English Renaissance," a judgement possibly echoed here in the slightly diminished figures associated with the fifteenth and sixteenth centuries. More important, Rampion's chart traces the decline of modern history from the beginning of the Reformation, a theoretical cornerstone of Huxley's philosophy of history as well. In *Point Counter Point* four major characters have, as it were, stepped down from Rampion's canvas: Illidge, Everard Webley, Lucy

Tantamount, and Maurice Spandrell. Collectively, they symbolize the presiding historicist values of post-Reformation history, while individually they each adopt a particular response to history that in turn is one of a limited range of attitudes available to Huxley's inverse romantic.

Illidge is the least complicated, trapped within the interstices of what Huxley viewed as an ideological distortion of history; he anticipates the more ambitiously conceived Marxists of *Eyeless in Gaza*, Mark Staithes, Ekki Giesebrecht, and Helen Amberley. Locked in an ideological struggle with the fascist Everard Webley, Illidge is a prisoner of "mechanist" science and the rigid formulas of class conflict. Despite his allegiance to progressive notions of history, he is betrayed by progress, emblematized by the scientific advances of "Einstein and Eddington," "Poincaré," and "Mach," all of which conflict with his "nineteenth Century materialism" (*PCP*, 213). As an inverse romantic he is associated with the "satirical romantics," eager to play a "Byronic part" in order to impress the upper-class guests attending the concert at Tantamount House. But his "Byronically superior" affectations (*PCP*, 70) are as outdated as his retrogressive scientific prejudices, outworn concepts that compel him for ideological reasons to "fight against any scientific theory that's less than fifty years old" (*PCP*, 213). His political inconsistencies, however, are not as radical as those of Mark Staithes in *Eyeless in Gaza*. His devotion to his mother is not, as Spandrell would have it, logically incompatible with Marxism; nor can his class loyalties be solely attributable to an irrationally intense hatred of the rich. As a "militant communist and a scientific materialist and an admirer of the Russian Revolution" (*PCP*, 212), he functions principally as the ideological adversary of Everard Webley. Lacking a passionate commitment to direct revolutionary action, never quoting Marx or Lenin or displaying any theoretical knowledge of communist ideology, Illidge is curiously unconvincing as an authentically realized Marxist. In a broader sense, however, he reflects the compromised impotency of the British Communist Party, ignored by the socialists and throughout the 1920s completely overshadowed by the more spectacular history of the Labour Party. Unlike the socialist Mr. Falx of *Those Barren Leaves* or the pseudo-Leninist Bojanus of *Antic Hay*, Illidge plays a central role within a more richly conceived context—but a context more insistently psychological than political. Long before Huxley, Friedrich Engels had complained that in England even the proletariat was bourgeois. Illidge is no exception; envious of the upper classes and eager to impress them, he is flattered when Lucy Tantamount, a woman whose existence he regards as symptomatic of a degenerate culture, shows him attention. Hoping for a revolution, he confines his activities to his immediate family, his mother in Lancashire and his brother Tom in Manchester. On one occasion he demonstrates at a gathering of Webley's fascists, the British Freemen, but shortly after he can only protest when Spandrell mocks his squeamish distaste for more direct revolutionary action.

As a "denouncing prophet" (PCP, 75) of the "gangrened insensitiveness" (PCP, 73) of the upper classes, he resembles Rampion to the extent that he is conscious of pervasive social decay and employs an imagery of disease and morbid growth to dramatize the historical process he sees at work everywhere around him. The "gangrened" sensibility of the rich is for Illidge concisely represented by the "putrefaction" of Lucy Tantamount, a woman whose historically inevitable appearance exemplifies the progressive decadence informing the economic history of Tantamount House itself. Illidge describes her in organic terms, as "the consummate flower of this charming civilization of ours," adding that her existence is "the logical conclusion" (PCP, 75) of the history of her family, a history that Huxley describes in detail.

The manner in which he reconstructs the historical bases of Tantamount House is of interest, as much for what it omits as for what it includes. Linked to sanctuaries of privilege and power like the "Reform Club" and the "Travellers' Club," as well as the "prison" ambiance of Raphael's "Cancelleria," it survives as a monument to the industrial revolution and the oppression of an entire class. The evolution of the Tantamounts is part accident—the acquisition of land at the dissolution of the monasteries—and part systematic exploitation: "Tantamount succeeded Tantamount. Elizabeth made them barons; they became viscounts under Charles II, earls under William and Mary, marquesses under George II." After marrying "heiress after heiress," acquiring "slaves in Jamaica" (PCP, 24), and amassing banks and land, they were swept up in the economic activity of "newly industrialized England" (PCP, 23). Obsessed with power, they are nevertheless dependent on the inventions of "obscure men" (PCP, 24), contributing little of their own and demonstrating no creative talents beyond an ability to capitalize on economic opportunities. As voracious consumers, they employ any method that contributes to their own profit, including child-labor, slavery, and theft. The economic history of the Tantamount family would seem to support Illidge's contention that the family represents a class "irrevocably corrupted" (PCP, 75), but while he traces the family fortunes in principally economic terms, Huxley refuses to accept a wholly economic explanation. He never suggests that the Tantamounts as factory owners may have contributed managerial skill or even the necessary investment capital in order to establish their factories; rather, he sees them as wholly parasitic and throughout *Point Counter Point* regards them as representative of the present state of English upper-class society. Indeed, they are close to being Marxist caricatures of the oligarchical capitalist. Yet Huxley does not wholly locate the "root of the evil" in an obsession with property and profit, nor does he invoke Hegelian or Marxist historical principles to account for the rise of the Tantamounts. For Huxley human greed and "the will to power" are psychological universals unconditioned by class or economic status. The millionaire Jo Stoyte and his historical counterparts, the old Earl in *After Many a Summer Dies the Swan* and the wealthy Mary Amberley with her stock investments and obsession with property in *Eyeless in Gaza*, are studies in psychological rather than economic behavior—where even Karl Marx is subsumed by the ubiquitous historicist logic of the Marquis de Sade.

Huxley places no value on labor as a commodity, nor does he regard "the proletariat" as a cohesive economic class, arguing in the essay "Revolutions" that modern capitalism has transformed the proletariat into "a branch of the bourgeoisie" (*DWW*, 219) and seeing in the activities of *all* social classes the same psychological traits. His insistence at the outset of *Do What You Will* that "to talk about religion except in terms of human psychology is an irrelevance" (*DWW*, 1) applies with equal force to economics and social history. "Bolshevism" is consequently defined in *Music at Night* as "romantic," its adherents betraying the same baroque-romantic aspirations as the Tantamounts embroiled in the "baroque of modern commerce" (*PCP*, 512). In this respect, Lucy Tantamount is correctly assessed by Illidge as displaying an intrinsically decadent sensibility but not for the reasons he confidently adduces.

Like Illidge, Lucy has adopted a definite, albeit superficial perspective on history. But her behavior accords to an unexpected degree with Huxley's characterization (in both *Music at Night* and *Do What You Will*) of the typically baroque-romantic Bolshevist. As a product of the Tantamount family and as a woman who displays not even a trace of social conscience, Lucy in this connection is perplexing so long as one looks for a socioeconomic rather than a psychological explanation. Huxley's assimilation of Marxism to inverse romanticism underlies this linking of Lucy Tantamount and the communist Illidge. Accordingly, the Bolshevist is defined by Huxley as inversely romantic as a consequence of four characteristics: his belief in progress, especially technological progress; his intense admiration for machines; a materialism so essentially lifeless that the historical process leading to the ascendency of the Bolshevist or the "new romantic" is metaphorically dramatized by Huxley in terms of a death-instinct; and a historicist repudiation of trans-historical or religious values. Despite her aristocratic and oligarchic heritage, Lucy Tantamount displays all of these traits, as well as a pronounced taste for sadistic aggression alternating with acts of masochistic submission. She exclaims, "I'm all for Progress" (*PCP*, 311), her admiration for machinery and her "scientific curiosity" (*PCP*, 114) being exclusively concentrated on modern aviation. She tells Walter Bidlake that "the moment I step into the aeroplane at Croydon I feel as though I had been born again—like the Salvation Army." Her eager endorsement of a society that offers "an almost unlimited supply of aeroplanes" (*PCP*, 311) is inseparable from her belief that her own carefully circumscribed personal world, which she metaphorically refers to as "my two-seater monoplane," cannot accommodate nonhistoricist ideas, warning Walter Bidlake that "in the aeroplane" there is "no room" for the "soul" (*PCP*, 282).

It is no accident, then, that Lucy abandons Walter Bidlake for a flight to Paris and "an aeronautical engineer" who "design[ed] aircraft engines" (*PCP*, 494). Lucy Tantamount's association with aviation and machinery is for Huxley a sign of cultural decadence that is swiftly approaching what Rampion calls a "gallop toward death." In his notebook Philip Quarles records Rampion's prediction of the outbreak of a major war by 1938 as a consequence of a society "infected with the love of death" which is in turn traced to the disastrous effect of a fanatical faith in technology and a materialist devotion to machinery: "It's as though the young were absolutely determined to bring the world to an end— mechanize it first into madness, then into sheer murder" (*PCP*, 437). In *Music at Night* Huxley maintained that "the new romanticism [was] headed straight towards death," a judgement that also underlies the essays of *Do What You Will*, despite its superficially optimistic celebration of the "life-worshipper." In "One and Many," for example, Huxley excoriates a culture wholly dedicated to what he calls "the Gadarene descent," a death-intoxicated "monomania" (*DWW*, 44) associated with the qualities he dramatizes in Illidge, Spandrell, and Lucy Tantamount: "turned against life, they have worshipped death in the form of spirituality, intellectualism, and at last mere efficiency" (*DWW*, 50).

The idea of an instinctive tendency towards entropic mechanism and finally death itself is a basic element in the plot-lines involving Illidge, Webley, Lucy Tantamount, and especially Spandrell. The "mechanist" Illidge becomes a murderer, Webley *is* murdered, Spandrell commits suicide, while Lucy Tantamount is repeatedly described as cadaverous. Dressed in mourning despite the fact that her husband Henry Tantamount had been dead for "more than two years" (*PCP*, 59), her obsession with death insinuates itself into her sexual behavior, including a candid preference for what she calls "the deathly sort of liveliness" (*PCP*, 214). Early in the novel she betrays a taste for extreme sensations and excessively violent experiences, perversely arguing that such practices are a sign of progress:

"In that case," said Lucy, "they must be stronger—progressively."
"Progressively?" Mrs. Betterton repeated. "But where would that sort of progress end?"
"In bull-fighting?" suggested John Bidlake. "Or gladiatorial shows? Or public executions, perhaps? Or the amusements of the Marquis de Sade? Where?"
Lucy shrugged her shoulders. "Who knows?" (PCP, 66)

Lucy Tantamount's connection with the Marquis de Sade further establishes her role as a representative figure and links her with Maurice Spandrell, the novel's presiding sadomasochist. She is aroused by Walter Bidlake only when his attentions are forced upon her and approximate "a rape" (PCP, 277) or when his body lying inertly in bed displays a "beautiful deadness" (PCP, 282). But if Lucy Tantamount is part of the "Weltanschauung" (DWW, 26) of "mechanized civilization" (DWW, 48), Maurice Spandrell is in Huxley's view its presiding spirit. The link between these two broadly symbolic figures lies with the Great War and its epochal significance for the postwar generation.

Huxley's essays contain numerous references to the impact of the war on the "historical moment" (DWW, 131), especially its effect on the compromise between socially imposed constraint and sexual self-expression. He notes a "recrudescence" of homosexuality in the years immediately following the war and a weakening of previously established sexual conventions under the onslaught of "modern psychology" reinforced by "the shock of the War" (DWW, 133). Huxley's estimation of the positive influence of "psychoanalysis" is twofold; he observes in "Fashions in Love" that its effect was to create a "rather inchoate and negative conception" of eroticism, while simultaneously releasing the postwar generation from "old taboos and repressions" (DWW, 136). Yet Huxley laments the shattering of "psychological or external restraints" (DWW, 138), which he sees as a potentially anarchic freedom traceable to the social and psychological upheavals of the war of 1914. In Point Counter Point Lucy Tantamount boasts that the Great War was for her the occasion of a profound metamorphosis: "I came out of the chrysalis during the war, when the bottom had been knocked out of everything. I don't see how our grandchildren could possibly knock it out any more thoroughly than it was knocked out then" (PCP, 186). Huxley never underestimated the cultural trauma fomented by the war and the social upheaval following in its wake, but he consistently viewed it as part of a broader process of decline beginning in the Reformation—although he customarily emphasized the romantic period as the watershed of modern decadence. Lucy Tantamount's belief in her own radical transformation is for the most part an illusion in which "the twentieth century is reproducing in a new form the error of the early nineteenth-century romantics" (*DWW*, 138). Convinced that where the norms of human nature are concerned, "history is too short for any change to be perceptible" (*DWW*, 130), Huxley assumed that "love's psychological and physiological material remains the same; but every epoch treats it in a different manner" (*DWW*, 132). Lucy's sadistic desire to inflict physical wounds, to dominate and torture or to be dominated in turn, is a symptom of a "lust for power" untrammeled by moral or social constraints. Individualism, anarchic subjectivity, and the will to power are constant elements in Huxley's theory of modern history as well as psychological universals present throughout the entire course of human history. Yet "the generation of the war" (*DWW*, 133) represents a final stage in a larger process of cultural decline in which the self expands to fill the vacuum created by the diminishing vigor of social conventions and communally imposed ethical restraints.

In accordance with the strong Blakean emphasis informing *Do What You Will* (as well as later works like *Ends and Means*), Huxley argues that in the absence of the "conflicting forces" of ethical imperatives and instinctive desires, romantic love degenerates into a "cold, unimpassioned indulgence." The "emptiness" (*DWW*, 137) created by the disappearance of the creative tension of Blakean contraries is symbolized in Huxley's novels by the prevalence of sadomasochistic behavior, violent political ideologies, and epistemological subjectivity. Not unexpectedly, the masochistic Maurice Spandrell resembles Lucy Tantamount to the extent of citing the war as a crucial factor in his own development. But Spandrell goes much farther, claiming, "the war, so far as I was concerned, was exactly like me" (*PCP*, 394). Spandrell's sense of total identification with the violence, romantic idealism, and corruption of the war is characteristic of his egocentric view of history. But his tendency to assimilate public historical process to private psychological development is traceable to an intricately worked out etiology of sadomasochistic behavior.

In a letter written in 1918 to his brother Julian, Huxley linked what he perceived as a widespread tendency among his contemporaries towards an extremely subjective religiosity—or what he described as an inclination to call "your whims and passions by holy names"—with "the spirit of Romanticism."[8] In "The Substitutes of Religion," published in *Proper Studies* the year before the appearance of *Point Counter Point*, he observed: "Defined in psychological terms, a fanatic is a man who consciously overcompensates a secret doubt. The fanatics of puritanism are generally bound to be overcompensating a secret prurience"—adding, significantly, that their influence "in the modern world is great" (*PS*,

220). The "spiritual sadisme" that Huxley associated with the romantics reappears in the sadistic spirituality of Maurice Spandrell, a composite figure whose origins can in some measure be traced to Huxley's studies of Alfred de Musset, Baudelaire, and the Marquis de Sade.[9] Spandrell is clearly "overcompensating a secret prurience," and as Huxley's language suggests, he is a figure drawn from Freudian psychology, although the degree to which the characterization of Spandrell is directly indebted to Huxley's study of Freud is difficult to determine. In the following discussion I have employed specific Freudian concepts in order to demonstrate a remarkable similarity between Huxley's study of a complex pattern of psychotic behavior and both Freud's and Wilhelm Stekel's analysis of moral masochism and the prostitute complex. In this regard, Huxley's repeated disparagement of Freud remains a vexing problem. His essays contain numerous references to covert psychological behavior; indeed, the existence of an "unconscious" level of irrational and appetitive energy is a persisting theme in them as well as an integral aspect of characterization in the novels. In the case of Maurice Spandrell, it is important to note that while functioning in *Point Counter Point* as a representative romantic within the broader context of Huxley's philosophy of history, his characterization—as I shall discuss further—is much more complicated than, for example, Lucy Tantamount's, a character who fulfills a similar thematic purpose.

Spandrell's chronic psychological instability raises a second, although related problem. A corollary of Huxley's interpretation of modern history, with its emphasis on the rise of romantic subjectivity and the cult of "personality," is his criticism of the notion of the self as an abiding unity in which a persisting identity or personality can be located. He consistently argues that "Human Personality" is "a mythological figure," an illusory abstraction derived from what is in fact "a vast colony of souls" (*DWW*, 141). This necessary fiction receives only halfhearted and temporary approval in *Do What You Will*. In *Point Counter Point* (and the rest of Huxley's canon as well), it is vigorously and repeatedly rejected. The difficulty lies with Huxley's equally persistent belief in the continuity of "those dark instinctive forces which consciousness rightly regards as its enemies," an hypothesis that is *not* confined to *Do What You Will*. Huxley's dramatization of etiologically complicated case histories in *Eyeless in Gaza* and *Point Counter Point* and his elaborate reconstructions of childhood or adolescent traumas related to parental influence, as well as their persisting effect well into maturity, suggest a stable and enduring "personality" that appears to complicate if not contradict his theory of the states. I shall reserve my analysis of Huxley's appropriation of Blake's concept of the states for the final section of this chapter; however, like the Freudian caste of so many of his studies in neurotic or

psychotic behavior, it remains a perplexing issue never satisfactorily resolved in Huxley's writing.

While previous critics of *Point Counter Point* have displayed remarkable unanimity in their regard for Maurice Spandrell as the novel's most
extraordinary figure, they have with few exceptions been equally at one
in their acceptance of Rampion's characterization of Spandrell as a self-
dramatizing "little Stavrogin"[10]—a naive but sinister egotist absorbed in
his own histrionics. But to label him a "diabolist"[11] and "inverted Christian,"[12] or a victim of "Baudelairian Satanism"[12] who delights in mere
"poses of evil,"[14] is to disregard the richly imagined depths of Spandrell's
character and to lose sight of the fact that his "poses" are really symptoms of an underlying psychological disorder that Huxley develops with
ruthless scrutiny. Accordingly, such broadly conceived and equivocal
designations as "satanist" skirt the central issue raised by Spandrell's
role, one sufficiently rich in content as to provide the organizing
psychological principle that helps to shape the crowded events of
Huxley's masterpiece into a relatively unified whole. Throughout *Point
Counter Point* Spandrell exhibits a cast of mind shattered by his sexual
attachment to his mother, a fixation that has been gradually transformed
into a disfiguring bias against the female sex as a whole. Insofar as his
relationship with Mrs. Knoyle is actually described in the novel, it is for
the most part limited to the past, to a time when Spandrell believed that
he fully possessed his mother—who in the present is enshrined as a
paralyzing ideal intimately connected with his attitude towards God and
his belief in a rigidly deterministic universe. In short, what is interesting,
indeed compelling, in Huxley's portrait of Spandrell is what lies hidden
beneath the specious diabolism that has engaged the attention of so many
of Huxley's critics.

In his "Contributions to the Psychology of Love," Freud defined the
origins of the neurotic condition that is covertly operative throughout all
of Spandrell's behavior in *Point Counter Point.* Spandrell's animus
against women, his quest for a proof of God's existence, even his belief in
a Calvinistic or Augustinian theology can all be traced to what Freud and
Wilhelm Stekel describe as the prostitute complex:

The adult's conscious thought likes to regard his mother as a person of
unimpeachable moral purity; and there are few ideas which he finds so offensive
when they come from others, or feels as so tormenting when they spring from his
own mind, as one which calls this aspect of his mother in question. This very relation of the sharpest contrast between "mother" and "prostitute" will however encourage us to enquire into the history of the development of these two complexes
and the unconscious relation between them, since we long ago discovered that
what, in the conscious, is found split into a pair of opposites often occurs in the
unconscious as a unity. Investigation then leads us back to the time in a boy's life-

at which he first gains a more or less complete knowledge of the sexual relations between adults, somewhere about the years of pre-puberty. Brutal pieces of information, which are undisguisedly intended to arouse contempt and rebelliousness, now acquaint him with the secret of sexual life and destroy the authority of adults, which appears incompatible with the revelation of their sexual activities. The aspect of these disclosures which affects the newly initiated child most strongly is the way in which they apply to his own parents.[15]

Like Freud, Wilhelm Stekel regards this condition as seriously disabling when joined by intense frustration due to the father's intervention during puberty. The result is the formation of what Freud described as a preference for "debased sexual objects" as well as what Stekel sees as a sadomasochistic desire to humiliate and torment such objects.[16] In Spandrell's case, not only do the conditions of his first initiation into adult sexuality closely resemble those described by Freud, but as a consequence of his mother's marriage to Major Knoyle, he is unable to accept normal sexuality, preferring instead a series of squalid affairs governed by what Huxley himself specifies as "masochistic prostitutions" (PCP, 301).

Spandrell's relationship with his mother is destroyed "in an uneasy moment of adolescence" (PCP, 301) by means of the unexpected intrusion of Major Knoyle. Spandrell does his best to suppress this period of his life, but in chapter thirteen a "long-dead memory" (PCP, 245) suddenly transports him back to the scene of his winter vacations in the company of his mother in the Italian Alps. He sees himself skiing over an eroticized landscape of rolling slopes "like the contours of a wonderful body" where "the virgin snow was a smooth skin, delicately grained" (PCP, 247). Looking back, he perceives his mother following him, "a strong tall figure, still young and agile." Spandrell insists that this is the happiest moment of his life and his mother "the most beautiful and at the same time the most homely and comforting and familiar of beings" (PCP, 247). His sudden displacement by Major Knoyle—whom he associates with a seducer of virgins from a pornographic novel—in what he regards as an act of betrayal by his mother, leaves him "ashamed of the body and its activities" (PCP, 162) and single-mindedly devoted to a career of sadistic revenge:

The corruption of youth was the only form of debauchery that now gave him any active emotion. . . . he could still feel a peculiar satisfaction in inflicting what he regarded as the humiliation of sensual pleasure on the innocent sisters of those too much loved and therefore detested women who had been for him the personification of the detested instinct. Mediaevally hating, he took his revenge, not (like the ascetics and puritans) by mortifying the hated flesh of women, but by teaching it an indulgence which he himself regarded as evil, by luring and caressing it on to more and more complete and triumphant rebellion against the conscious soul. And the final stage of his revenge consisted in the gradual insinuation into the mind of his victim of the fundamental wrongness and baseness of the raptures he himself had taught her to feel. (*PCP*, 301-2)

Spandrell selects as his prey the "innocent sisters" of "the detested women" (i.e., prostitutes), who have become in his eyes the "personification" of the sexual instinct. He does this in order to repeat over and over again the pivotal fact of his life, his betrayal by the mother whom he has come to regard as a prostitute. Harriet Watkins is robbed of her innocence by Spandrell, much as his mother had been by the major who had walked straight out of the pages of a "Girls' School in Paris" (*PCP*, 393), to create a unbridgeable abyss between Spandrell's feminine ideal and the reality of adult sexuality. And more important, Harriet is made to experience shame and guilt in much the same way as he would like to see his mother suffer, while Spandrell himself shares in this humiliation: "Seduced in the manner he had described to the Rampions, Harriet had adored him and imagined herself adored. And she was almost right; for Spandrell did genuinely care for her, even while he was deliberately making her his victim. The violation of his own feelings as well as of hers gave an added spice of perversity to the proceedings" (*PCP*, 302). Spandrell, bound to the harrowing demands of his "pubescent imagination" (*PCP*, 394), cannot conceive of human sexuality apart from intense humiliation and guilt, a sadistic negation of life that will ultimately lead to his suicide.

Spandrell's adolescent idealism and its resultant metamorphosis into a paralyzing sexual neurosis is upon examination emblematic of the fundamental themes of *Point Counter Point*. Like Spandrell, the majority of the characters of Huxley's novel suffer from an unsatisfactory relationship with their parents, are incapable of sexual satisfaction due to a highly cerebral way of approaching physical sexuality, and in some cases as a consequence are engaged in a search for God—a proof of God's existence or a way of living an ascetic life divorced from the world. In what I would argue is a central iconic representation of one of the basic themes of Huxley's novel, Spandrell enters a woods accompanied by a prostitute and finds himself confronted by what he describes as a clump of "pleasingly phallic" (*PCP*, 479) foxgloves. Connie, the prostitute, is outraged by the comparison and asks Spandrell how he can make so odious an identification in such a pastoral setting:

"In God's country," he mocked. "How can I?" And raising his stick he suddenly began to lay about him right and left, slash, slash, breaking one of the tall proud plants at every stroke. The ground was strewn with murdered flowers. "Stop, stop!" She caught at his arm. Silently laughing, Spandrell wrenched himself away from her and went on beating down the plants. "Stop! Please! Oh, don't, don't." She made another dash at him. Still laughing, still laying about him with his stick, Spandrell dodged away from her.

"Down with them," he shouted, "down with them." Flower after flower fell under his strokes. "There!" he said at last, breathless with laughter and running and slashing. "There!" Connie was in tears. (*PCP*, 479)

This is the second eroticized landscape that Huxley has used in connection with Spandrell—the first being the cold and virginal winterscape of his adolescence. The phallic spikes of the foxgloves symbolize more than sex or natural fecundity, just as Spandrell's destructive rampage is symptomatic of something more than a generalized animus against nature or life. The key to the scene lies in Spandrell's neurotic sense of having been insulted by the potency and vigor of the plants: "Do you think I'm going to sit still and let myself be insulted? The insolence of the brutes! (*PCP*, 480). The presence of the "aging prostitute" and the brutelike "phallic" energy of the foxgloves acts as a catalyst on Spandrell's neurotic sensibility. The flowers suggest, in their "insolence," the sexual rivalry of Major Knoyle (who in turn regarded Spandrell as an example of irresponsible "insolence"—*PCP*, 114), the man for whom Spandrell felt his mother had prostituted herself.

Huxley has, I believe, borrowed this scene from Ford Madox Ford's *Some Do Not . . .*, first published in 1924 as the opening volume of the *Parade's End* tetralogy. Christopher Tietjens, like Spandrell, is incapable of achieving a harmonious sexual relationship with either his wife or the woman whom he would like to enjoy as his mistress. His life is rigidly governed by "self-suppression in matters of the emotions"[17] and in a manner that Ford regarded as broadly representative of his society. In a pivotal scene Tietjens enters a garden after breakfasting with the Rev. Mr. Duchemin, a repressed Ruskinian aesthete given to uncontrollable outbursts of violent obscenity. Tietjens, accompanied by a young woman to whom he is sexually attracted, suddenly begins to attack the yellow mulleins with his walking stick.

"God's England!" Tietjens exclaimed to himself in high good humour. "Land of Hope and Glory! . . . Tietjens paused and aimed with his hazel stick an immense blow at a tall spike of yellow mullein with its undecided, furry, glaucous leaves and its undecided, buttony, unripe lemon-coloured flowers. The structure collapsed, gracefully, like a woman killed among crinolines!

"Now I'm a bloody murderer!" Tietjens said. "Not gory! Green-stained with vital fluid of innocent plant. . . . And by God! Not a woman in the country who won't let you rape her after an hour's acquaintance!" He slew two more mulleins and a sow-thistle![18]

Tietjens's "God's England," like Spandrell's "God's country" with which he begins his attack on the foxgloves, is a society that encourages both sexual repression and as a consequence sadistic neuroses. Tietjens, who aspires to Anglican sainthood, is like the equally idealistic Spandrell the product of the upper-middle class. He is described as a "good public school boy," a man who like Spandrell has undergone "the normal upper-middle-class training in refinement and gentlemanly repression" (*PCP*, 301). In attacking the yellow mulleins, Tietjens achieves a momentary release for his fiercely repressed eroticism while at the same time he is able to strike out against his wife Sylvia, who has betrayed him both before and after his marriage. Spandrell's attack on the foxgloves is similarly motivated in that the flowers are associated with Major Knoyle. Both scenes throw into greater relief the theme of repression and psychological abnormality that by and large constitutes the heart of Huxley's and Ford's criticism of Edwardian and early modern English society.

Spandrell's preoccupation with his mother's betrayal morbidly insinuates itself into his attitude towards religion, even to the point of usurping his belief in free will and a benevolently providential divinity. Indeed, his mother figures so predominantly in his discussions of God that as the novel progresses it becomes increasingly clear that for Spandrell God is, at least in part, a substitute parent who in fact resembles the youthful ideal of his mother. Huxley writes of Spandrell's early attempts to discipline his erotic instincts: "What shame he had felt and what remorse! Struggled how hard, and prayed how earnestly for strength. And the god to whom he had prayed wore the likeness of his mother. To resist temptation was to be worthy of her" (*PCP*, 393). Once this "pubescent" idol was overturned by Major Knoyle, Spandrell began his long masochistic decline towards suicide, a descent interrupted by the sadistic interlude with Harriet Watkins but governed chiefly by a masochistic urge to punish his mother by destroying his own life. Freud describes this condition as "moral masochism" and maintains that

masochism creates a temptation to perform "sinful" actions, which must then be expiated by the reproaches of the sadistic conscience (as is exemplified in so many Russian character-types) or by chastisement from the great parental power of Destiny. In order to provoke punishment from this last representative of the parents, the masochist must do what is inexpedient, must act against his own interests, must ruin the prospects which open out to him in the real world and must, perhaps, destroy his own real existence.[19]

This is precisely what Spandrell has done:

Ever since his mother's second marriage Spandrell had always perversely made the worst of things, chosen the worst course, deliberately encouraged his own worst tendencies. It was with debauchery that he distracted his endless leisures. He was taking his revenge on her, on himself also for having been so foolishly happy and good. He was spiting her, spiting himself, spiting God. He hoped there was a hell for him to go to and regretted his inability to believe in its existence. (*PCP*, 299)

Spandrell's motivations are complex, but insofar as they can be coherently synthesized, his "masochistic prostitutions" (*PCP*, 301) involve a sadistic desire to humiliate women as an act of revenge directed against his mother, the tainted prostitute, as well as a masochistic urge to be chastised by his mother, the original untainted goddess of his adolescence. In his treatment of Harriet Watkins, he usurps the role of Major Knoyle in the performance of, to use Freud's terminology, "sinful actions"—which in turn must be expiated by the activities of a "sadistic conscience."

Spandrell's willing acquiescence in the face of Freud's "great parental power of Destiny" is equally patent in his belief that "events come ready-made to fit the people they happen to" (*PCP*, 389). Spandrell associates the formation of this theory with his adolescent disillusionment: "I feel sure that everything that has happened to me was somehow engineered in advance. As a young boy I had a foretaste of what I might have grown up to be, but for events. Something entirely different from this actual Me." He adds, referring to his mother's marriage to Major Knoyle: "But from the time that I was fifteen onwards, things began happening to me which were prophetically like what I am now" (*PCP*, 392). After brooding on the physical features of Major Knoyle, Spandrell goes on to confess his admiration for St. Augustine and Calvin, ominously noting that "God means to save some people and damn others" (*PCP*, 394).

His sense that after his fifteenth year "things began happening" to him that were "prophetically" part of a series of characteristic events is another way of describing his own decision to "deliberately" encourage his "own worst tendencies" (*PCP*, 299), to make the worst of things as a response to what he regards as his mother's betrayal. In his discussion of determinism and its role in his own dissipated life, Spandrell introduces a hypothetical argument that predictably is based on emotional rejection—in his example by a man one has deeply loved and admired. He maintains that the proper response to a total rebuff of the kind he describes is sadistic violence: "You'd knock him down. At least, that's what I would do. It would be a point of honour. And the more you'd admired, the more violent the knock and the longer the subsequent dance on his carcase." He adds, "That's why the whores and the alcohol weren't avoidable. On the contrary, it became a point of honour never to avoid them!" (*PCP*, 398). Spandrell's peculiar argument is designed to justify both his wasted life and his taste for prostitutes as a response to an earlier act of emotional rejection. Of equal interest, however, is the fact that it precisely foreshadows his murder of Webley as well as his dance on Webley's corpse. Through this remarkable foreshadowing, Huxley is not asking his reader to accept Spandrell's sense of profound rejection by his mother with his character's decision to throw away his life and his interest in prostitutes, and then associating them both with his future murder of Webley. As I hope to show later, there is a reasonable basis to this association of Spandrell's belief in his rejection by his mother and his decision to kill Webley.

It has become commonplace in the criticism of *Point Counter Point* to note the various juxtapositions of parallel plots and characters employed by Huxley as well as the theoretical pronouncements made by Philip Quarles (especially in chapter twenty-two). But the "sufficiency of characters and parallel, contrapuntal plots" (*PCP*, 408) that Philip Quarles recommends does not preclude the presence of a centrally significant plot and character. In his notebook Philip Quarles observes that a "novelist modulates by reduplicating situations and characters. He shows several people falling in love, or dying, or praying in different ways—dissimilars solving the same problem. Or, *vice versa*, similar people confronted with dissimilar problems" (*PCP*, 408). Huxley has employed both techniques, but such a method does not prevent Spandrell from establishing not only the basic paradigmatic plot of "falling in love, or dying, or praying" but in terms of thematic significance the central narrative line that—if not causally, at least thematically—dominates the remaining parallel plots and to which all in various ways are referred. Like Myra Viveash in *Antic Hay*, Maurice Spandrell is, to employ Huxley's terms, "a social symbol," and *Point Counter Point* a "novel of social history." As "a paradigm of the whole life of the community,"[20] Spandrell's sadomasochistic behavior is a satirical exaggeration intended to heighten and define the irrational self-absorption and neurotic self-destructiveness that Huxley associated with both the modern romantic and the figure of de Sade, especially de Sade as described in *Ends and Means* (see my chapter one). Spandrell's sadomasochism is reflected in much of the behavior of Lucy Tantamount, but as in the latter's case, he is not merely a carefully probed study in aberrant behavior so much as a modern anarchic individualist, a typical example of Huxley's "Sadean sociology" (*CE*, 204) and a romantic egoist, suicidal to the extent that the new romanticism itself was "headed straight towards death" (*MN*, 220). As a product of "the late, degenerate days" (*AH*, 254) of the 1920s Spandrell's obsession with "the philosophy of meaninglessness" that Huxley claimed to have come once more "triumphantly into fashion" after the Great War (*EM*,

274) links him to de Sade, Huxley's archetypal proponent of intellectual nihilism. And as a paradigm of the "whole life" of his generation, the emphasis on Spandrell's psychotic behavior corresponds to Huxley's emphasis on the psychological factor in history. Both Spandrell and de Sade are self-absorbed egoists, "uncompromisingly consistent" in their opposition to "the value of non-attachment" (*EM*, 5). In Spandrell's case, his suicidal Shelleyian idealism masks an attachment to his own past—his mother and his idealized childhood. His religiosity is a neurotic stance, and as a victim of his own protracted childhood, his entire life a persistent vendetta directed against his mother and her second husband. On a more representative level, Spandrell is a typical Huxleyan romantic, estranged from those around him, incapable of love, politically nihilistic, and powerless to free himself from the neurotic exigencies of personality or discrete selfhood. As the kind of socially emblematic character that Huxley termed a "social symbol," his various impairments and weaknesses appear to varying degrees in the behavior of most of the other characters in *Point Counter Point*.

Huxley's novel is thematically structured around the four fundamental relationships (with parent, lover, death, and God) that govern a man's life and, in their unfolding, define his character. In *Point Counter Point* all of the parental relationships are inherently unsatisfactory: John Bidlake despises his son Walter; Lord Edward Tantamount is incapable of communicating with his daughter Lucy; Sidney Quarles is an object of ridicule in the eyes of his son Philip, who in turn ignores his own son; while Spandrell, as we have already seen, believes himself betrayed by his mother. Similarly, the sexual and marital unions are equally fragile: Walter Bidlake is disgusted with his idealistic mistress, Marjorie Carling, and forced to almost rape the woman he physically desires, Lucy Tantamount; while Burlap's lubricious religiosity and Beatrice's frigidity reflect the intense cerebration that characterizes most of the sexual relationships in the novel. Elinor Quarles is frustrated by the emotional sterility of her marriage to Philip Quarles, while Spandrell is incapable of a normal sexual attachment. Philip, Spandrell, Marjorie, and Beatrice are for various reasons and to varying degrees disgusted with the body, while Lucy Tantamount can be sexually aroused only when raped or physically violated—"Letting oneself be hurt, humiliated, used like a doormat—queer. I like it" (*PCP*, 493). In addition, all of the older marriages (the Tantamounts', Bidlakes', and Quarles') are equally bankrupted by a remarkable series of infidelities. This profound impairment of both parental and marital relationships reinforces the desperate search for either a religious solution (Spandrell, Rachel Quarles, Marjorie Carling, Lord Gattendon, Burlap, and Lord Edward Tantamount) or a social one (Rampion, Illidge, and Everard Webley). The "Truth-Searchers" (*PCP*, 443), as Philip Quarles describes them, are with the exception of Rampion characterized by excessive intellectuality and are busily engaged in "substituting simple and therefore false abstractions for the living complexities of reality" (*PCP*, 444).

Within these three categories of child, lover, and "Truth-Searcher," one feature stands out with special significance, namely the fact that of all the characters in *Point Counter Point*, only Spandrell is present in each category. Walter Bidlake, for example, is described as son and lover but not as a seeker after God. Burlap, while a major figure in the grouping of God-seekers and clearly one of the chief examples of perverse sexuality, has not been given a complete biography—we know nothing of his childhood; accordingly, he does not figure in the parent-child grouping. Spandrell's narrative, however, dominates each thematic category. His relationship with his mother is probed more thoroughly than that of the others, while his sexual life is described in greater detail. Moreover, his quest for God is more intensely evoked than that of Marjorie Carling or Rachel Quarles. Spandrell's centrality in *Point Counter Point* can be demonstrated in other minor ways as well. Like Spandrell, Beatrice has suffered a serious psychological trauma during her youth. Burlap, again like Spandrell, manages to seduce an innocent young woman, and significantly his "ardours were those of a child for its mother" (*PCP*, 232), a state of mind clearly linked to Spandrell's arrested development. Marjorie Carling also despises the body and is pointedly associated with Shelley, a poet admired by Spandrell, while Lucy Tantamount rivals Spandrell in her perversely masochistic behavior. More than any other character in Huxley's novel, it is Spandrell who embodies in his own life and in particular in the ending of that life the corruption of "the whole man" (*PCP*, 555) that Huxley saw as endemic in a "collapsing" society, one about to succumb to the "nihilist revolution" discussed in my opening chapter.

Spandrell's death, one of the four deaths that conclude the novel (the others being Webley's, little Phil's, and Ethel Cobbett's), is further evidence of Spandrell's centrality in the novel's thematic structure. It is intimately connected with the murder of Everard Webley and is the final link in a chain of events stretching back to Spandrell's youth and the appearance of Major Knoyle. Echoing Peter Bowering, George Woodcock has suggested that Spandrell's "poses of evil are shot through with glimpses of an essential decency; when he decides to kill, it is a potential monster of violence, the quasi-fascist Webley, that he chooses as his victim, afterwards atoning for his act by a virtual self-execution."[21] This interpretation loses sight of the harrowing consistency of all of Spandrell's actions in *Point Counter Point.* His decision to enlist Illidge in a plot to murder Webley shows no trace of social or political motivation. Rather, it is another stage in Spandrell's masochistic decline, murder having been significantly prefigured in the foxglove scene where Spandrell slashes at the "phallic" plants, thus establishing a connection between Webley and Major Knoyle. Webley himself bears a significant resemblance to Major Knoyle in that both men are militaristic and aggressively masculine. In addition, Spandrell clubs Webley in much the same way as he levels the foxgloves that symbolize to him Knoyle's masculine "insolence" (*PCP,* 480). Spandrell's behavior after the murder confirms his sadomasochistic bent as he places his foot on Webley's face to complete the act of unconscious revenge directed against Major Knoyle and at the same time, by its very audacity, to invite the chastisement of the "great parental power of Destiny." His attempts at corruption are in essence endeavors to bring this Absolute into existence, and accordingly it would be an error to regard Spandrell's suicide as a moral gesture or the act of atonement Woodcock terms it.

For Spandrell God is "a felt experienced quality of personal actions" (*PCP,* 588), in short an immediate presence, just as his mother's had been during his adolescence when "those delicacies of feeling, those scruples and sensitivenesses and remorses of his boyhood . . . were all—the repentence for a bad action no less than the piercing delight at the spectacle of a flower or a landscape—*in some way bound up with his sentiment for his mother,* somehow rooted and implied in it" (*PCP,* 393—italics mine). Spandrell's attempts to conjure God into existence, to force "him to come out of his lair" (*PCP,* 588), are essentially attempts to resurrect his adolescent idol, the god who "wore the likeness of his mother" (*PCP,* 393). But his "piercing delight at the spectacle of a flower" that he associates with his mother's presence has been transformed into the rage he fears when confronted with the reality of the spiky "phallic" foxgloves. Nevertheless he consistently endeavors to reincarnate this "pubescent" idol; indeed, it is the dynamic psychological factor behind his quest for God.

Spandrell offers a second definition of this God as "simply the absence of dust-bins" (*PCP,* 587), a more significant definition than it might at first appear. Spandrell identifies sex with filth as the most sordid level of human activity that after his boyhood disillusionment both attracts and repels him: "All I know is that, when I discovered the reality [sex], I found it disappointing—but attractive, all the same. Perhaps so attractive just because it was so disappointing. The heart's a curious sort of manure heap; dung calls to dung, and the great charm of vice consists in its stupidity and sordidness" (*PCP,* 395). Similarly, he describes the murder of Webley as "a piece of squalid knockabout among the dust-bins, a piece of dirty dung-beetle's scavengering" (*PCP*, 588). The connection between Spandrell's attitude towards sex and his murder of Webley is, as I pointed out above, his attack on the "phallic" foxgloves which takes place prior to the murder. In killing Webley, he is in essence destroying General Knoyle, the man, now promoted, who introduced him to the "manure heap" of adult sexuality; by killing Knoyle, he expects that God, defined as the "absence of dust-bins" (i.e., a God associated with the virginal, untainted mother of his youth) will suddenly make his existence felt "as a providence . . . the giver or withholder of grace . . . the predestinating saviour or destroyer" (*PCP*, 589). Consequently, Spandrell's chastisement by such a God will guarantee the existence of absolute goodness and by extension the reality of his adolescent state of grace under the benign and pure influence of his mother.

Spandrell is for Huxley (and Rampion) the "modern aesthete," the product of an "excessive intellectual and aesthetic refinement" (*PCP*, 301) that has rendered him sexually and socially sterile. Accordingly, he is broadly representative of the "strange emotional degeneration" (*PCP*, 301) that is the fundamental theme of *Point Counter Point*. The excessive cerebration (D. H. Lawrence's "sex in the head") that characterizes Burlap, Philip Quarles, Marjorie Carling, Beatrice, and Lucy Tantamount is the chief feature of Spandrell's character—an inability to achieve a harmonious relationship between intellect and body. Spandrell's suicide exemplifies this tendency, and consequently his perception of a "Lydian Heaven" (*PCP*, 597) is strategically placed between the torpid mysticism of Marjorie Carling's "peace of God" (*PCP*, 495) and Burlap's "Kingdom of Heaven" (*PCP*, 601), a nihilistic revel in the bathtub with his mistress. Frustrated in her attempt to possess Walter Bidlake, Marjorie retreats into the ostensible perfection of an "infinite and eternal nothing" (*PCP*, 496). Like Spandrell, her religious quest is motivated by romantic disappointment and reinforced by her Shelleyan idealism. Of equal importance, her God like Spandrell's is characterized primarily by absence. Burlap's religiosity is also sexually inspired, while his "romp" in the bathtub with Beatrice like "two little children" (*PCP*, 601) is equally a commentary on Spandrell's neurotic fixation on his adolescent sexual experience.

Spandrell's death is carried out with such Gothic intensity that on the surface at least it justifies Rampion's disgust with what appears to him as mere histrionics. After playing Beethoven's A Minor Quartet in the hope that the Lydian melody of the *heilige Dankgesang* will convince Rampion of God's existence, Spandrell becomes totally absorbed in the music that in its final phase is identical in significance to Marjorie Carling's sterile mysticism. Huxley's critics have disregarded the fact that the slow movement of the quartet is described in three distinct stages. The first and third descriptions correspond to Marjorie Carling's experience of the "peace of God," a state of "vacant lifelessness" that in its "translucent" perfection (*PCP*, 495) is as much a negation of life as Spandrell's suicide. The first phase of the movement is similarly described as "transparent, pure and crystalline" (*PCP*, 595). It expresses the "serenity of the convalescent"—that is, "the peace of God" (*PCP*, 595), a state of mind identical in tone and substance to Marjorie's supine spirituality—while in its abstract and spotless purity, it reflects Spandrell's unconscious desire to resurrect the immaculate female ideal of his youth.

But just before the moment of Spandrell's total commitment to the music, the latter is described in pointed contrast to Marjorie Carling's languorous revelation of the "marvellous nothingness of God" (*PCP*, 496). The quartet, at least momentarily, exhibits "something new and marvellous": "It quivered, it was alive, it seemed to grow and intensify itself, it became an active calm, an almost *passionate* serenity. The miraculous paradox of eternal repose was musically realized" (*PCP*, 598—italics mine). Prior to this moment Rampion had dismissed the music as "just a hymn in praise of eunuchism" (*PCP*, 596). Now he is almost persuaded, using the same formula ("Almost thou persuadest me") that Spandrell had used at the beginning of the novel in his rejection of Rampion's ideal of marriage (*PCP*, 133). But once Spandrell has completely surrendered to the music, Huxley's description of the movement is subtly altered as he reemphasizes its connection with Marjorie's life-denying idealism. The "active" vitality of the quartet does suggest a level of reality, harmonious and ideal, that at least on the surface appears to affirm Spandrell's spiritual quest; but Huxley appears to be saying that such a level of being is achievable only in art and even there only fitfully. Spandrell's role as a "modern aesthete" (*PCP*, 301) is to confuse art with life or in Philip Quarles's terms, "Art before life; *Romeo and Juliet* and filthy stories before marriage or its equivalents. . . . In the good old days poets began by losing their virginity; and then, with a complete knowledge of the real thing and where and how it was unpoetical, deliberately set to work to idealize and beautify it" (*PCP*, 395). Beethoven's music is an endorsement of Quarles's aesthetic, but Spandrell's interpretation of it is not. Spandrell remains in essence a virgin. His career is the reverse of Quarles's description in that he remains devoted to a poetic ideal that has rendered him helpless in the face of a less than poetic reality.

Consequently, at the moment of his most intense enthrallment, when neither the world nor Rampion's judgment any longer matter to Spandrell, his death occurs and the music becomes once more "the place of absolute rest, of still and blissful convalescence" (*PCP*, 599). It has often been argued, most persuasively by Peter Firchow,[22] that the scratching of the needle that occurs shortly after Spandrell's suicide is Huxley's comment on the significance of Spandrell's death. But the careful description of the music itself and its obvious resemblance to Marjorie Carling's idealism provides a richer and more telling gloss on the nature of Spandrell's suicidal aestheticism and its masochistic foundation. Huxley's final comment on the significance of Spandrell's suicide is Burlap's whistling of Mendelssohn's "On Wings of Song" (*PCP*, 600), a reference to the "soaring" notes of the final movement of the A Minor Quartet as well as Shelley's "To a Skylark" that Rampion had earlier associated with "suicide" (*PCP*, 166). Spandrell's "Lydian heaven" is as empty of significance as Marjorie Carling's ideal of nebulous transcendence, while its psychological roots extend downwards to Burlap's sensual "Kingdom of Heaven," a world of childish eroticism and adolescent spirituality. Accordingly, Burlap's bathtub "romp" is another facet of Spandrell's ideal of puerile sexuality, while the whistled "Song" testifies to the futility of Spandrell's masochistic gesture.

The fact that Spandrell's idealized conception of his mother has been an incubus on his own psychological development, transforming him into a moral masochist, does not set him apart from the other characters of *Point Counter Point*. Rather, it reflects the psychological degeneration that Huxley saw as a universal affliction within his society and consequently is inseparable from Spandrell's centrality in the thematic structure of the novel. Spandrell, then, is a psychological microcosm of that society, while his "Lydian heaven" embodies its values, both neurotically spiritualized and intrinsically suicidal. In his analysis of the masochist's personality, Freud observes that the typical masochist resembles "so many Russian character types,"[23] a comparison also made by Rampion when he associates Spandrell with the Marquis de Sade as well as Dostoevsky or Stavrogin and describes him as "Smiling like all the tragic characters of fiction rolled into one!" (*PCP*, 564). However, Spandrell's theatrical diabolism is symptomatic of his neurotic sensibility, a predatory psychological impairment that reflects the wider paralysis of instinctual life in his society as a whole. All of which is to say that what Philip Quarles is intent on observing, and Mark Rampion bent on exposing, is symbolized in the values and behavior of Spandrell. In *Point Counter Point* Huxley has woven a complex net of complicity within which all of his characters are caught. In Spandrell he has created a protagonist who embodies the essential pattern that underlies the novel's complex and episodic surface.

*Point Counter Point* marks the consolidation of Huxley's philosophy of history and its effective merging with his aesthetic of the social novel. As a kind of social history, it embraces a broad range of economically defined classes and is notable for its inclusion of a detailed study (with mixed results) of lower-class characters, a category that Huxley had skirted in the earlier novels. Despite the continuity of satirical aim and style with his earlier novels of the twenties, *Point Counter Point* exhibits a confident marriage of theory and practice, more exigently political in emphasis, more insistent on the psychological basis of history, and for the first time placing peculiar stress on anarchic sadomasochism—a satirical formula that came to dominate his novels of the following decade. Equally significant, Huxley's fourth novel is haunted by the memory of the Great War and the approaching menace of a new conflict. The society he depicts is pervaded by a Spenglerian ambiance of decay and dissolution, addicted to "sadistic *frissons*" (*PCP*, 435) and systematically vulnerable to the emerging ideological fanaticism of fascist, communist, and nihilist. In a letter written to John Middleton Murry in March, 1925, Huxley speculated on the connection between history and psychology, remarking that society had entered a phase of increasing disintegration: "And then the alarming results in [the] present days of the collapse, for an ever widening circle of individuals, of the social system—the uncomfortable results of an utter scepticism about society in its present form."[24] Illidge, Webley, and Spandrell are of course the principal voices of skepticism regarding the social system of class privilege and economic instability dramatized in *Point Counter Point*. Yet it is Spandrell, the Sadean nihilist, who overshadows the others, insinuating himself into the lives of fascist and communist alike as the death-intoxicated presiding spirit of a "collapsing" culture.

## 2. The Molecular Theory of Personality in *Point Counter Point, Eyeless in Gaza,* and *After Many a Summer Dies the Swan*

Accompanying Huxley's increasingly pessimistic view of history as a romantic odyssey of radical dimensions is a correspondingly complicated but cautiously optimistic theory of personality that is also rooted in his thinking about romanticism. However, to understand the relationship between Huxley's philosophy of history and his concept of the self, it is necessary to explore briefly the link between his assessment of D. H. Lawrence and his use of concepts derived from the romantic poet William Blake. In *The Olive Tree* Huxley observed of Blake that "in a certain sense he was a contemporary of D. H. Lawrence," an identification he based on the similarity between Lawrence's and Blake's theories of the impersonal self. In *Do What You Will*, the title of which he borrowed from Blake, he described the poet in terms of the ubiquitous balance metaphor as one of "those who live fully and harmoniously with their whole being" and who would encounter "almost certain social disaster" (*DWW*, 36) in the neurotically aimless society of *Point Counter Point*. He then singles out Blake's *Marriage of Heaven and Hell* as a reliable index to the "life-worshipper's metaphysic" (*DWW*, 277), quoting from the third and fourth plates where Blake first announces his dialectical philosophy and then, in the voice of the Devil, clarifies the relationship between body and mind. But Blake, a precursor of Lawrence and according to Huxley the one romantic poet to espouse an ethic of mind-body unity, appealed to the latter for another and potentially more complicated approach to the subjective nature of the personality and its relationship to the external world.

In *Point Counter Point* Mark Rampion praises Blake as "the last civilized man," civilization being defined as a mental equipoise of "harmony and completeness" (*PCP*, 144). After citing this encomium in *Fearful Symmetry*, Northrop Frye remarked that "had Blake heard himself so described in his life-time, it might have been the one thing that could have broken his spirit."[25] Frye's reservations about Rampion's use of Blake in his theory of "Atavismus" or "noble savagery" (*PCP*, 157) stems from the critic's awareness that the classical ideal of mind-body harmony or the romantic obsession with cultural primitivism praised by Rampion was essentially static and therefore fundamentally un-Blakean. The degree to which Huxley was aware of this is difficult to determine, but it is clear that he regarded the Lawrencian-Blakean ethic of Miles Fanning and Mark Rampion as an advance on the self-divisiveness of the baroque-romantic. Yet this progress was only of provisional value as Huxley became increasingly critical of any attempt to defend a theory of the unified personality at a strictly empiricist or psychological level. In this regard, it is Blake, in alliance with Wordsworth rather than Lawrence, who emerges as a decisive influence on Huxley's thinking and in an unexpectedly complex way.

In *Do What You Will* Huxley carried a stage further the problem first raised in *Proper Studies* concerning the possible coherency of a self or personality (Huxley uses these terms interchangeably) defined as "discontinuous in time" (*PS*, 235) and subject to the covert "offices of the unconscious" (*PS*, 241). Huxley regarded the personality as essentially atomistic, composed of discrete elements requiring some kind of organizing framework "so that the discontinuous states may reveal themselves as part of a whole developing in time" (*PS*, 243–44). The troublesome question of a "framework" remained unresolved in *Proper Studies*, although Huxley does turn to Wordsworth's "techniques for association-making" as potentially capable of providing the grounds for a "deliberately chosen continuity" (*PS*, 250). He returns to this vexing issue in *Do What You Will*, where he defines the self as "a series of distinct psychological states, a colony of diverse personalities" (*DWW*, 300). Just as the universe has "no single, pre-established meaning" (*DWW*, 293), man reflects this diversity as a psychological entity intrinsically "multifarious, inconsistent, self-contradictory" (*DWW*, 81). Huxley's dilemma, however, is the result of two tendencies inherent in his thinking about the self. On the one hand, he will argue for the ethical-emotional unity of the conscious personality, while on the other he insists on its fundamental fragmentariness. In short, axiological solutions repeatedly collide with ontological doubts.

Beginning in *Antic Hay* and culminating in the writings of the late 1920s, Huxley insists on the viability of his "complete man," a Huxleyan-Lawrencian moral ideal of the "man in whom all the elements of human nature have been developed to the highest pitch compatible with the making and holding of a psychological harmony within the individual and an external social harmony between the individual and his fellows" (*DWW*, 72). Such a harmony is premised on the essentially rhetorical meaning of such phrases as "balanced contradictions" (*DWW*, 72) or "unstable equilibrium" (*PCP*, 81). But ontologically the basis for such a moral-psychological ideal does not exist except, Huxley argues, as "a kind of Hydra—many as well as one, numerous in its uniqueness." Huxley's writings from 1921 to 1939 were dominated by an increasingly articulate sense of the radical discontinuity of all experience. History is fragmented and chaotic, the universe essentially pluralistic and profoundly complex, and not surprisingly the ontological basis of the self inevitably a mirror of this atomized world. Huxley's aversion to the monistic impulse of Shelleyan romanticism is inextricably wedded to his metaphysical pluralism and sensitivity to a universe characterized by flux and change. The romantic's aspiration towards "a consistent perfection" (*DWW*, 74) is an illusion designed to compensate for the "inconsistent" basis of personality. Thus Marjorie Carling's quest for mystical illumination results in an ecstatic union with "nothing" (*PCP*, 496), the Shelleyan romantic's idealistic counterpart of the "void" of a "reverse romantic" like Francis Chelifer.

In *Eyeless in Gaza* Anthony Beavis, whom I regard as Huxley's spokesman (the character's ideas conform closely to those of *Ends and Means*), clarifies the ontological—as opposed to Mark Rampion's essentially moral—concept of personality:

Now, human experience is analogous to matter. Analyze it—and you will find yourself in the presence of psychological atoms. A lot of these atoms constitute normal experience and a selection from normal experience constitutes 'personality.' Each individual atom is unlike normal experience and still more unlike personality. Conversely, each atom in experience resembles the corresponding atom in another. Viewed microscopically a woman's body is just like a washstand, and Napoleon's experience is just like Wellington's. (*EG*, 104)

Thus the answer to the question as to "why we imagine that we have coherent experience and personality" lies with the fact that although we don't, "our minds work slowly and have very feeble powers of analysis" (*EG*, 104). Although Beavis's theory permits him to avoid accountability for his moral and emotional failings, it must always be kept in mind that in the late twenties Huxley is dealing with two *distinct* perspectives on the self, one moral and psychological and the other ontological and ultimately mystical. Beavis will learn to integrate his personality on the moral-emotional level, but his basic premise of the inherently molecular structure of the self remains for Huxley an indisputable axiom.

In the eleventh chapter of *Eyeless in Gaza*, Huxley attempted to synthesize his thinking on the subject of the self or "personality" in a lengthy meditation recorded in Anthony Beavis's notebook. Anthony Beavis, after citing F. H. Bradley's *Appearance and Reality*[26] and Hume's *Treatise*, turns to Blake and his doctrine of the states to resolve the problem of identity and the possibility of a more holistic conception of self:

It was left to Blake to rationalize psychological atomism into a philosophical system. Man according to Blake (and, after him, according to Lawrence), is simply a succession of states. Good and evil can be predicted only of states, not of individuals, who in fact don't exist, except as places where the states occur. It is the end of personality in the old sense of the word. (*EG*, 107)

He adds unexpectedly that Blake's concept of the states argues the appearance of a new kind of personality, the "total man" who exhibits two major traits: first, he is "the antithesis of . . . the fundamental Christian man of our history" and, second, he is nevertheless "the realization of that ideal personality conceived by the Jesus of the Gospel" (*EG*, 107). In short, ontologically "the individual" does not exist except as a locus for the functioning of "states," but in the very same paragraph a "new kind of personality" is scrupulously defined in intensely moralistic and decidedly Victorian terms. The new personality is a very sharply contracted self conceived as inherently disinterested, passive in its receptivity to immediate experience, and characterized by humility and honesty. The important element in this concept of the self is its resounding negativity. The new man is "not interested," evinces a "refusal to exalt himself," lays "no lasting claims on anything," and is "not pharisaic" (*EG*, 107). This of course would be a good description of one of George Eliot's or Dickens's self-renunciatory protagonists.[27] Moreover, Huxley's ideal of a sensitive but passive alertness to immediate experience, coupled with a self-effacing humility, is profoundly un-Blakean in its neglect of the creative imagination and Blake's spirited endorsement of energy and self-assertion. There is, however, a subtle strategy behind Huxley's use of Blake.

Huxley's interpretation of Blake's concept of the states (set forth in Blake's *Milton* and *Jerusalem*[28]) is somewhat skewed, emphasizing not only the transiency of the states but the disappearance of the individual as well. Blake vigorously stressed the potential infinity latent yet imperishable in every human being. Nevertheless, Blake did conceive of the self as constituting a series of states; that is, of static conditions that individuals are capable of transcending. For Blake a state is a fixed mental configuration, shaped and informed by specific societal, psychological, or political pressures, and as such can be recognized and then rejected by the individual. The personality or self, then, is governed by "the limitations of the given psychological socioeconomic state that a man inhabits at a certain time in a certain place,"[29] and is often emblematized in Huxley's novels by carefully circumscribed symbolic landscapes like the "realist's" Gog's Court, the romantic's Brighton Pavilion, or Mark Staithes's barren house. Huxley's adoption of Blake's theory of the states permits him to argue for the deliberate creation of an enduring matrix of associated memories and feelings (i.e. personality) but *to limit* the integrity of that creation on the ontological level. Thus by defining the self in negative, sharply circumscribed terms, he avoids the inflated egoism of the baroque-romantic and the equally egocentric self-pity of the reverse romantic, whom Calamy in *Those Barren Leaves* condemns as hopelessly "sentimentalist" (*TBL*, 371). And in denying the absolute integrity of the individual on the ontological level, he has opened a window onto the absolute—so to speak. Just as life may exhibit a surface of diversity and flux, so too the mind is conceived as essentially dynamic. But underlying both is a *tertium quid* that only makes its presence felt when the exigent self disappears.

In *Point Counter Point* Philip Quarles also draws on Blake's theory, substituting the term "moulds" for "states." He observes that the essential trait of the self is its malleability, a protean capacity to immerse itself in the welter of thought, feeling, and emotion that constitutes human experience. This dynamic conception of a fluid self capable of adapting to "all contours and yet remain[ing] unfixed in any form" (*PCP*, 269) is on one level self-serving, permitting Quarles like Beavis to justify his moral and emotional disengagement from those around him. Thus the ability of the self "to take, and with equal facility efface impressions" preserves what for Quarles is an irresponsible freedom, but what for Beavis and earlier for Calamy is potentially the basis for a mystical detachment from the empirical level:

> To such moulds as his spirit might from time to time occupy, to such hard and burning obstacles as it might flow round, submerge, and, itself cold, penetrate to the fiery heart of, no permanent loyalty was owing. The moulds were emptied as easily as they had been filled, the obstacles were passed by. (*PCP*, 269)

Not surprisingly, Quarles identifies himself with the "essential liquidness that flows where it would"; that is, a passive self that conforms to its world guided only by the nature of that world as it flows in an "indifferent flux of intellectual curiosity" (*PCP*, 269). It is not hard to find romantic analogues for this conception of an impersonal, chameleon self. Keats's theory of negative capability is, as Jerome Meckier has suggested,[30] an obvious source. While often expressing doubts concerning Keats's poems, Huxley was an admirer of the letters, and Quarles's theorizings are clearly indebted to Keats's theory of creative anonymity. But while Keats's impersonal aesthetic worked against the egoism of the baroque-romantic sensibility, it did not solve the problem of achieving even a degree of unity within the atomized personality. Quarles's fluid consciousness is not an integral entity so much as a motion or process that resists stasis in any form, including the existence of a stable and determinant self. The intellectual leap from the molecular theory of self based on Blake and resulting in a flat denial of personal unity to a more richly conceived self, marked by an emotional and moral concord that stretches vertiginously over the "abyss" of inverse romantic despair, is precariously achieved by an appeal to Wordsworth's theory of memory —a theory previously satirized in *Those Barren Leaves*.[31]

Shorn of his "pantheistic hypotheses" (*DWW*, 122), Wordsworth reemerges with Blake as one of the cornerstones of Huxley's dualistic theory of the self. The evolution of Huxley's thinking can best be illustrated by comparing three quotations, each of which paraphrases Wordsworth; when taken together, they represent an important strand in Huxley's endeavor to establish the theoretical "framework" for a tenuously integrated personality on the level of empirical experience —but not, it must be emphasized, that of absolute reality. In *Proper Studies* Huxley maintained that in order to overcome mental discontinuity and to consolidate the, at least, contingent existence of a central consciousness presiding over sequences of memory, it is necessary to "devise a technique for association-making" in order to transform a normally recalcitrant world into a humanized one "charged with associations" (PS, 250). For Huxley, to endow the world with such subjective associations is to create a mirror for the self, shoring up its sense of a holistic identity as well as providing an edge to its moral reactions. Huxley then quotes from Wordsworth's "My Heart Leaps Up" and concludes that by systematically employing memory, the discrete fragments of past and present feelings and thoughts constituting the self "shall not be discontinuous" but "bound each to each by natural piety" (PS, 250). Similarly, in *Point Counter Point* Elinor Quarles accuses her husband of deliberately refusing to draw on his powers of associating ideas: " 'That's true,' said Philip. 'I don't often try to remember. Hardly ever, in fact. I always seem to have too much to do and think about.' " Elinor, paraphrasing the same Wordsworth lyric, replies, "you have no natural piety" (PCP, 373). Quarles, who insists on the "molecular theory" of self and the absence of any supporting substructure, lacks the moral will or inclination for emotional association.

In this respect, he resembles Anthony Beavis of *Eyeless in Gaza* who boldly proclaims, "I would wish my days to be separated each from each by unnatural impiety" (EG, 7) and prefers to believe in a "lunatic" who, deep "in the mind," merely "shuffled a pack of snapshots and dealt them out at random" (EG, 17). But if the lunatic who presides over "a succession of more or less incongruous states" (EG, 109) can be restored to some kind of associational sanity, controlling sequences of thought, feeling, and emotion in such a way as to promote and enrich the moral life— as well as provide a basis for a self persisting in time—such an achievement is for Huxley merely the creation of a provisional "framework" (PS, 249). It may be possible to organize Blake's states by means of Wordsworth's theory of memory and association, but between the interstices of such a "framework" lies a "void" (EG, 472), alien to the exigencies of personal desires, thoughts, or values. To attempt to possess, or more accurately to fill, this void through the intrusion of the ego is to pursue the path of the baroque-romantic. The associational linking of the present with the past, however central to the sense of a persisting moral-emotional matrix of personal identity, does not constitute a uniquely monadic personality. Huxley was consistent in his rejection—on the ontological level—of an absolutely "coherent and enduring soul" (AMS, 309).

In *After Many a Summer* he will continue to conceive of the self in Quarles's and Beavis's terms, as an essentially "molecular" entity based on Blake's theory of the states. Huxley employs two related metaphors: first, the individual is described as "a swarm of constellated impulses and sentiments and notions . . . contradictory thoughts and desires" and, second, is conceived as a "spatiotemporal cage, within which the swarm is enclosed" (*AMS*, 309). This judgement does not constitute a decisive revision of the concept of the self set forth in *Eyeless in Gaza*. Quarles's "moulds," Beavis's "states," and Huxley's "swarms" and "cages" are identical in meaning. Indeed, Huxley does not so much add a new dimension to his concept of self as clarify an old one in reaching back to *Point Counter Point* and Quarles's emphasis on the self as intrinsically intellectual, a dynamic motion or fluid point of view as opposed to a rigidly static entity. Huxley argues with increasing emphasis that the atomized "self" or "soul" is simply a necessary fiction, a verbal construct—in essence, language itself:

The nature of our "souls" and of the world they inhabit would be entirely different from what it is, if we had never learned to talk. . . . Madness consists, among other things, in imagining that our "soul" exists apart from the language our nurses happen to have taught us. (*AMS*, 310)

Unlike Anthony Beavis, who seeks "a unity" where there are "no more words" (*EG*, 472), the blindly self-assertive romantic like Casimir Lypiatt desires only to reify the anarchic babble of Shelley's West Wind (the "great wind that is in me"—*AH*, 94), just as Francis Chelifer attempts to impose his "Wordsworthian formulas" on the world around him. Such egoistic endeavors are essentially projections of language, of a self whose atomized constitution amounts to a babble of words too often regarded as "reality" and substituted for the silence that Anthony Beavis and, much earlier, Calamy have grown progressively conscious of—and in relation to which they adopt a poised and alert sensitivity. The contentious garrulity of the baroque-romantic who, like Casimir Lypiatt, behaves like a noisy Cain bearing the stigmata of his own egoistic formulations is not too far removed from the obstreperous Mark Rampion, who confesses in the final chapters of *Point Counter Point*, "The way I've been talking—it's really non-human. Really scandalous. I'm ashamed. But that's the trouble: when you're up against non-human things and people, you inevitably become non-human yourself" (*PCP*, 564). Rampion is closer to the truth than he realizes, just as Spandrell's and Marjorie Carling's quest for silence and peace contains an element of genuine insight.

In *After Many a Summer Dies the Swan*, the "cage of flesh and memory" (*AMS*, 310) would appear to mark a shift in Huxley's assessment of Wordsworth's associational theory of memory, but this is only an apparent contradiction. Just as William Propter condemns all history as romantic and corrupt yet insists on the limited endeavor to achieve some degree of "progress" based on past experience, so Huxley is consistent in his view that the conscious sense of an enduring personality is—provisionally—a viable concept necessary to the moral life of man and at the same time an illusory "cage." Ultimately the self is only a conditional or tentative network of language, an affiliated web of words that functions contingently as an imprisoning "swarm" obscuring the reality that lies beyond the exigencies of ego and personality. Accordingly, at the conclusion of *Eyeless in Gaza*, Anthony Beavis achieves not only a morally enriched sense of identity that owes much of its substance to Wordsworth and Keats but also, on the ontological level, the awareness that such an achievement, however valuable, is a severely circumscribed one and that only as the linguistic pattern of self recedes can "the silence" emerge and somehow deepen into "the serene activity which springs from the knowledge that our 'souls' are illusory" (*AMS*, 312). Anthony's momentary immersion in the "dark void beyond all personal life" (*EG*, 472) transcends not only the "images" and "words" of discursive reason but the discursive self as well. Such an experience represents, among other things, the radical effacement of the baroque-romantic impulse in which the essential discontinuity of self (the "void" spanned by the "framework" of personality) is not a defect but a fragility necessary to the appearance of the numinous "light" and "serenity" (*EG*, 472) that in *After Many a Summer* is conceived as wholly dependent on "the complete absence of what we call our humanity" (*AMS*, 311). Yet at the same time Beavis must paradoxically embrace an ethic of direct action and self-sacrifice in a world where there is "no remedy except to become aware of one's interests as a human being" (*EG*, 343). For Huxley a secular ethic of self-renunciation points inevitably towards a mystical self-transcendence in which the self-aggrandizement of the romantic or the dour capitulation of the new have no place.

It should be clear, then, that much of Huxley's speculation on the nature of history, art, modern society, and finally the personality or self is intimately bound up with his interpretation of romanticism. To mark his progress from *Antic Hay* to *After Many a Summer* is to become increasingly aware of an essential continuity in his thought in which the secular is never far from the sacred. His quest for a human ethic based on an organically integral and enduring self remains inseparable from his gradually evolving belief in the mystical self-effacement of a molecular and thus illusory personality. The context for these developments is pervasively romantic, specifically derivable from Blake's prophecies, Wordsworth's criticism, Keats's letters, and Shelley's poems; but as always with Huxley his approach was invariably selective, choosing whatever conformed to his own ideas and rejecting everything else. His early and systematic repudiation of the major English romantic poets was succeeded by a qualified approval, but his fundamental assessment of the baroque-romantic aesthetic remained essentially the same. Blake's theory of the states and Wordsworth's associational theory of memory became the cornerstones of Huxley's theory of selfhood, while the mystical experience of Anthony Beavis in *Eyeless in Gaza* owes much to Shelley's *Adonais*. These conclusions are by no means exhaustive of Huxley's debt to English romanticism,[32] but they do establish the broader lineaments of that debt as well as the subtler oscillations between tentative rejection and an approval always edged with mistrust. There are other dimensions to his philosophy of history, his aesthetic, and his psychology that cannot be measured in terms of specifically romantic categories, yet there is little doubt that the issues raised by these categories formed the philosophical context for much of Huxley's work from 1923 to 1939.

### 3. *Brave New World:* Huxley's Dystopian Dilemma

The world of the seventh century after Ford is a projection of Huxley's increasingly somber assessment of the course of modern history—an alternative world systematically conceived as an anti-utopia or, more precisely, a dystopia in which the course of history has been diverted to apparently rational ends. While drawing on many of the traditional utopian conventions, the literary ancestry of *Brave New World* can be traced back to the evolutionary romance,[33] an Edwardian genre for the most part played out by 1914. H. Robert Huntley has characterized the Darwinian controversy insofar as it affected this genre in the late Victorian and Edwardian periods as one "that implanted the notion of 'process' indelibly on the Western mind, while leaving it free to interpret the end of that process as either promise or threat for the well-being of mankind."[34] The distant evolutionary good of the greatest number, or in Huxley's terms the "Higher Utilitarianism" of Mustapha Mond's World State, was a recurrent theme in novels like Bulwer-Lytton's *The Coming Race* (1871), W. H. Hudson's *A Crystal Age* (1887), or the various evolutionary romances of H. G. Wells. *Brave New World* can be described as a literary descendent of the evolutionary romance to the extent that it analyzes the behavior of a future race in the context of radically evolved biological types; but in this later variant of the genre, the arbitrary and unpredictable processes of natural selection have been supplanted and rationalized by eugenics. The striking opening scene in the Central London Hatchery is a satirical tableau in which the Fordean production line merges with the scientific laboratory where Mond's apprentice sorcerers concoct, nurture, and decant a witch's brew of artificially evolved types. But if evolution has been brought under the control of social engineering and eugenics, history too has been nullified by the scientists and technicians of the "World State," where both "historicism" and "developmentalism" have become archaic concepts bereft of any trace of meaning.

Throughout the twenties Huxley repeatedly expressed his misgivings concerning not only the methodological principles underlying the study of the past but the actual course taken by modern British and European history. By 1928 he had become increasingly aware of the threat posed by the two principal variants of modern totalitarianism, Italian fascism and Russian communism. While neither as overtly political nor as sensitive to contemporary developments in Europe as *Eyeless in Gaza* or *After Many a Summer Dies the Swan*, *Brave New World* is an implicit condemnation of collectivist absolutism, despite the fact that in Huxley's dystopia, coercion is exercised in an ingratiatingly mild and benevolent form. The inhabitants of the World State are condemned to a life of discreetly stimulated apathy, and as Huxley argued in a letter to George Orwell,[35] he firmly believed that his gently paternalistic form of despotism was much more likely to evolve out of current historical conditions than the systematically violent alternative envisaged in *Nineteen Eighty-Four*. Of equal significance, however, the autocratic utilitarians governing the World State have succeeded in solving the problem of the meaning and direction of history that had exercised Huxley throughout the 1920s; they have simply banished it by fiat.

In *Ends and Means*, published five years after *Brave New World*, Huxley speculated on the path of "regression" taken by modern history, contrasting it to a conceivably "non-Euclidean history" with its potentially utopian line of development: "it would be interesting to construct a historical 'Uchronia' (to use Renouvier's useful word), based upon the postulate that Robespierre and the other Jacobin leaders were convinced pacifists. The 'non-Euclidean' history deducible from this first principle would be a history, I suspect, innocent of Napolean, of Bismarck, of British imperialism and the scramble for Africa, of the World War, of militant Communism and Fascism, of Hitler and universal rearmament" (*EM*, 145). *Brave New World* is the darker antithesis of such a hopeful Uchronia, a satiric dystopia based on a rejection of current European ideology, including its ancillary belief in limitless technological innovation. And while history is denied in Huxley's Fordean society, the World

State is the direct outgrowth of, in his terms, a bleakly "Euclidean" series of historical undulations. In *The Olive Tree*, which appeared four years after *Brave New World*, Huxley speculated on the existence of collective trends shaping and informing the flow of historical events but never manifesting themselves in such a way as to be susceptible to scientific formulation.

As I observed in chapter one, Huxley's "historical undulations" are not nomological entities operating according to scientific laws but rather broad cultural tendencies, heterogenous in form and psychological in nature. Equally important, Huxley on occasion associated them with a rhythmic oscillation between alternating states of "decadence" and cultural vigor: "The history of any nation follows an undulatory course. In the trough of the wave we find more or less complete anarchy; but the crest is not more or less complete Utopia, but only, at best, a tolerably humane, partially free and fairly just society that invariably carries within itself the seeds of its own decadence" (*CE*, 277). Throughout the interwar period Huxley consistently disparaged theoretical generalizations regarding historical process, but in the essays and satirical narratives of the 1930s, he did occasionally introduce the concept of cyclical process. Moreover, his playful use of the term "Euclidean" does hint at a nomological emphasis; that is, a history proceeding according to laws and axioms systematically and logically deducible from each another. The "trough" and "crest" of Huxley's historical wave finds its antecedent in *Point Counter Point* where Rampion revised Wellsian theories of linear "progress" in terms of a pattern of "peaks and declines" (*PCP*, 291). Similarly, Mark Staithes of *Eyeless in Gaza* will employ Gibbon's *Decline and Fall* as a touchstone in his attempt to gauge the current status of British and European history. However, I believe the bleakly Spenglerian caste of Huxley's assessment of events in Europe and England is symptomatic less of a shift in his estimate of history's comprehensibility than of his despair regarding a series of events which, as he informed E. M. Forster, seemed to be moving irrevocably toward "some fantastic denial of humanity" and in a discernibly *"straight, un-dulating trajectory"* (italics mine). The "inward decay" of *Point Counter Point* had become in the thirties outright "regression" in a society where the forces of history had outstripped even Rampion's prophecies of an apocalyptic "gallop toward death" (*PCP*, 437).

In *Brave New World* Huxley attempted to envisage a very distant development of the society depicted in *Antic Hay* and *Point Counter Point*. The liberal "Utopia" of tolerable humaneness and partial freedom described in *The Olive Tree* was rejected in favor of a more likely alternative, a collectivist dystopia. Occupying neither the "crest" nor the "trough" of the wave, Mustapha Mond's World State is a massive socioeconomic improvisation marking the termination of history, an apocalyptic ushering-in of a society so authoritarian and immobile that historical process has been halted, rather like a river frozen in its bed. As an attempt to dam up the forces of history, such a society is founded on fear and revulsion, specifically a dread of those libidinal and sadomasochistic drives that Huxley had previously dramatized in the irrational urges and violent attitudes of socially emblematic characters like Maurice Spandrell, Lucy Tantamount, Everard Webley, and Illidge of *Point Counter Point.* Throughout the period 1928 to 1939, Huxley's letters and essays illustrate his belief that he could detect social processes at work that seemed vaguely and only conjecturally lawlike in their pervasive effect and apparent inevitability. This intractably "Euclidean" set of conditions he associated with social fragmentation, increasingly irrational behavior, moral "decadence," and a kind of social death-wish. In *Brave New World* Mustapha Mond's government had come into being only after a period in which these forces or tendencies (i.e. Huxley's "undulations") had been given unlimited play during the "Nine Years' War."

The World State, then, is premised on the futility of history, specifically a denial of the concept of progress and a revulsion for "the remote past" (*BNW*, 112), any mention of which is regarded as an unforgivable solecism. The inhabitants of the seventh century after Ford are "taught no history" (*BNW*, 39) in compliance with Ford's dictum that "history is bunk" (*BNW*, 38). *Brave New World,* however, is provided with a schematic past, the salient events of which emerge gradually in the course of the novel and when summarized form a sequence of events that conform to Huxley's "deteriorationist" perspective. The chronology of Fordian and pre-Fordian history begins with a period of increasing violence and widespread social instability:

A.F. 141: Outbreak of "The Nine Years' War" followed by "the great Economic Collapse." A period of Russian ecological warfare including the poisoning of rivers and the anthrax bombing of Germany and France.

A.F. 150: Beginning of "World Control."
The "conscription of consumption" followed by a period of social restiveness and instability.
The rise of "Conscientious objection and [a] back to nature movement."
The reaction to liberal protest movements.
The Golders Green massacre of "Simple Lifers."
The British Museum Massacre.

Abandonment of force by the World Controllers.
Period of an anti-history movement and social reeducation in-
cluding intensive propaganda directed against viviparous
reproduction as well as a "campaign against the Past."
Museums closed.
Suppression of all books published before A.F. 150.
A.F. 178: Government subsidization of special programs in pharma-
cology and biochemistry.
Stabilization of the World State.
A.F. 473: The Cyprus Experiment: establishment of a wholly Alpha com-
munity.
A.F. 478: Civil war in Cyprus.
Nineteen thousand Alphas killed.
A.F. 482 (approx.): The Ireland Experiment (increased leisure time and
four-hour work week).
A.F. 632: The present of *Brave New World*.

The achievement of, in Mustapha Mond's words, "the stablest equilibrium in history" (*BNW*, 272) is attributable to a paralysis of historical
process that extends to the individual citizen in a world where birth leads
immediately to arrested development. For Mond the clamant needs of his
society, indeed the exigencies of history itself, have finally been provided
for by a pantheon of cultural heroes including Henry Ford, Freud,
Pavlov, Marx, and Lenin. The World State is a wholly secular culture,
dominated by economics, supported by technology, and dedicated to
the—within carefully set limits—Freudian pleasure principle with its emphasis on libidinal appetite. In brief, Mond's carefully controlled society
involves an immersion in the present in which Pavlovian conditioning,
Marxist collectivism, Fordean technology, and a calculated indulgence of
Freudian infantile appetitiveness combine to rigidly stabilize society and
undermine the concept of linear progress.

Cut off from the past and heedless of a future that no longer beckons
with the promise of an enlargement of knowledge or a further refinement
of consciousness, the inhabitants of Mond's Fordean culture no longer
aspire to a good "somewhere beyond, somewhere outside the present"
(*BNW*, 211). As the names of many of the characters suggest (Bernard
Marx, Hubert Bakunin, Sarojini Engels, Lenina Crowne, and Polly Trot-
sky), the Fordean dystopia is a workers' paradise where the state, instead
of withering away, has metastasized into a benevolent despotism that in
a very general sense Huxley extrapolated from the secularist materialism
of Marx and Lenin. The hinted connection with Marxism and Leninism is
tenuous at best, but it does serve to remind the reader of Huxley's iden-

tification of Russian socialism with the new romanticism and its "disparagement of spiritual and individual values" (MN, 216). For Huxley "the Bolsheviks are romantic in denying that man is anything more than a social animal, susceptible of being transformed by proper training into a perfect machine." In essence this is the fundamental postulate of Mond's perverted socialism, a new romantic preoccupation with "human biology and economics" (MN, 215) culminating in the transformation of human beings into reliable and predictable mechanisms. To that extent *Brave New World* prophesies the ultimate triumph of the new romanticism.

Flying over the New Mexico landscape, Bernard Marx notes the presence of an electric fence demarcating the boundary between civilization and the "savagery" of the reservation: "the fence marched on and on, irresistibly the straight line, the geometrical symbol of triumphant human purpose" (BNW, 123). But such New Romantic linearity had reached its terminus in the World State, and despite the sleep-inculcated principle that "progress *is* lovely" (BNW, 118), no further development is contemplated by the World Controllers. Mustapha Mond firmly repudiates the notion of "scientific progress" and its corollary "that it could be allowed to go on indefinitely, regardless of everything else" (BNW, 273). Having reached its apotheosis in the World State, history has been displaced by a static present founded on a carefully selective approach to technology and science; as a result, progress has become a noun lacking a meaningful referent. Keith May has observed that "*Brave New World* is a portrait of a dilemma," the quandary being an ambiguous polarization between the utopian and the primitive, or "between the minimization of suffering and the positive search for suffering."[36] In large measure this is the case, but the Savage Reservation is as much an insulated time capsule as the Fordean World State. The former is a weird agglomeration of ancient religious and barbaric customs. Thriving on supernatural rituals that in turn are founded on the presumed efficacy of suffering, the Savage Reservation is a small dystopia existing within what purports to be a larger utopian state. Carefully quarantined, it is an unnatural survival from "the Bottomless Past" (BNW, 116), part museum for the benefit of prudently chosen tourists, part concentration camp for those who cannot be smoothly assimilated into Mond's ideal state. But the atavistic suffering that it offers is without meaning, compounded equally of religious violence and a broad range of physical ailments, including disease, arbitrary violence, and the aging process. Admittedly, the pain that pervades the reservation does hold out the promise of rousing Bernard from the soma torpor of the World State, but it remains an unsatisfactory alternative as a consequence of its essential barbarity. Indeed, these two apparently contrasting cultures actually mirror each other in a number of ways. History is no more relevant to the inhabitants of the reservation than to the citizens of Fordean civilization. Both societies are morally coercive, while the debasing violence of the fertility ritual finds its attenuated counterpart in the repressed violence of the communal orgies of Bernard's London.

Like *Point Counter Point*, *Brave New World* achieves closure with an act of calculated yet futile rebellion followed by a sexual orgy and a suicide. Spandrell's murder of the fascist Everard Webley finds its distant echo in the climactic scene at the Park Lane Hospital, where John the Savage, spurred by the Fascist regimentation of the Delta workers, attempts to foment a social uprising. Burlap's private bathroom tryst with Beatrice is expanded at the close of *Brave New World* to an appropriately public sadomasochistic saturnalia, while the suicide of Spandrell is reenacted by John the Savage. Both suicides proceed from similarly complicated sources. As I argued earlier, Spandrell's self immolation is motivated only in part by his inability to discover meaning in the secularized and atomistic society of *Point Counter Point;* it is also, perhaps even principally, a masochistic gesture directed at his mother as a consequence of his belief that she had prostituted herself by betraying him to his rival, Major Knoyle. John the Savage is also deeply scarred by his memories of what he regards as his mother's promiscuity. Singled out by the savage community as sexually profligate, she is enshrined in his consciousness as a woman who surrendered herself to a hostile masculine interloper who literally shuts the young John out of his mother's life. The memory of "Linda and Popé" (*BNW*, 156) in bed is a trauma from which John never recovers. It is linked to his mother's whipping by the Indian women and expresses itself in his own desire to be whipped during the fertility ceremony. Both the public exposure of Linda and her beating are reenacted by John when, years later, he whips Lenina Crowne at the airlighthouse and inadvertently provokes a mass scene of erotic flagellation. As I have argued in earlier chapters, the ideas and erotic practice of the Marquis de Sade were an important element in Huxley's philosophy of history, bracketed in his mind with what he referred to as the nihilist revolution, cultural decadence, and a final historical period of complete moral bankruptcy—an association of ideas that accounts for the pervasive presence of sadism and references to de Sade throughout Huxley's satire from 1928 to 1939.

The Savage, then is a virtual avatar of Maurice Spandrell, consumed by the same anxieties and fears, similarly obsessed with female promiscuity as well as what he takes to be his mother's unchastity, and bent with the same neurotic intensity upon self-destruction. The Freudian family romance, despite Huxley's repeatedly expressed misgivings concerning Freud's emphasis on erotic behavior, is one of the principal satirical conventions of his social satire. *Brave New World* is no exception to this practice, and Huxley will employ it again but in much greater detail in both *Eyeless in Gaza* and *After Many a Summer Dies the Swan.* For Huxley these strangely troubled sadomasochistic figures were satirical types (part of his "Sadean sociology") as well as psychological studies, and in the former role were intended to reflect the historical conditions of a gradually deteriorating society. The Savage's suicide cannot be attributed solely to the pernicious impact of Fordean civilization on a mind umprepared for such an onslaught. Therefore his death significantly complicates the satirical direction of *Brave New World*, implicating both the irrational freedom of the Reservation as well as the oppressive regimentation of the World State.

The dilemma confronting Bernard Marx is equally ambiguous. By introducing a young man already psychologically crippled into the libidinal freedoms of Fordean London, Huxley deliberately skewed the satiric clarity of *Brave New World*. Bernard Marx is a similarly compromised character. As a self-conscious individual swallowed up in a social body numbed by drugs and permeated by conformist categories of response, he must confront the implications of his egocentric aspirations. No revolutionary and at best only a moderate opponent of Mond's paternalistic despotism, he oscillates between a despairing conformity and a servile endorsement of Fordean values. Moreover, he never fully comprehends the nature of the choices facing him, while the mainspring propelling much of his behavior lies with his sense of sexual inadequacy. His aimless peregrinations in the company of Lenina Crowne is another Huxleyan satiric convention, establishing Bernard as a typically intimidated Huxleyan protagonist, uncertain as to his social role, anxious regarding his relationship with women, and bemused by his own promptings to resist the pressures of a society the intellectual or spiritual postulates of which he can neither endorse nor reject. Like Theodore Gumbril of *Antic Hay*, Bernard resists the demands of his profession and yearns to realize an elusive goal of romantic monogamy, a predilection that links him to the Savage. But his progression from social outcast to social lion corresponds to his gradual adoption of an increasingly condescending role of patron and mentor to the Savage whom he had previously discovered at the New Mexico Reservation. Unwittingly adopting the role of Mustapha Mond, he instructs his protégé in the customs of Fordean culture, only to become progressively outraged by the Savage's nonconformist objections. Similarly, his deliberate exposure of his superior at the Central London Hatchery as the father of the Savage is less an act of social rebellion than a spiteful act of personal revenge. The sequence of events following his return from the Savage Reservation, instead of leading to his gradual emancipation from the regimentation of the World State, feeds his eager insecurity, binding him closer to the values of Mustapha Mond. In short, in a manner characteristic of the social satire of the twenties, Huxley refuses to permit a significant degree of development in his major satiric protagonist. Bernard Marx fails to transcend the values and customs of Fordean society, while John the Savage—the one character whose fresh perspective is capable of reinforcing Bernard's insurgent iconoclasm—is undermined at the very outset by his psychotic response to female sexuality. John the Savage gradually displaces Bernard Marx as Huxley's principal protagonist in the latter half of the novel. Usurping the affection of Lenina Crowne and winning the friendship of Helmholtz Watson as well as the grudging respect of Mustapha Mond, the Savage's reactions to the radical simplifications of Fordean Utilitarianism seem especially designed to expose the self-contradictions of Bernard Marx's character. On the other hand, the Savage's choice of suffering and isolation is not an unalloyed good; indeed, in *Eyeless in Gaza* the choice of pain as a concomitant of individual identity is in large part denounced by Huxley as a potentially degenerate impulse. Similarly, Helmholtz Watson's choice of Promethean isolation and Shelleyan romanticism is equally unacceptable to the author of *Music at Night* and *Ends and Means*.

In their endeavor to direct the course of history to apparently rational ends, Huxley's World Controllers fostered the development of a society that cherished above all else collective stability and historical stasis. In the novel this revolutionary exercise in control over populations and economic processes had begun after the Nine Years' War, but in actual history, in Soviet Russia—although Huxley insisted that traces of the same processes could be detected in Europe, Great Britain, and North America. Huxley associated such unwelcome developments with the New Romantic fascination with technological progress, and yet the absence of suffering in Mustapha Mond's utopia is attributable to the systematic eradication of precisely those attributes of human nature that Huxley himself found most objectionable. It is this fact that accounts for the curiously ambiguous quality of Huxley's social criticism in *Brave New World*. In this respect, it can be said that Huxley has created his dystopia in order to frame a complicated question in the guise of an apparently simple juxtaposition of contending points of view. A significant number of Mustapha Mond's principal beliefs, including his repudiation of history, disavowal of the value of the individual ego, dismissal of unlimited historicist progress, rejection of art, and aversion for the family, were shared at this time by Huxley. Indeed, they form the staple subjects of his satirical fiction throughout the interwar period. Mond's political and sociological hypotheses, however, proceed from a corrupted source, one Huxley will explore in greater detail in *Eyeless in Gaza*, while Mond's neurotic quest for absolute material security will reach its psychotic apotheosis in Joseph Stoyte's castle-museum in *After Many a Summer Dies the Swan*. Most important, his consuming passion for a completely regulated society involved an assault on mind and intelligence that Huxley could never countenance.

The secular and material values of the World State represent a massive projection of Lucy Tantamount's insistence in *Point Counter Point* that in the "aeroplane" there is "no room" for "the soul" (*PCP*, 282). Just as John the Savage is a variation on Maurice Spandrell, Lenina Crowne is a damped-down version of Lucy Tantamount, shorn of the latter's neuresthenic restiveness and sadomasochistic violence. Like Lucy, Lenina is a fervent admirer of machinery, a believer in progress, and a promiscuous sensualist. To create a secure society for neurotic hedonists like Lucy Tantamount, to purge them of their libidinally destructive drives in an environment of carefully stimulated apathy, is in essence the *raison d'être* of the World State. For Huxley this was a goal of sorts, indeed the only one he could envision for the Europe of the late 1920s. As Mustapha Mond observed, "liberalism . . . was dead of anthrax" (*BNW*, 57), a casualty of the Nine Years' War.

Huxley associated liberalism with the old romanticism and its stress on individuality, unlimited historical development, and political freedom. Like "history," it is a concept that has no relevance to Fordean paternalism and its monolithic embodiment in the World State. The World Controllers are not presented as charismatic leaders, nor do they require an electoral consensus in order to act. The end of history necessarily implies the death of politics in a world where the rulers have become faceless technocrats, worshipping efficiency and regulation, and administering a complex social system that has no need of ideological justification beyond sleep-taught clichés. Despite these objections to the despotic paternalism of the World Controllers, Huxley permits Mustapha Mond to formulate in the final chapters a detailed apology for Fordean collectivism, including systematic governmental intrusion into and domination of all spheres of human existence. Mond's objections to the psychological and economic anarchy that he believes informs the entire gamut of human history are essentially Huxley's, and his collectivist materialism was if not the most desirable answer to Sadean anarchy, at least a conceivable solution. It should be stressed that the sadistic irrationality Huxley linked with the society of *Point Counter Point* was for the most part a trait of John the Savage, not Mustapha Mond; and while

Huxley consistently repudiated Marxist collectivism, he nevertheless observed in a letter written in 1931, approximately two years before the appearance of *Brave New World*, that "the Marxian philosophy of life is not exclusively true: but, my word, it goes a good way, and covers a devil of a lot of ground."[37] A month later he observed in another letter that history was an incurable disease and Marxist economics merely another symptom of social decay: "the human race fills me with a steadily growing dismay. I was staying in the Durham coal-field this autumn, in the heart of English unemployment and it was awful. If only one could believe that the remedies proposed for the awfulness (Communism etc.) weren't even worse than the disease—in fact weren't the disease itself in another form, with superficially different symptoms."[38]

Mond of course is not a Marxist; however, his ideas are similar enough, in the broadest sense, to suggest the scope and depth of the philosophical dilemma in which Huxley found himself in the early thirties. In his next novel, *Eyeless in Gaza*, Huxley will turn to the theme of political engagement—a subject, with the exception of *Point Counter Point*, noticeably absent from the satires of the twenties. Its exigent presence in the world of Maurice Spandrell and Anthony Beavis signals Huxley's departure from the familiar terrain of Eliot's *Waste Land* and his long-postponed incursion into Auden country.

# CHAPTER FOUR

# History and Ideology in Eyeless in Gaza

## 1. Historicism, Politics, and the Drainpipe of Weltanschauung

*Eyeless in Gaza* marks a radical departure in narrative technique from Huxley's novels of the twenties, substituting for the customary sequential structure a subtly patterned fusion of past and present. The result is a novel that resembles a temporal collage shaped by a complex interplay between the "dramas of memory" and the urgencies and vagaries of an intractable present. Anthony Beavis's attempt to take stock of his past, in order to bring to the surface what has been buried in the swirl of time and to unravel its import for his present life, is a cautious revision of the pervasive pessimism of the earlier novels. In this respect, Beavis is Huxley's first major protagonist to undergo a discernibly complete transformation. His "journal," unlike Francis Chelifer's in *Those Barren Leaves*, is the record of his endeavor to take control of his life, to seek out a pattern of moral causality that bridges past and present and thus allows for the creation of a moral identity, if not a persistingly personal one. The elegiac subtlety of Huxley's art is the result of an analytic vision of the connections and relationships that no matter how deeply buried in the past, can be made to influence moral behavior—a conception of memory, as I shall show, deepened and complicated by a conflicting emphasis on the psychologically deterministic affiliation of past to present. In *Eyeless in Gaza* all of the familiar thematic categories employed by Huxley in his earlier novels are subsumed by the concept of time. Romanticism, inverse or Shelleyan, the concept of selfhood or personality, the speculative significance of history, language, apocalyptic vision, and sadomasochistic eroticism are intertwined themes within a montage juxtaposing intimately personal memories with present public experiences. These are in turn placed against an historical background involving the approach of the first world war in 1914, the rise of Mussolini, and Hitler's seizure of power in 1933. Anthony Beavis's attempt to order chronologically his own chaotic past is at least in part a further and more useful extension of his work as a sociologist concerned with "historical facts" (*EG*, 15). Equally important, most of the major characters whose lives impinge on Anthony's enact conflicting, sometimes contradictory but always specific attitudes towards temporal experience.

In the 1930s Huxley's interest in history and contemporary politics took on an added depth and urgency, influencing the tone and thematic complexity of both *Eyeless in Gaza* and *After Many a Summer Dies the Swan* and culminating in a final assessment of history begun almost two decades earlier in *Crome Yellow* and *On the Margin*. In a letter written in October, 1931, he complained, "It's a bad world; at the moment worse than usual. One has the impression of being in a lunatic asylum—at the mercy of drivelling imbeciles and dangerous madmen in a state of frenzy —the politicians."[1] The metaphor of the lunatic asylum was taken up with a vengeance by Huxley in *After Many a Summer*, but in *Eyeless in Gaza* he made a final attempt to come to grips with the chaotic array of historical data and the strange causal demons plaguing modern society. Mark Staithes, for example, is one of the "dangerous madmen" referred to in the letter quoted above, while his political ideas are defined and developed against a sinister backdrop of political allusions to the world "of Poincarés, of Mussolinis, of Northcliffs" (*EG*, 150), who in turn stand in the foreground of a more comprehensive analysis of the Europe of the thirties, an Audenesque "Vision of frightened faces, of abject gestures of servility" (*EG*, 500). Huxley's references to contemporary political events form a panoramic montage, never examined in detail but always present, setting the tone and providing the historical context for much of the action. The continual references to "the General Strike" (*EG*, 233), to "Campbell-Bannerman" and "Arthur Balfour" (*EG*, 501), as well as other "governments, even Hitler's, even Stalin's, even Mussolini's" (*EG*, 228), are directly related to the detailed psychological studies of Mark Staithes, Helen Amberley, and Anthony Beavis. The reason for this lies with Huxley's insistence that "to-day's national behaviour" is essentially "a large-scale projection of to-day's individual behaviour." Politics, even "international policies," are not merely reflections of the conscious behavior of individuals but, Huxley argues, can be conceived as projections "of the individual's secret wishes and intentions" (*EG*, 228–29). The individual is always responsible; he cannot stand outside of history because he cannot claim to be innocent—that is, to be a helpless element within a larger, uncontrollable whole. Accordingly, Huxley's philosophy of history, at least at the time of the writing of *Eyeless in Gaza*, is inseparable from his psychology to the extent that the two areas of inquiry overlap within his analysis of modern culture.

In the novels of the thirties, Huxley's attitude towards historical process tends to reflect his increasing anxiety over events in Europe, an apprehensiveness especially evident in *After Many a Summer Dies the Swan.* In *Eyeless in Gaza* he approaches history from a number of conflicting perspectives (usually related to a specific character) that define it alternately as a "game," a process of arbitrary change, the record of collective neurosis, a temporally linked series of "conventions" or "psychological undulations," a discernible pattern of either Wellsian progress or Gibbonesque decline, a deterministic juggernaut, or finally a chronicle of freedom and self-energizing political action. And just as the values and actions of professional historians dominate the narrative logic of *After Many a Summer Dies the Swan*, the protagonist of *Eyeless in Gaza* is a sociologist "surrounded by history," whose obsession with discrete "historical facts" masks a covert fear of human relationships, especially as they extend back into the past, as well as an indifference to social or political experience in the present. Anthony is surrounded, not only by the violent events of the Europe of the 1930s but by a circle of friends, mistresses, and relations who collectively testify to the pervasive desire "to break out of contemporary history" into a "purely private life" (*CE*, 219). In a letter written at the end of 1933, Huxley described the germinal idea for *Eyeless in Gaza:* "I am thinking now about a novel. The theme, fundamentally, is liberty. What happens to someone who becomes really very free—materially first (for after all liberty must depend very largely on property) and then mentally and emotionally. The rather awful vacuum that such freedom turns out to be."[2]

During this period Huxley was increasingly conscious of contemporary history as something more than a mere aggregate of events governed by contingency and chance. In his attempt to grasp the operative factors in history, he rejected the notion of "Wellsian Progress," arguing instead that the flow of political, economic, and diplomatic events seemed to trace a more complicated, less discernible path. In a letter to E. M. Forster, he expressed an idea first defined in *The Olive Tree*, where he observed that "History pursues an undulatory course; and these undulations are the result, to some extent at least, of the tendency displayed by human beings to react, after a certain time, away from the prevailing habits of thought and feeling towards other habits," adding that "The autonomous nature of psychological undulations is confirmed by the facts of history" (*OT*, 20). In the 1935 letter to Forster, he writes:

> I share your gloom about the period, and add to it a considerable gloom about myself. Bertie Russell, whom I've just been lunching with, says one oughtn't to

mind about the superficial things like ideas, manners, politics, even wars—that the really important things, conditioned by scientific techniques, go steadily on and up . . . in a straight, un-undulating trajectory. It's nice to think so; but meanwhile there the superficial undulations are, and one lives superficially: and who knows if that straight trajectory isn't aiming directly for some fantastic denial of humanity.[3]

It is not surprising to find the author of *Brave New World* displaying little confidence in a simplistic and precariously selective view of historical causation in which a privileged class of events, here presumably the work of scientists, are so conditioned by scientific method that they inevitably advance in a rationally progressive way, while other socioeconomic phenomena, including political activity, can be safely left to look after themselves. But as Huxley observed in *The Olive Tree*, the "mistake of all propagandists [even those espousing the orderly progress of science] has been to suppose that the psychological movement which they observe in the society around them is destined to go on continuously in the same direction" (*OT*, 22–23). The exigency of the "undulations" of history are for Huxley a menacingly decisive fact. Furthermore, he tends to psychologize history, regarding social phenomena even at the macroscopic level of "national behaviour" or "international policies" as "large-scale projection[s]" of "individual behaviour" (*EG*, 228). In *Eyeless in Gaza* characters like Anthony Beavis, Mark Staithes, or Helen Amberley exemplify the "individual behaviour" that energizes and informs the broader "psychological undulations" of contemporary history. As I will show later, Huxley is not arguing for a naively conceived form of methodological individualism, a major problem in the philosophy of history and one that he was familiar with (in its technical formulation), as the essay on Maine de Biran demonstrates.[4] But during the early thirties, he did believe that a significant link existed between the actions of the individual and the broader "psychological movement" of historical process and that the novelist could dramatize such a relationship in what Huxley called "the novel of social history."[5] Accordingly, his interest in the individual elements that constitute "the Weltanschauung of 1933" extends in *Eyeless in Gaza* to a series of characters whose lives are touched in various ways by the political events of the early 1930s but who in turn help to create the psychological and social matrix of those events.

Most of the characters of *Eyeless in Gaza* are incurably self-regarding, their lives exemplifying a narcissism become habitual. Yet all of the major characters undergo a crisis that either impels them beyond the circumscriptions of the self towards a more inclusive social world or forces them deeper into a self-stultifying state of aggressive conceit. This turning away from social empathy, moral responsibility, and the candor and emotional openness necessary to both personal and public well-being is the central theme of *Eyeless in Gaza*, particularly as it forms the psychological matrix of "secret wishes and intentions" that Huxley believed underlie historical process:

"For we should all like to behave a good deal worse than our conscience and respect for public opinion allow. One of the great attractions of patriotism—it fulfills our worst wishes. In the person of our nation we are able, vicariously, to bully and cheat. Bully and cheat, what's more with a feeling that we're profoundly virtuous. Sweet and decorous to murder, lie, torture, for the sake of the fatherland. Good international policies are projections of individual good intentions and benevolent wishes . . ." (*EG*, 229)

This entry from Anthony Beavis's journal defines his concept of the axis upon which history moves, a reciprocal motion involving "the periphery and the centre" (i.e. the people and their government): "States and nations don't exist as such. There are only people. Sets of people living in certain areas, having certain allegiances. Nations won't change their national policies unless and until people change their private policies. All governments, even Hitler's, even Stalin's, even Mussolini's, are representative" (*EG*, 228). The principal political and historicist assumption of *Eyeless in Gaza* is that our modes of thought fatefully condition history, that "historical facts" are in some way reducible to discrete psychological ones, uniquely located in a specific time and place and radically temporalistic in nature. In short, "historical trends" are synonymous with broad "psychological movements" which raise the fundamental question of *Eyeless in Gaza*: "What are, and what should be, the relations between the personal and the historical, the existential and the social?" (*CE*, 217).

If the events of the late twenties and early thirties appeared to Huxley to be moving in a troubling "undulation" towards "some fantastic denial of humanity," such a trend could be authentically depicted in the lives and values of representative individuals. As Huxley has observed, "each generation has its private history," and in *Eyeless in Gaza* that private history is dramatized and explored against the backdrop of "recent history" (*EG*, 450), "English politics" (*EG*, 451), and "the depression . . . the Nazis, [and] the New Deal" (*EG*, 289). *Eyeless in Gaza*, as its title suggests, is a study of blindness and imprisonment. Its thematic lucidity—despite what at first appears to be a temporally snarled if not anarchic narrative structure—is the result of the care with which Huxley embodied his appraisal of English society from 1914 to 1934 in a number of imagistic configurations that in turn are coherently aligned with the novel's principal subject, the moral and political reformation of Anthony

Beavis. The formal dimensions of this complex work are rooted in a recurrent pattern of dirt and disease imagery closely allied to a symbolic landscape of subterranean enclosure and repressive confinement. And equally important, these patterns of imagery are of pivotal significance in relation to Huxley's attempt to explore an endemic social malady, the "spiritual onanism" (*DWW*, 42) previously defined in *Crome Yellow*, *Antic Hay*, and *Those Barren Leaves*. However, in the new novel this is expanded to the level of pervasive social and political disorder symbolized primarily by the pointless dynamism of Mark Staithes, the moribund scientism of Anthony Beavis, and the chronic anomie of Helen and Mary Amberley. The seemingly irresistible tendency to withdraw into a securely private universe that governs all of the characters of *Eyeless in Gaza* is a variation on a similar theme first introduced in *Crome Yellow* and steadily refined and developed in the novels of the twenties. But in *Eyeless in Gaza* the risks attendant on such epistemological maneuvering have become much graver. The "vision of frightened faces, of abject gestures" that for Anthony forms the background to the posturings of Hitler, Stalin, and Mussolini during the "thirties of the twentieth century" (*EG*, 86) is also an apocalyptic panorama of a society moving aimlessly towards the tragedy of Munich and the "fantastic denial of humanity" that Huxley postulated in his letter to E. M. Forster in 1935. In this respect, *Eyeless in Gaza* is a much more prophetic work than *Brave New World*.

Anthony's antagonistic relationship with Mark Staithes is the central drama of *Eyeless in Gaza*, around which the subordinate plots gradually unfold and in contrast to which the second principal narrative line, Anthony's betrayal of Brian Foxe, takes on additional meaning. Anthony's life is organized by Huxley into three periods: the years from 1902 to 1904, during which Anthony attended the prep school Bulstrode; the years 1912 to 1914, pivoting mainly around his affair with Joan Thursley and the death of Brian Foxe; and a much greater span of time from 1926 to 1935, centering on Anthony's psychological and political paralysis and his moral reformation under the combined tutelage of Mark Staithes and Dr. Miller, one of Auden's healing heroes. This third stage, occupying much of the book, also includes the subordinate plots involving Anthony's affair with Helen Amberley, the basis not only for an additional perspective on Anthony's psychological inertia but on English and European society in general; Huxley accomplishes the latter by amplifying the roles of important minor characters like Hugh Ledwidge, Gerry Watchett, or Mary Amberley as well as introducing new characters like the political refugee Ekki Giesebrecht (minor figures, of course, appear and reappear in more than one phase). However, the three stages of Anthony's development are thematically interrelated to the extent that the pro-gressive momentum of each period is generated by the intrusion of death; in the first the death of Anthony's mother, Maisie Beavis; in the second the death of Brian Foxe; and in the third the near-death of Anthony himself. Each period also involves a specific challenge to Anthony's moral integrity; first, Anthony's response to the cruel treatment of Hugh Ledwidge at Bulstrode (including Brian Foxe's moral example); then Anthony's profoundly immoral betrayal of John Thursley and Brian Foxe; and finally Anthony's reaction to the moral complexities posed by Mark Staithes's violently aggressive asceticism and Dr. Miller's idealistic pacifism. Equally important, each phase is a dramatization of Anthony's capacity for love as well as his sense of alienation and rejection. The three periods are subtly linked by Anthony's evolution in terms of his search for and estimation of different kinds of love. In the first period, denied the love of his mother as a consequence of her death and deeply alienated from his father, he seeks out a substitute family in Rachel and Brian Foxe. In the second period he exists in psychological thralldom to his mistress, Mary Amberley; the problems of family love have been displaced by a morally and emotionally anarchic "eroticism" that debases Anthony and destroys Brian Foxe—whose own neurotic aver-sion for physical sexuality is as much to blame for his death as Anthony's betrayal in seducing his fiancee, Joan Thursley. In the third phase Anthony moves from a frustratingly unsatisfactory affair with Helen Amberley to a more widely conceived social love. In this stage the dif-ficult challenge of loving human beings on the basis of both a political and ontological "unity" supersedes his own preoccupation with familial or erotic love.

In short, the three periods are on the one hand sharply demarcated by the types of love sought by Anthony and on the other united by his prog-ress from emotional dependency to spiritual autonomy. The bulk of the book is given over to the second and third periods (the first being primarily introductory), where Huxley attempts to connect Anthony's psychologi-cal and political education with the major events of European and English history from 1912 to 1935. References or allusions to contempo-raneous European history do not occur in the first stage (1902 to 1904). In this respect it is important to note that Anthony's great crime, his treacherous seduction of Joan Thursley and the resulting death of Brian Foxe in 1914, are roughly coincident with the events following the assassination of Archduke Franz Ferdinand at Sarajevo in June of 1914 and the mobilization of "Russia and Austria and Germany" during July, while Anthony's act of atonement in the third section of the novel takes place against the background of Hitler's seizure of power, his withdrawal of Germany from the League of Nations, and Germany's rearmament. Anthony's moral irresponsibility and the outbreak of the Great War in 1914 (Brian commits suicide on the day that Austria-Hungary delivered its ultimatum to Belgrade) are carefully balanced against the approach of a second war and Anthony's spiritual atonement as a self-sacrificing pacifist. This connection, while not to be pressed too hard, testifies to Huxley's optimistic belief (in the early 1930s) that broad historical undulations are the holistic effect of discrete "psychological" causes, that the individual can stimulate historical process, and that, in Anthony's words, authentic "changes in social organization" are the outcome of a process that begins with "a change in personal relations" (*EG*, 418). The chronological and thematic structure can be arranged as follows:

| | |
|---|---|
| *First Stage 1902-1904:* | *Chapters IV, VI, IX, XV* |
| | Anthony's childhood |
| 1. Death: mother | Maisie Beavis's funeral |
| 2. Love: child for parent | Bulstrode schooldays |
| 3. Ethical Crisis: persecution of Hugh Ledwidge | Mark Staithes's exposure of Hugh Ledwidge and Brian Foxe's intervention |
| | |
| *Second Stage 1912-1928* | |
| 1. Death: Brian Foxe | 1912: Chapters X, XVI, XIX |
| 2. Love: sensual-erotic | Oxford |
| 3. Ethical Crisis: seduction of Joan Thursley | 1914: Chapters XXVII, XXX, XXXIII, XXXVI, XLIII, XLVIII, LII |
| | Anthony's affair with Mary Amberley |
| | Anthony's betrayal of Brian Foxe |
| | Brian Foxe's suicide |
| | 1926-28: Chapters V, XI, XIV, XVIII, XX, XXII, XXIV, XXXIV, XXXIX, XLV |
| | Mary Amberley's party |
| | Mary Amberley's affair with Gerry Watchett |
| | Helen Amberley's affair with Gerry Watchett |
| | Helen's abortion |
| | Mark Staithes's communist activities |

*Third Stage 1931–1935:*
1. Death: Anthony threatened with assassination
2. Love: social
3. Ethical Crisis: political commitment to pacifism

Chapters XXV, XXIX, I, III, VIII, XII, XXI, XXVI, XXXI, XXXVII, XLI, XLVI, XLIX, LI, LIII, II, VII, XIII, XVII, XXIII, XXVIII, XXXII, XXV, XXXVIII, XL, XLII, XLIV, XLVI, L, LIV
Anthony's affair with Helen Amberley
Helen's rejection of Anthony
Mark Staithes's intervention in Anthony's life and the trip to Mexico
Anthony's conversion by Dr. Miller
Anthony's pacifist activities

I began this analysis of the formal structure of *Eyeless in Gaza* with the observation that Anthony Beavis's antagonistic relationship with Mark Staithes is the central drama of the novel. Staithes's role in Anthony's political and psychological education is complicated, becoming even more opaque when removed from the novel's historical context. Mark Staithes is Huxley's representative European, part communist, part fascist, at once a political anarchist careless of social stability and a reactionary who helps to prop up a South American oligarch, a capitalist who hopes for a revolution and a communist who owns a perfume factory and who loathes people both individually and in the mass. His shifting allegiances and sadistic taste for violence reflect a society in the process of becoming increasingly unstable. His first appearance in the novel is that of the school bully, hectoring the school pariah, Hugh Ledwidge, and patronizing Anthony Beavis. When brought to the test of choosing between Brian's moral indignation and Mark Staithes's domineering aggressiveness, Anthony sides with the latter while grudgingly recognizing the truth of the former.

Staithes's second stormy appearance (June 18, 1912) inaugurates the second period of Anthony's education. His materialization in Anthony's room is brief but characteristic, in that his rivalry with Brian Foxe over the leadership of the Fabians has led to Brian's withdrawal as a candidate, thereby robbing the election of any value in Staithes's eyes. The scene does not progress beyond the latter's complaints, but it reinforces his role as a neurotically anarchic egotist constantly on the watch for an adversary. The irrationality and cynicism of Staithes notwithstanding, he is the most politically involved and politically ambiguous of all the characters of *Eyeless in Gaza*. According to Anthony, he "notices every-thing" (*EG*, 170), observing the world around him "with sharp, in-quisitorial movements" (*EG*, 233). Equally significant, not only do most of the political judgments and historical allusions emanate from Staithes, but until Anthony becomes an active pacifist, he is the only character to involve himself directly in political affairs.

At Mary Amberley's party Staithes introduces a minor historical motif that further establishes his role as an emblematic figure, a personification of the "Weltanschauung" of the decade and a half following the Great War, both in terms of his will to power as well as his sense of contempo-rary decadence. Like both the fascists and the communists of this period, Staithes regards bourgeois Europe with Spenglerian disdain. Taking stock of the assembled hedonists, upper-class dilettanti, and jaded sen-sualists at the party, he observes: "You people—you're survivors from the Age of the Antonines," adding, "imagining you're still in the first volume of Gibbon. Whereas we're well on in the third" (*EG*, 236). Earlier in the novel Mary Amberley had remembered her husband's remark about Gibbon and his distaste for "the Middle Ages" (*EG*, 224), while after the death of Brian Foxe, Anthony discovers "a note-book half-full of jottings about the economic history of the Roman Empire" (*EG*, 585). The theme of cultural decline, first clearly invoked by Mark Staithes, surfaces repeatedly in *Eyeless in Gaza*, in for example Anthony Beavis's reference to "Sorel's *Reflexions sur la Violence*" (*EG*, 504) and Helen Amberley's meditation on the river of history as she contemplates the bending course of the Rhine (an undulating path that symbolizes Huxley's idea of historical undulations) prior to Ekki Giesebrecht's kid-napping by Nazi agents. I shall discuss both of these incidents in more detail later, but it is crucial to note here that they form part of a series of references to historical process and cultural decadence. Mark Staithes is both a Gibbonesque ironist, sardonically observing a cultural undulation from what he believes to be a position of superiority and at the same time a characteristic product of a declining culture, deeply self-conscious, haunted by the past, politically contradictory, and ultimately anarchic in his social alienation and carefully developed taste for violence and domination.

Staithes repudiates Mary's guests as corrupt exemplars of a debased culture that extends beyond the socio-historical conditions of the upper ranges of English society from 1912 to 1935 to embrace the Weimar Republic and in particular the example of Weimar Berlin. Germany is a pervasive theme in *Eyeless in Gaza*. Brian Foxe, the nascent historian of the Roman Empire's economic decline, plans a trip to Germany in order "to learn the language" (*EG*, 246). Beppo Bowles journeys to Berlin as an erotic pilgrim approaching a Mecca of sexual freedom and perversity. The communist Ekki Giesebrecht escapes from Germany and is later taken forcibly across the frontier by Nazi agents, while Helen Amberley meditates on the river Rhine as a symbol of irreversible historical process and Germany as a death-intoxicated "Gothic" world (*EG*, 599). This reference to a Gothic world of barbaric violence is linked to an earlier allusion to Gibbon's despised "late Gothic" (*EG*, 224), reinforcing the Gibbonesque theme of widespread cultural decline. Mark Staithes describes Berlin as a political arena of contending "monarchists, fascists, Junkers, Krupps," and "communists" (*EG*, 235). Beppo Bowles sees it from a different but related angle of vision, lovingly cataloguing its "masochists," "Lesbian bars" (*EG*, 231), "transvestitists" (*EG*, 233), "top-booted tarts" (*EG*, 281), and particularly its "Museum of Sexology" (*EG*, 231)—an inventory of aggressive, at times sadistic eroticism that parallels, with its sadomasochistic emphasis, Staithes's more conventional inventory of political violence. The cultural instability of the Berlin of the Weimar period reaches its end with the election of Hitler, an event that consolidates and redirects the earlier violence and which eventually impinges directly on Anthony's world in the form of the communist refugee Ekki Giesebrecht. The response of Mark Staithes to Ekki's ideological purity and the latter's optimistic view of human perfectibility is to label him "an ass with the moral qualities of a saint" (*EG*, 297). Staithes's own peculiar brand of socialism is clouded by a sadomasochistic impulse that Huxley saw as the accompaniment of the fascist "will to power."

At Mary Amberley's party, despite his Spenglerian view of contemporary history, Staithes clings to the possibility of a communist revolution in England. He rejects what he calls "the imbeciles of the T.U.C." and "the rank and file of the Unions" (*EG*, 239), dismisses "the Labour Party" (*EG*, 238) as numerically weak yet paradoxically hopes that "a revolution might succeed" if the English "bourgeoisie" follow the example of "the German republicans" (*EG*, 239) and not use their superior strength and training to crush what he regards as the intrinsically helpless "proletariat" (*EG*, 238). Staithes has no confidence in the working classes; indeed, he seems to have no direct knowledge of them. Like Anthony Beavis's father, he responds to the hymn-singing of the workers during "the General Strike" in a naively class-ridden manner, while his activities as a member of the Communist Party are evoked with an underlying languor that betrays his real attitude:

"One joined the Party, one distributed literature, one financed pressure-groups out of the profits on synthetic carnations, one addressed meetings and wrote articles. And perhaps it was all quite useless. Perhaps, on the contrary, the auspicious moment might one day present itself . . ." (*EG*, 316)

This is not George Orwell's socialism any more than Beppo Bowles's Berlin, despite an outward resemblance, is Christopher Isherwood's. In the first place, Staithes's political disposition is fundamentally passive, his activities while a member of the Party appearing to have no causal relationship with "the auspicious moment" that in the course of time will simply "present itself." Huxley ironically employs the same phrase to expose Anthony Beavis's cowardly evasiveness as he waits in 1914 for "the auspicious moment" (*EG*, 504) to confess his treachery to Brian Foxe. Equally significant is Staithes's unconscious use of the personal "one," never betraying a sense of belonging to the cooperative "we" of the Party.

The key to the snarled web of Staithes's political allegiances lies with Anthony Beavis's reference to "Sorel's *Reflexions sur la Violence*," a text that he refers to as "uncomfortable reading for Fabians!" (*EG*, 504). In *The Olive Tree* Huxley linked Sorel with Mussolini, recognizing in Sorel's disillusioned socialism (and consequent Nietzschean bias in favor of a ruling elite)[6] a perhaps only apparent connection with the rise of Italian fascism. George Sorel's political philosophy involves three primary tenets, each of which informs Mark Staithes's political behavior as well as his assessment of the course of contemporary history. Like Sir Oswald Mosley, who also lies behind Huxley's characterization of Staithes, Sorel began his career as a Marxist, only to abandon orthodox socialism in favor of the most revolutionary wing of the French labor movement, the anarchosyndicalists—eventually transferring his interest to right-wing politics, including ultranationalists and monarchists. He had predicted an important career for Benito Mussolini, "who, in turn called *Reflections on Violence* his bedside book."[7] Sorel's political philosophy was based upon, first, a complete repudiation of bourgeois culture, especially what he regarded as the linked illusions of parliamentary democracy and the idea of progress. He believed that discernible parallels could be traced in what he saw as contemporary bourgeois decadence and the ruin of the ancient world (the title of one of his early books). Second, he advocated the necessity of sociopolitical "myths," principally the myth of the "General Strike," as a means of galvanizing a politically lethargic working class and stirring it to action through the appeal of an image of collective heroism and triumphant morality. Sorel admitted that a totally successful general strike was a practical impossibility but adhered to the ideas as a necessary fiction. The third and most important element was Sorel's concept of the ruling elite, what he referred to as a class of ascetic elitists or "producers," whose lives involved both moral isolation and hard discipline amidst a mass of inferior "consumers." This small class of creative, energetic egoists he felt provided the stimulus necessary to energize a culture and provide the necessary economic and scientific advancements to satisfy the passive demands of the mass of consumers. Sorel believed, however, that violence was a legitimate expression of social unrest, a necessary and even logical extreme of a spectrum of violent attitudes all designed to force a confrontation with the bourgeois forces of parliamentary democracy and ultimately to defeat them.

Mark Staithes is *not* a spokesman for Sorel's political beliefs, but as a composite "paradigm"[8] intended to dramatize the irrational political tendencies of the interwar period, he reflects Huxley's attitudes toward the rampant egotism underlying fascist *and* communist aggressiveness and their emphasis on a ruling elite. Like Sorel, Staithes is a perplexing combination of communist revolutionary and ascetic elitist. He opposes "bourgeois" society and, again like Sorel, sees it as literally decadent, drawing on Gibbon's *Decline and Fall* for a suitable analogy. In addition, while he rejects conventional socialism (as did Sorel), he cites "the General Strike" as a portent of revolutionary success: "And think of what happened here, during the Strike? Even the majority of industrialists were ready to compromise" (*EG*, 239). More important, his vehement repudiation of parliamentary democracy—"It's childish to think you can get what you want by constitutional methods"—and his rejection of the British Labour Party as "naturally bourgeois" echo the biases of Sorel. Even his belief that the middle classes (more educated and disciplined) are "potentially better soldiers than the proletariat" (*EG*, 238) places him closer to the elitist impulse that underlay Sorel's belief in the special status of a creative, highly disciplined minority. Finally, Staithes's rejection of "social progress" within a "safe urban world" (*EG*, 280–81), his sardonic disgust with "the larger hopes, the proliferating futures" of a "progress" that "is still progressing" (*EG*, 409), is a staple of Sorel's political philosophy.

Mark Staithes also reflects Huxley's interest in the possibility of ruling elites—but a possibility warped and twisted by the political climate of the late twenties and early thirties. The specific historical context for Huxley's conception of Staithes as a superior Sorelian "producer" turned fascist is best defined by Huxley in *Ends and Means*, where he observes that "by the end of the twenties a reaction had begun to set in—away from the easy-going philosophy of general meaninglessness towards the hard ferocious theologies of nationalistic and revolutionary idolatry." He adds, "meaning was reintroduced into the world, but only in patches"

(*EM*, 274). If as Anthony Beavis insists, national and international policies are reflections of individual behavior, including "secret wishes and intentions," then Staithes as a character functions as the "paradigm of the whole life of the community" that Huxley referred to in his letter to Russell Green. However, Staithes's ferocious egotism is tempered by a debilitating skepticism, and while it is easy to detect in him the "ferocious theologies" of *both* fascism and communism that Huxley saw as new political idolatries, he is also a typical Huxleyan inverse romantic, whose literary lineage can be traced back to Maurice Spandrell and Francis Chelifer. Despite his flirtation with communism, Staithes has found it increasingly difficult to sustain his interest in an historical process which displays a depressingly cyclical pattern. By 1933 he is forthright on the futility of violent political revolution, a significant revision of his tempered optimism of 1926 (and reminiscent of Bojanus's cynical formulation of the course of modern history in *Antic Hay*): "What did the French peons get out of their Revolution? Or our friends the Russians, for that matter? A few years of pleasant intoxication. Then the same old treadmill. Gilded, perhaps; repainted. But in essentials the old machine" (*EG*, 467–68). When he advises Helen Ledwidge to "look at history," he holds out a cyclical theory (a belief held by Sorel) in which "Hitler or Mussolini" (*EG*, 298) represent inevitable phases of oppression, just as Don Jorge's "revolution" is merely another turn of the Viconian wheel that Anthony Beavis first defined in 1926: "A revolution to transform common humanity into common humanity of another variety . . . To detect, after your catastrophic reform of everything, the same old uniformities working themselves out in a slightly different way. . . ." At this point in the twenties, Staithes is tempted to endorse Anthony's bleaker version of historical change, worrying that "if that's all that revolution can do, the game isn't worth the candle" (*EG*, 312). But he refuses to relinquish his fragile dream that "in Russia they haven't yet had the chance to be pigs" (*EG*, 317), a hope tempered by his suspicion that while "Revolutions are delightful in the preliminary stages" (*EG*, 316), what follows is possibly nothing more than self-indulgent materialism: "Millions and millions of soft, piggish Babbitts, ruled by a small minority of ambitious Staitheses." Nevertheless, Staithes rejects "orthodox Marxism" (*EG*, 317) with its deterministic formula of base and superstructure[9] and finally accepts the futility of violent revolution, seeing it as a cycle of insurrections in which the proletariat is simply manipulated into replacing one form of oppression for another: "Tyranny under commissars, tyranny under *Gauleiters*—it doesn't seem to make much difference" (*EG*, 413). For Anthony Beavis prior to his conversion by Dr. Miller, history is an "endlessly shifting game" whose outcome is determined by "fixed rules" and covert "uniformities" (*EG*, 312). Staithes cannot share Anthony's delight in historicism, or worse his belief in endlessly alternating periods of oppression, and once he perceives the pattern of cyclical violence underlying modern history, he has no scruples in shifting his ideological stance from revolutionary to counterrevolutionary.

This fundamental pessimism was present in Staithes from the outset, and its egoistic roots reinforce his inherent fascism. When he appears at Mary Amberley's party in 1926, his belief in the efficacy of the general strike and the possibility of a successful revolution in England exists side by side with a misanthropic impulse of Swiftian dimensions, a trait that complicates Staithes's politics by introducing the psychological features of the Huxleyan inverse romantic. In *Ends and Means*, Huxley repeatedly insisted on the psychological basis of history, claiming that theory of government or political science is best approached by "psychologists" (*EG*, 58). He argued that contemporary problems of government could only be explained by "psychological facts," that no reform could be separated from, among other things, its "psychological contexts," and that the causal explanations of modern history, while nominally political or economic, "are ultimately psychological in their nature" (*EM*, 49). Similarly, "the causes of war are not solely economic, but psychological" (*EM*, 45), while the characteristic "association of progressiveness and aggressiveness" in modern history had its causal explanation "in the depth of human psychology" (*EM*, 23). When he discusses the baneful influence of the Versailles settlement on modern European history, Huxley maintains that it was historically inevitable because an alternative was "psychologically all but impossible" to the framers of the treaty (*EM*, 140). Similarly, the Spanish Civil War was determined in part by the "working-class psychology of 1931 Spain" (*EM*, 145). In his systematic attempt to elucidate the "historical situation" of the 1930s and the "ferociously ideological" conflicts of European politics, he repeatedly turned to psychological explanations, emphasizing the relationship of large-scale social movements to their psychological roots in the behavior of the individual. The chief psychological factors informing much of the ideological "fanaticism" that Huxley perceived in "the contemporary philosophers of Fascism and dictatorial Communism" (*EM*, 6) was "the lust for power" that while often "deflected from one channel to another channel" (*EM*, 19), remained one of the—to use Anthony Beavis's terms—"uninformities" evident everywhere in contemporary European history.

This irrationally self-assertive impulse was linked by Huxley with the rise of historicism, or what he called the "historical" (*EM*, 66), to create an aberrant or eccentric "undulation," a "psychological movement" informed by a uniquely "primitive" level of political discourse that he traced back to Hegel. While Huxley's analysis is by no means exhaustive, nor is it as intellectually rigorous as it ought to have been in order to justify a number of his conclusions, its relevance to *Eyeless in Gaza* is immediately apparent. Just as Huxley stressed the role of psychological motivation (by which he means primarily the egocentric will to power) as the principal element underlying nationalist, fascist, or communist ideology, "the historical" was both the medium in which such ideologies clashed with increasing violence as well as their metaphysical justification. Huxley rejected "the appeal to history," especially when it was made in the modern historicist context, where "in Hegelian language, the real is the rational—that what happens is ultimately the same as what ought to happen." This basic allegiance to historical process, to the idea that because events "occur; they are therefore historical" (*EN*, 67), is for Huxley an undiscriminating emphasis on the radical temporality of human experience. This fundamental adherence, first, to sheer chronicity as man's defining trait and, second, to values only as they declare themselves in time, is a pervasive feature of modern culture: "For ever-increasing numbers of men and women, 'historicalness' is coming to be accepted as one of the supreme values" (*EM*, 68). The "dictatorship of the proletariat" is, he writes, defended as the outcome of "historical necessity"; the violence of revolution is excused as an inevitable part of the "ineluctable 'historical' process," while "Fascism" justifies itself in terms of its "'historical' mission" (*EM*, 67). Huxley's position is to deny historicism by undermining its apparent autonomy through the introduction of nontemporal experience and trans-historical values. His opposition to historicism is by 1938 unequivocal: "one word is common to all the dictatorial vocabularies and is used for purposes of justification and rationalization by Fascists, Nazis and Communists alike. That word is 'historical'" (*EM*, 66). But, he insists, "'historicalness' is not a value" (*EM*, 69).

Mark Staithes is a further development of the Huxleyan inverse romantic, disguising his fear of Francis Chelifer's "void" (what Staithes refers to as "Nothing—absolutely nothing"—*EG*, 207) by embracing the world of time and change, and filling the vacuum with historicist ideology. As early as 1926 he viewed humanity with Swiftian revulsion. He joined the Communist Party as part of a pattern of rootless wandering, rebelling first against his family by enlisting in the army as a private and refusing his father's offer of a career "in the City" (*EG*, 315). He thus rebels against society by joining the Party and finally rebels against the Party by repudiating the proletariat and becoming a counterrevolutionary in support of Don Jorge. His neurotic "asceticism," rooted in part in his revulsion for bodily processes (he refers obsessively to excrement) and the senses, as well as for the bourgeois luxuries of what he regards as his family's exploitative materialism, can be traced to this pattern of chronic rebellion. The result is a masochistic personality defined principally by negatives, a fragile sense of identity that he attempts to shore up with a self-renunciatory asceticism that gradually transforms itself into a debilitating sadomasochism. His ethic of fanatical self-discipline is directed not outwards towards society—despite his conscious political affiliations—but inwards towards an inhuman ideal that, stripped of human traits, enables Staithes to overcome his nausea of humanity. His aesthetic opposition to just about everything is a parody of Anthony Beavis's concept of what he believes to be a new kind of self-renunciatory "total man," the "realization of that ideal personality conceived by the Jesus of the Gospel" (*EG*, 145).

Staithes's "dingy house" is an emblematic setting intended to further define the covert aggression that even in 1926 is slowly eroding his sense of socialist solidarity. As a creation of his moral masochism, the stark austerity of the interior is "intentional"; that is, deliberately calculated to satisfy his need "to punish himself" (*EG*, 311). Like Francis Chelifer's Gog's Court, the house is "hideous on purpose" (*EG*, 322), functioning as a symbol of the inverse romantic's historicist despair in which the sterile banality of Chelifer's "void" is sought for its own sake. But Staithes's house suggests a further refinement of the inverse romantic's cynicism, in that it embodies his sense of puritanical superiority, the covert motive for all of his actions. Even Miss Pendle, an impoverished spinster rescued by Staithes and employed as his housekeeper, is in fact kept as an exhibit of the self-flagellatory depths to which he has sunk—or in Anthony's words, "the most monstrous of the knick-knacks" (*EG*, 322) that fill his rooms. Anthony correctly diagnoses Staithes's subterfuge, recognizing "that Mark's asceticism was undertaken for its own sake . . . that he might feel himself more separate, more intensely himself" in order that he might "look down on other people" (*EG*, 480).

Despite his astringent self-denial, Staithes is pursuing what Huxley regards as an illusory concept, the personality conceived as a persisting entity, and consequently an historicist phenomenon rooted in ideas of chronicity and process. However, in Staithes's case persistence of self is measured by if not synonymous with persistence of pain. This absurd reduction of selfhood to the savored endurance of mortification and suffering explains his clinging to his untreated wound in the final chapters of *Eyeless in Gaza*, as well as his masochistic efforts to make it bleed and his stubborn resistance to Dr. Miller's efforts to save his leg. Pain awakens and intensifies Staithes's numbed sense of being, the psychological experience of pain and the resulting exercise of will being all that remains to him of his sense of identity. Moral and psychological identity is dependent on separation and superiority, and superiority is measured by a punishing but nevertheless willed self-denial that extends to the endurance of acute physical torment—Huxley's satiric reduction of the historicist personality to the level of a masochistic residue of pain. Anthony Beavis will also confront the challenge of physical pain, "sharp, excruciating" (*EG*, 610), but an agony directed outwards towards his fellow man and ultimately towards a non-historicist perception of reality. Suffering is for Anthony an inevitable part of his attempt "to cultivate the painful art of loving people" (*EG*, 606), itself a necessary stage in a process of spiritual development. But Anthony's regimen is directed towards the creation of an ethically provisional selfhood, a more rationally coherent entity because it does not rest on historicist illusion.

Staithes's search for meaning, both in terms of ideology and personal identity, is an expression of his allegiance to temporality and process, a bias shared by most of the novel's characters. In *Eyeless in Gaza* Huxley set himself the task of creating a "psychological landscape" in which he expanded and developed many of the formal motifs first introduced in *Crome Yellow* and elaborated in *Those Barren Leaves* and *Point Counter Point*. The defining feature of this landscape is the "magic circle" (*EG*, 340), the "burrow" or what Anthony Beavis refers to as "our Poonas" (*EG*, 503), emblems of a "neurotic" withdrawal from social and political life as well as a turning inward to a claustrophobic selfhood. *Eyeless in Gaza* is organized around an incrementally developed series of references to sepulchers, vaults, ossuaries, crypts, walled gardens, locked rooms, cubicles, compartments, cocoons, galleries, monasteries, private boxes, tubes, dolls' houses, and warrens that collectively constitute a metaphoric landscape through which Anthony Beavis must carefully thread his way. When we first encounter him as a child, he is so encompassed by adults dressed in mourning that "their blackness hemmed him in," inducing the suffocating feeling that he was walking at the bottom of a moving well" (*EG*, 35). Similarly, John Beavis, Anthony's father, lives like a marmot securely tucked away in the "subterranean burrow" of domesticity (*EG*, 207). Mark Staithes's "dingy house" finds its counterpart in Hugh Ledwidge's retreat, "the long gallery of the Ethnographical Collection" in the British Museum (*EG*, 514). Hugh's sense of himself as a man confined to a "dingy little kennel" (*EG*, 487) reappears concretely in Mary Amberley's Paris apartment, where she lives on drugs in the cramped squalor of a "dog-kennel" (*EG*, 288), crawling through a hole in the door to her filthy bedroom like an animal entering a "dirty burrow" (*EG*, 24). Anthony Beavis prefers the "haven of the London Library" (*EG*, 354) and the familiar surroundings of the British Museum to a world grown increasingly anarchic. A similar impulse drives Beppo into "the Museum of Sexology" (*EG*, 231) and confines Mr. Thursley to "his study" (*EG*, 357). Anthony's moral and spiritual growth is accompanied by the perception that the social landscape is pitted with carefully excavated "boltholes from unpleasant reality" (*EG*, 503), that he himself is "a man in a burrow" (*EG*, 469) of his own construction, and that "half the population of Europe live[d] in a universe that's entirely home-made" (*EG*, 162). Anthony conceives of hell as a "crypt-like room" (*EG*, 496) resembling the bar at Tapattan and imagines Beppo Bowles's hell as "an underground lavatory" (*EG*, 230). John Beavis retreats into his dead wife's bedroom like a mummy in "his own sepulchre" (*EG*, 196), while the scholarly life is compared by Anthony to a retreat into "a monastery" (*EG*, 171), and his perspective on society as a practicing sociologist to that of an observer occupying a "private box" (*EG*, 611). Hugh Ledwidge also conceals himself in a "private room" (*EG*, 185), just as Anthony dwells in an "aquarium fastness" not essentially different from his father's "private world of silence" (*EG*, 96). At Bulstrode Hugh Ledwidge continues to dwell in a "squalidly tender little Eden of enemas and spankings" (*EG*, 79) that will later extend into his sexually crippled marriage, where he retreats into a fantasy world of "invisible solitude," leaving his wife to occupy a bedroom resembling a "family vault" (*EG*, 291–92). Similarly, Ledwidge's friend Croyland pursues an equally constricting illusion, claiming that "with the highest art one enters another world" (*EG*, 302). Anthony Beavis's attempt to rise above "the drain pipe of *Weltanschauung*" (*EG*, 145) to become the "good man" who is "merely a less completely closed universe" (*EG*, 615)—neither the victim of the anarchy within "the cellars of his mind" (*EG*, 24) nor a captive of the "prison" (*EG*, 124) of knowledge—is a movement from spiritual confinement and psychologically crippling enclosure towards a new freedom in relation to time, history, and death. The motif of enclosure pervades almost every chapter of *Eyeless in Gaza*, differing both in intensity and scope from its employment in earlier novels.

A false perspective on time can be made to serve the cloistral mentality of the burrower, when it does not actually constitute it. John Beavis, safely immured within the "connubial burrow" (*EG*, 468), observes that "our time scale is all wrong" and insists that the problems confronting Europe in "the thirties of the twentieth century" can be ignored as soon as one realizes that modern history is merely "a point between two ice ages" (*EG*, 86). John Beavis has expanded Mark Staithes's Gibbonesque view of history to embrace geological time, thereby minimizing the significance of contemporary events and justifying his social and political inertia. Mary Amberley, on the other hand, is conscious only of "the boring nothingness of . . . time" (*EG*, 399), an anomie that also informs Joan Thursley's sense of "the prosaic world of time" (*EG*, 376). Mrs. Foxe, dependent on her son to endow her life with meaning, finds "time" to be "strangely empty," however "tightly crammed" with a "succession of committee meetings" (*EG*, 246). In *Eyeless in Gaza* time can also function as a form of enclosure. Anthony's uncle, James Beavis, seeks shelter under the notion of linear time, or what Anthony refers to as "the self-sufficient, the atomic present" (*EG*, 25).

For James, a severely repressed homosexual, accurate measurement and the comforting illusions fostered by a rigid adherence to the present constitute a strategy designed to forestall thoughts about his past or his even bleaker future. When the reader first encounters James, he is traveling by train to his sister-in-law's funeral and anxiously preoccupied with the train's schedule: "as though to a sore, to an aching tooth, his fingers traveled again to the chronometer in his waistcoat pocket. Time for its own sake. Always imperiously time, categorically time—time to look at one's watch and see the time. . . ." James Beavis cannot truly "see the time" but only experiences it as a "mystical ulcer" (*EC*, 30), a source of unrelenting pain and anxiety. Similarly, his brother's attempt to recreate the past by preserving his wife's bedroom as it had been during her life is both a moral and psychological evasion of the truth, an attempt to circumvent the effects of the linear flow fatally measured by James's "chronometer." Anthony Beavis will also attempt to hide from the past, insisting that his memories exhibit "no chronology" (*EG*, 23) while actively pursuing "the discrete, the self-sufficient, the atomic present" into a morally insipid state "beyond the past and the future, beyond right and wrong" (*EG*, 25).

Anthony's relationship with his own past, his views on the nature of time, and his assessment of contemporary European history are subtly intertwined. His fear of epiphanic flashes illuminating his own past is also a measure of his detachment from modern history. For Anthony, despite his ostensible interest in "historical facts," time is an anarchic tangle of "atomic" instants beyond control or comprehension. He actively fears the past and loathes memory as an alien phenomenon imbued with an arbitrary treachery: "Even the seemingly most solid fragments of present reality are riddled with pitfalls. . . . Nothing was safe" (*EG*, 22). A memory for Anthony is a violent shock that precipitates him into a past that he would prefer to regard as psychologically and morally extinct. He fears emotional involvement and shrinks from active political action. His metaphorical indictment of memory, like his hysterical harangue on the subject of Proust—Mary Amberley observes that he talks of Proust "as if he were a personal enemy" (*EG*, 8)—is symptomatic of Anthony's aversion for experiencing anything beyond the present instant. Haunted by a past, the most notable features of which are death, suicide, betrayal, and slavish sensuality, he prefers a present in which he can assume the superiority of the "preoccupied man of science" (*EG*, 4). Accordingly, Anthony's metaphor of the interior lunatic is at best a half-truth: "Somewhere in the mind a lunatic shuffled a pack of snapshots and dealt them out at random, shuffled once more and dealt them out in different order, again and again, indefinitely. There was no chronology. The idiot remembered no distinction between before and after. The pit was as real and vivid as the gallery" (*EG*, 23). The final observation tips Anthony's hand, revealing his anxiety over his role in Brian Foxe's suicide and his consternation when confronted with a memory that not only dredges up a picture of the chalk-pit in which Brian's body was found but connects such an event with an apparently unrelated and essentially harmless flirtation with Mary Amberley in a Paris "gallery." Yet if his "thirty-five years of . . . conscious life" appear to Anthony "as a chaos" (*EG*, 23) that obeys no associative process, this is because Anthony has refused to acknowledge the moral and emotional affiliations that connect his slavish infatuation with Mary Amberley to Brian Foxe's suicide. Anthony is wrong and the pit and the gallery do belong together, just as both are linked to his present affair with Helen Amberley. It was at Mary's instigation that Anthony seduced Joan Thursley, Brian Foxe's fiancee, a train of events that culminated in Brian's suicide. The "lunatic within" Anthony's mind has thus brought to the surface a causal pattern that he cannot afford to recognize because such a concession to the past would force him out of the "atomic" present and expose him to a moral chronology of devastating implications.

John Beavis's persistent endeavor to create a secure space (his deceased wife's bedroom or the "connubial burrow" of his second marriage) that would function as a sanctuary within the stormy social landscape of the Europe of the 1930s is equally present in his attitude towards history. As a philologist, he is also an historian, his work dealing principally with the English Renaissance. His speciality is Jacobean English, and he plans an "exhaustive essay on Jacobean slang" (*EG*, 55), a meaningless historicist exercise in the context of *Eyeless in Gaza* because it reinforces his conception of the past as a scholarly shelter from the present. However, his philological history, when linked to his habitual quest for emotional security, introduces a third aspect of time that pervades *Eyeless in Gaza*—the role of the parental past in shaping the filial present.

Time in Huxley's novel is thematically ordered like a series of Chinese boxes, one concept hidden inside the other. Universal time becomes the more comprehensible geologic time, which narrows to the Gibbonesque sweep of history, which in turn contains "the thirties of the twentieth century" (*EG*, 86) comprised of both tiny fragments of memory and the sequential instants of the "atomic present." The various ways of conceiving time are all drawn into a complicated historicist web, not the least important of which is the continuing influence of childhood and especially the barren examples of Huxley's parental figures, whose behavior deeply scars the lives of most of the characters of *Eyeless in Gaza*. The two defining traits of John Beavis—his preference for secure "bolt-holes," either scholarly or domestic, and his emotional immaturity—are both passed on to his son, where they directly inspire Anthony's chronic moral apostasy. The role of Anthony's mother, however, is more complicated. Chiefly defined by her absence, she introduces her son to the mystery of death and the idea of an incomprehensible termination to sequential, linear time. Anthony's obsessive counting of the "OX IN THE TEA-CUP" advertisements while traveling by train to the church where his mother's funeral services will be held is an attempt to confront and control linear time. The counting game induces a shameful sense of impropriety, but in spite of his mounting embarrassment, he continues it, surrendering to his covert anxiety over a temporal succession that points to death as the culminating sum.

Yet Maisie Beavis's influence is not confined to the concept of death. During her life she deeply marked her son in one important respect, provoking Anthony to a morbid fastidiousness with physical process by emphasizing the likelihood of infection in a germ-infested world and as a result prompting him to feelings of near universal loathing for physical contact: "Always spit when there's a bad smell about," she had warned him. "There might be typhoid germs in the air" (*EG*, 36). His "sickening disgust" (*EG*, 37) with the dusty smell of the church and his acute consciousness of a "disgusting wet place on his cheek" after he is kissed by Lady Champernowne (*EG*, 33) are symptoms of a deeply ingrained revulsion for physical contact that continues to haunt him as an adult, rigidly curtailing the range of normal responses to other human beings. For example, he finds the lower-class children invited to stay at Rachel Foxe's home "insidiously disgusting": "'Reeking with germs!' he heard his mother's angrily frightened voice repeating. 'Reeking with germs!'" (*EG*, 111). Earlier in the church during the service for his mother, he is "forced to . . . swallow his spittle" (*EG*, 37), despite his fear of contamination. Huxley intensifies this childhood deformation at the hands of a neurotic parent by extending it into adulthood, where it not only inhibits Anthony's ability to form deep and lasting relationships but wells up repeatedly in the form of a recurrent nightmare.

After burying the dog that had fallen from a passing airplane onto Anthony and Helen Amberley as they lay on the roof of Anthony's villa, "he went to bed early, and, at two, was woken by that horribly familiar dream that had haunted his boyhood and plagued him from time to time even as a grown man." This dream establishes a connection with Anthony's past that significantly complicates, if it does not directly contradict, Huxley's theory of the states. It introduces a carefully developed etiology that firmly unites the child and the adult in a matrix of psychic causality. The dream, "always the same," is part of a motif involving swallowing and regurgitation first introduced in the earlier church scene. In Anthony's nightmare,

He took a mouthful of some indeterminate food and instantly it expanded between his teeth, became progressively more rubbery and at the same time stickier, till it was like a gag smeared with a kind of gum that dried in a thick film on the teeth, tongue, palate. Unspeakably disgusting . . . asphyxiating. . . . He tried to swallow, tried, in spite of the obscure presence of strangers, to disgorge. Without effect. In the end he was reduced to hooking the stuff out with his finger—lump after ropy lump of it. But always in vain. For the gag continued to expand. . . . (*EG*, 167)

Anthony's neurotic antipathy for a world so repellent that he cannot tolerate physical contact without his gorge rising is pointedly emphasized both at the beginning of *Eyeless in Gaza* and at the conclusion. The following passages, describing Anthony in 1902 and 1934, are almost identical:

But Anthony hardly heard, because he could think of nothing except those germs . . . and of the spittle that kept flowing into his mouth and that he had to swallow in spite of the typhoid and influenza, and of that horrible sick feeling in his stomach. (*EG*, 38)

At the sight of those broad flaps of skin turned back, like the peel of a huge banana, but from a red and bleeding fruit, Anthony was seized with a horrible sensation of nausea. The saliva came pouring into his mouth and he had to keep swallowing and swallowing to get rid of it. Involuntarily, he gave vent to a retching cough. (*EG*, 562)

Anthony's nausea is clearly a symptom of a neurotic fear inspired by his unhealthily fastidious mother and at the same time an element within a wider motif that extends to other characters. It seems intended to express what Huxley regarded as a legitimate attitude towards experience and is closely tied to a shift in Huxley's view of nature that aligns itself with his attack on historicism. But to return to Anthony's psychological development, it is obvious that Huxley has introduced and then systematically amplified a crippling, parentally induced neurosis that while enriching the theme of time and its various aspects, is also at cross-purposes with his denial that the personality is a unified, continuously developing entity.

Anthony's father appears to be equally decisive at inducing in his son a set of psychological "tics and tropisms" (*EG*, 521) that reappear in later life. Continually mortified by his father's foolish jokes, clumsy attempts to draw him out, and egregious sentimentality, Anthony shifts allegiances to Rachel Foxe and her son Brian. But Anthony cannot so easily escape his father, adopting an identical pattern of behavior in both his professional and personal life. Equally important, in turning to Rachel Foxe, he in fact substitutes an ineffectual parent with a positively dangerous one. Mary Amberley describes Rachel Foxe's love for her own son as a compensatory passion: "All the love she never got from her husband, all the love she never gave him—it's being poured out on that miserable boy" (*EG*, 227). Huxley reintroduces and intensifies the theme of parental dominance and destructiveness by means of Brian Foxe's stutter and his dread of sexuality. His fiancee Joan Thursley insists that his sexual anxieties are "mostly his mother's doing" (*EG*, 374). Similarly, Mary Amberley confesses that her own parents made her a "mental cripple" and a "deformity" (*EG*, 222), and her daughter Helen attributes her own fears "to the unreliability of her mother," whom she dismisses as "a very bad practical joke" (*EG*, 186–87). Not unexpectedly, Anthony's final awakening in *Eyeless in Gaza* is accompanied by the realization that "having spent all his life trying to react away from the standards of his father's universe, he had succeeded only in becoming what his father was . . ." (*EG*, 469). Furthermore, the insidious effect of parental influence clouds the question of responsibility in relation to Brian Foxe's death. Anthony's betrayal of Brian is the catalyst that directly motivates his suicide, but Rachel Foxe has smothered her son 'like a vampire, fastened on poor Brian's spirit. Sucking his life's blood" (*EG*, 586). Subjected since childhood to Rachel's possessive, suffocatingly idealistic love, Brian has been rendered incapable of enjoying normal sexuality. In her own marriage Rachel Foxe felt only loathing for her husband, spurning his physical advances as an "outrage" (*EG*, 248) and communicating this morbidity to her son, who makes his fiancee feel "dirty and criminal" when she asks for physical attention (*EG*, 375).

The theme of debilitating parental influence—especially as it twists and distorts the emotional life of the child and extends into adulthood, where it prohibits participation in normal sexuality and marriage—not only pervades *Eyeless in Gaza* but is so ubiquitous as to be an accepted norm, a fact of life on the level of time and process. Huxley has so fashioned his fictional social world that no alternative seems to be possible. Anthony cannot reach beyond the circumscriptions of the "magic circle," his only prolonged affair being shallowly rooted in a physical attraction or what he calls "irresponsible sensuality, rather than love" (*EG*, 323–24). Conversely, Brian Foxe can experience love but cannot endure its physical expression. The second phase of Anthony's education (1912–1928) introduces the theme of love within a "psychological landscape" of failed marriages, sexual perversion, infidelity, and sadomasochistic eroticism. The various affairs of the second phase are, in a manner of speaking, exhibits in Beppo Bowles's "Museum of Sexology." Just as Mark Staithes had reduced personality to a residue of pain, so love is debased to the level of intense but unfulfilling agony. As the detached Anthony makes love to Helen Amberley, he studies her face and sees only "intolerable suffering": "Distorted, the face was a mask of extremest grief. It was the face, he suddenly perceived, as he bent down towards those tormented lips, of one of Van der Weyden's holy women at the foot of the Cross" (*EG*, 20).

The role of pain as an inevitable, even preponderate element in wholly erotic relationships is best illustrated in John Beavis's masochistic ritual designed not only to preserve the memory of his wife but to induce a discernibly sensual response as well. After handling his dead wife's dresses, inhaling the "faint sweet essence of her body" and carefully cataloguing the contents of her dresser, he performs the final act of "the sacrament of communion" (*EG*, 194):

The night-gown refolded and once more shut away, it was the turn of the two smaller drawers on the right—of the gloves that had encased her hands, the belts that had girdled her body and that now he wound round his wrist or tightened like a phylactery about his temples. And the rite concluded with the reading of her letters—those touchingly childish letters she had written during their engagement. That consummated the agony for him; the rite was over and he could go to bed with yet another sword in his heart. (*EG*, 194–95)

This emphasis on masochistic suffering combines with the theme of time to create a bleak image both of a failure to recapture time past (a parody of the Proustian epiphany) and a developed taste for masochistic self-stimulation. The private nature of this masturbatory act further reinforces Huxley's insistence on the subjective futility of erotic pleasure. The eventual failure of John Beavis's onanistic ritual is accompanied by an image of detumescence: "He buried his face in the scented folds of her dresses, he spread out the lace and lawn she had worn next to her skin, he blew into one of her gloves and watched the gradual deflation of this image of her hand—dying, dying, till the skin hung limp and empty of even the pretence of life" (*EG*, 195). The close connection between death and sexuality is a constant motif in Huxley's novels, often dramatized in sadomasochistic scenes that stress the onanistic imprisonment of the participants (a theme that will occupy the thematic foreground of *After Many a Summer Dies the Swan*).

Mary Amberley also betrays a desire for masochistic humiliation when she submits to Gerry Watchett. The scene is essentially a pornographic fantasy in which Mary encourages Gerry to rape her. At the outset she experiences "an obscure pleasure in her helplessness," and her feelings continue to intensify to the point where she begins to enjoy her sense of violation for its own sake:

> the consciousness was intoxicating in its shamefulness—in fact, she really wanted to be treated as he was treating her—like a prostitute, like an animal; in her own house, what was more, with her guests all waiting for her, and the door unlocked, and her daughters wondered where she was, perhaps at this very moment coming up the stairs to look for her. Yes, she really wanted it. Still struggling, she gave herself up to the knowledge, to the direct physical intuition that this intolerable degradation was the accomplishment of an old desire, was a revelation marvellous as well as horrible, was the Apocalypse, the whole Apocalypse at once, angel and beast, plague, lamb and whore in a single, divine, revolting, overwhelming experience. . . . (*EG*, 280).

Like John Beavis's onanistic ritual, Mary Amberley's masochistic surrender is a carefully orchestrated, essentially solitary experience, the element of exhibitionism only intended to intensify her sense of degradation. And just as John Beavis hoped to stimulate the past into existence, she possesses the future "Apocalypse" in a violent present of ecstatic pain.

Mary Amberley's role in *Eyeless in Gaza*, in terms of chronological structure, is that of a link between generations. She was present at the funeral of Anthony's mother; she competed (unknowingly) with her daughter for the attentions of Gerry Watchett. As Anthony's mistress, she recklessly encouraged him in his seduction of Joan Thursley; and her hovel in Paris is the grimmest of the novel's burrows. As a figure that embodies the spirit of anomie pervading English society, she is the final version of the Nancy Cunard figure,[10] a Huxleyan convention first introduced in *Antic Hay* in the person of Myra Viveash and reappearing in *Point Counter Point* in the character of Lucy Tantamount. Her masochistic pleasure in the scene described above finds its sadistic counterpart in her psychological dominance of Anthony Beavis, whom she manipulates into betraying his closest friend—but only after forcing him to assume a posture of submission by ordering him to "kneel down on the floor." Anthony complies and "felt humiliated by her almost contemptuous assumption of the dominant role." Yet he passively "abandoned himself" (*EG*, 385), much as Mary surrendered to Gerry Watchett. In *Eyeless in Gaza* sexual relationships are informed by an almost gladiatorial eroticism. The emotional intensity of an affair or a marriage is generated by aggression and combative rivalry, a self-assertiveness in a private sphere that finds its counterpart in the clash of warring ideologies in the public realm of international politics. The "special tarts for masochists" (*EG*, 231) that Beppo Bowles encountered in Berlin are a sexual extension of the activities of those who "torture for the sake of the fatherland" (*EG*, 229). Accordingly, it is not surprising to discover a growing indifference to romantic love and physical eroticism in Anthony as the second phase of his education draws to a close. In the third phase, prior to Anthony's break with Helen Amberley (after the rooftop episode), he notes in his journal that he no longer finds "physical desire" to be compelling or even interesting, observing, "I don't think much in erotic terms now" (*EG*, 324). His disgust with the violent eroticism of an increasingly turbulent world is one of the lasting results of his experience in Mexico. Anthony's revulsion for aggressive sexual behavior and his sense that such behavior is widespread is evident in his rather morbid inventory of the "lunatic" desires of his contemporaries, especially their compulsion "towards young men, towards little girls in trains, towards exhibitionism, . . . towards being whipped, towards all the innumerable crazy perversions" (*EG*, 521). Beppo Bowles's Berlin, with its "Museum of Sexology," applies as much to English as to German society, its comic side (the rubber breast of the transvestite) surfacing in John Beavis's philological pun on his "teeny weeny penis" (*EG*, 407) or Hugh Ledwidge's "mystical mouse" (*EG*, 395) and its darker, more malevolent aspect flaring up in the sadomasochistic behavior of Mary Amberley or John Beavis.

According to Anthony, "the Marquis de Sade" is "the ultimate and absolute revolutionary" (*EG*, 84), his political radicalism and lust for power broadly representative of the vulgar infamies of modern history and the neurotic waywardness of its constituent individuals. Accordingly, most of the characters in *Eyeless in Gaza* who profess a specific attitude towards political experience are marked by sadomasochistic patterns of behavior, a conjunction of politics, power, and eroticism that reaches its most sterile intensity in the perversely heroic decorum of the Sorelian Mark Staithes. The self-torture of Brian Foxe laboring up mountains and hiking for miles in order to discipline his body is a more serious development of John Beavis's self-punishment in his deceased wife's bedroom, and culminates in the even more luridly fanatical sadomasochism of

Mary Amberley and Mark Staithes, who cherishes the agony of his infected leg as evidence of his moral identity. In *Eyeless in Gaza*, the principal monument to the ubiquity of both social and sexual violence is "the long gallery" in the British Museum housing "the Ethnographical Collection" (*EG*, 514), an anthropoligical assemblage that introduces another perspective on history—man's primitive past and its survival into the present. Ironically it is the gentle and epicene Hugh Ledwidge who as curator supervises the collection, although as the product of a violent childhood regimen of "enemas and spankings," his presence is not wholly inappropriate. The array of grotesque objects comprising the collection serves as a backdrop to his encounter with Helen Amberley, whom he has transformed in his mind into a "virginal . . . but melting" image of spiritual love. The irony of the situation is compounded by the fact that unknown to Hugh, Helen has just recovered from an abortion in Paris. Moreover, she has returned to England in the hope of finding a husband in the sexually impotent Hugh. The gallery, however, is a torture chamber bristling with "the trophies of . . . Papuan headhunters" (*EG*, 515), obsidian spears of "human bone," wooden bonito fish containing human skulls, musical instruments using skulls for resonators, and shrunken heads hanging from the belts of warriors (*EG*, 516). Standing in the midst of this sadistic collection of primitive weapons and trophies Helen exposes the wound on her arm (where her mother Mary Amberley had bitten her) to the astonished and frightened Hugh. Like Anthony's discovery of Brian Foxe's body in the chalk-pit, the confrontation of Helen and Hugh in the museum is one of the novel's culminating images of futility, a fruitless attempt to overcome the sadomasochistic aggression of a society given over to what Anthony Beavis describes as "tics and tropisms, lunatic and unavowable cravings" (*EG*, 355).

The explanation for Huxley's use of the Marquis de Sade can be found in *Ends and Means*, published two years after *Eyeless in Gaza*. Huxley's use of sadomasochism as a metaphor for erotic antagonism in a "degenerate" society in *Point Counter Point*, *Eyeless in Gaza*, and *After Many a Summer Dies the Swan* stems from his belief that "the behaviour of the insane is merely sane behaviour, a bit exaggerated and distorted." Accordingly, sadomasochistic behavior has both a particular and a representative role in *Eyeless in Gaza*: "The abnormal casts a revealing light upon the normal. Hence the interest attaching, among other madmen, to the extravagant figure of the Marquis de Sade" (*EM*, 270). As I observed earlier, Huxley's philosophy of history tends to stress "psychological" explanations, while significant trends or movements in cultural history are described as "psychological undulations" or "psychological movements." In *Eyeless in Gaza* Anthony records in his diary a number of observa-

tions that shed light on the representative social and psychological meaning of sadomasochistic activity throughout the novel, especially as it
touches on Huxley's philosophy of history: "Each age has its psychological revolutionaries. La Mettrie, Hume, Condillac and finally the Marquis
de Sade, latest and most sweeping of the eighteenth-century de-bunkers.
Perhaps, indeed, the ultimate and absolute revolutionary. But few have
the courage to follow the revolutionary argument to Sade's conclusions"
(*EG*, 84). While Huxley admitted that de Sade's behavior was governed
by "a strictly sexual perversion" (*EM*, 271), he stresses the latter's
significance as an epistemological skeptic: "De Sade's philosophy was the
philosophy of meaninglessness carried to its logical conclusion. Life was
without significance. Values were illusory. . . . Sensations and animal
pleasures alone possessed reality and were alone worth living for" (*EM*,
270).

## 2. Historical and Trans-Historical Apocalypse
### in *Eyeless in Gaza*

*Eyeless in Gaza* is a satirical reduction of a culture whose values are
derived principally from historicist assumptions. De Sade is its presiding
genius, the representative of a bankrupt intellectuality and its attendant
violence—both sexual and political. Huxley's fascination with de Sade
stems from the latter's consistency in acting on his skeptical principles:
"His books are of permanent interest and value because they contain a
kind of *reductio ad absurdum* of revolutionary theory. Sade is not afraid
to be a revolutionary to the bitter end" (*EM*, 271). De Sade interests Huxley because he is the ultimate skeptic, preaching an ideology of violence
that refuses to confine itself to "the field of politics and economics" but
insists on insinuating itself into every area of human experience, including "that of personal relations, including the most intimate of all, the
relations between lovers" (*EM*, 271). In Huxley's philosophy of history,
the Marquis de Sade is his fallen Adam, the universal symbol or "paradigm" of the collapse into historicism. The sexual sin of de Sade, the uncontrollable penchant for violence, manifests itself in the irrationality of
a methodical "will to power" that rends and finally destroys the fabric of
both private and political life. For Huxley it is the final and inevitable
symptom of historicist disillusionment, hence its association with "Apocalypse." Its seemingly outrageous logic as displayed in de Sade's writings
is in Huxley's eyes its single valuable truth: "De Sade is the one completely consistent and thoroughgoing revolutionary of history" (*EM*, 272).
As the adamic skeptic who has plucked "the fruits" from "the philo-

sophical tree" of historicism (*EM*, 273), de Sade can only be opposed by an equally radical revolutionary, but not a modern ideologue like "Karl Marx," whom Huxley associated with de Sade's "personal will to power" (*EM*, 272). Instead, Huxley turned to the Audenesque healing hero, in this case literally a medical doctor who embodies what Anthony Beavis calls "the total man," a concept traceable to the "ideal personality" of "the Jesus of the Gospel." However, Anthony is careful to distinguish what he hopes is a revolutionary revision of a traditional concept from the merely historicist "variants on the fundamental Christian man *of our history*" (*EG*, 145—italics mine).

As the disciple of Dr. Miller, Anthony Beavis is pursuing such an ideal based, as I shall show later, upon a curiously empiricist-idealist psychology of love that culminates in a personal act of self-sacrifice for what is only apparently a political ideal of universal pacifism. The role of de Sade in Huxley's attempt to reenvision a sanely tempered alternative to the irrationally appetitive historicist values of modern culture is to provide a psychological basis for Huxley's idea of evil. At this point trans-historical values are beginning to enter and shape Huxley's fiction, albeit in a tentative and exploratory form. The sadomasochistic turbulence that agitates the atomistic society of *Eyeless in Gaza* is, when it expresses itself in the will to power systematized into political ideologies, the only generative force immanent in history. Such a force, however, is traceable to neither a Hegelian rational Spirit nor a Christian providence but manifests itself as an increasingly unstable, ultimately nihilistic phenomenon, without direction or purpose. Accordingly, the "philosophy of meaninglessness" finally embraced by Mark Staithes, and which Huxley associated with the coalescence of "political *and erotic*" (*EM*, 275—italics mine) violence in the modern period, is symptomatic of the terminating phase of historicist culture. It can only be opposed by an equally extreme denial of the egoistic personality and its substitution by a provisional entity existing principally if not solely for the sake of moral accountability. I shall show that Anthony Beavis's pacifist heroism is much more of a religious gesture than a political one, despite the obvious political context of *Eyeless in Gaza*. Anthony, as the title implies, is a Samson come to his senses. In Milton's *Samson Agonistes* Samson, whose pride had been wounded by his captivity and degradation at the hands of his enemies, underwent a process of transformation in which self-pity and self-assertion gave way to an acceptance of God's will—and a resulting act of heroic martyrdom. Anthony Beavis's attempt to rise above the Gaza of historicist values is motivated by a repudiation of both personality and history and by an almost Platonic theory of love.

Almost all of the characters of *Eyeless in Gaza* are incapable of love.

Maternal affection, marital love, healthy sensuality, even friendship, fail to take root in the stony ground of Huxley's Gaza. At the outset of the novel, Anthony defines the problem as simply: "how to love." The word itself is suspect as a result of repeated usage, of "being fingered" by endless "generations" (*EG*, 15) who have twisted its meaning to serve discrete historicist ends. But for Huxley and eventually for Anthony, the word appears to have a self-evident tenor that raises significant, possibly insurmountable difficulties for the reader. For example, despite the evidence crowding in from all sides, Anthony serenely maintains that "we are all capable of love" but "we impose limitations on that love." Such self-imposed constraints, he adds, can be set aside "if we choose to" (*EG*, 229). Huxley's insistence on the deep and pervasive influence of parents on their children, especially in the matter of love, would seem to contradict if not falsify such an optimistic assessment. It is hard to see, for instance, how Hugh Ledwidge, raised on a regimen of "enemas and spankings," can be other than he is—a deterministic causality far more elaborately dramatized in Brian Foxe's life and death, not to mention Anthony's own experience as a child. In this regard, Anthony's uncomplicated rationalism fails to align itself with the "historical facts" as conceived by Huxley. It seems too neat and simplistic, just as Dr. Miller's moral precepts are unconvincing against the background of Hitler's seizure of power and Stalin's Russia. The answer to this thorny problem lies with Huxley's concept of love and the paradoxical resolution of *Eyeless in Gaza*.

Huxley's theory of self-renunciatory love is elaborately set forth in chapter forty-two. It forms, along with Anthony's meditation on "unity" in chapter fifty-four and his definition of "the total man" in chapter eleven, the moral system that lies at the heart of *Eyeless in Gaza* and encourages Anthony to accept the risk of political assassination by attending the Battersea pacifist meeting. In chapter forty-two Anthony offers a single historical fact to buttress his argument concerning the effects of a political policy informed by love. After an inventory of the various forms of fascist violence and the effects of "economic coercion," he cites as an example the debate over reparations after the Boer War: ". . . the translation of love into terms of politics. Campbell-Bannerman's insistence that reparations should be made in South Africa—and in the teeth of the protests, the Cassandra-like prophesyings of such 'sane and practical men' as Arthur Balfour. Love gains even in the clumsy, distorted form of a good political constitution." Anthony goes on to note that no moral progress has been made "since the last war, because no combatant has yet forgiven those by whom he has been wronged or those he has wronged" (*EG*, 501). Such a judgment echoes Huxley's account of the Versailles Treaty in *Ends and Means* as historically inevitable because the participants were "psychologically" unable to conceive of an alternative settlement. The problem facing Huxley is simply whether or not he can bring himself to endorse the liberal idea of moral and thus historical progress—whether the "total man's" appearance is part of an evolutionary process. Through much of *Eyeless in Gaza*, history has been thoroughly discredited, and in *After Many a Summer Dies the Swan* Huxley will reject it altogether. But in the earlier novel, Huxley is making a final attempt to see in history the possibility of a revolutionary change in the moral-psychological sphere sufficiently powerful to confront de Sade's revolutionary nihilism. Anthony's theory of love is intended, when combined with the new "total man," to provide the basis for such a process of historical recovery. In terms of its effects, when applied consistently to "any given situation," love always "gains," according to Anthony; the progressive nature of love is "an empirically determined fact" (*EG*, 501). But it is hard to see how such a naive assertion corresponds, for example, to Huxley's analysis of the chain of events that culminate in Brian Foxe's suicide. The moral and psychological causality that Huxley has dramatized in *Eyeless in Gaza* is much more subtly conceived than Anthony's blithe assurances that we have only to choose properly. The dramatic situations conceived by Huxley usually (but not always) preclude the possibility of choice. Anthony, for example, could have chosen not to seduce Joan Thursley, but such a decision would run counter to the kind of man Anthony is, a product of his parents' regressive disgust with the world. And while such a choice would remove the immediate cause of Brian's death, it would have no influence on the deterministically conceived sexual crippling that had marred his life so deeply and thoroughly. Similarly, the sadomasochistic behavior of Mark Staithes is not amenable to the teachings of Dr. Miller, as Huxley admits, while characters like Beppo Bowles, Croyland, Hugh Ledwidge, and Mary Amberley are caught up in patterns of behavior whose symptoms suggest complicated etiologies beyond the range of simple choices. In this respect, *Eyeless in Gaza* would seem to dramatize the opposite truth, that love *seldom* gains.

Anthony's meditation on love results in seven distinct propositions:

1. Love always gains.
2. The progressive beneficial nature of individual acts or government policies inspired by love is "an empirically determined fact."
3. Love is self-energizing. Once it is chosen as the moral basis for action, it creates[11] its own "means whereby its policy can be carried out" (*EG*, 501).

4. The object of love is "Goodness and the potentialities for goodness in all human beings."
5. Love can overcome "fear," even the terror of "malevolently active enemies."
6. The "process of loving" appears to be a spiritual discipline: "in order to go on loving, one needs patience, courage, endurance"; but Anthony adds that loving will generate these moral qualities of its own accord. Once the process is chosen and set in motion, other virtues will follow as effects.
7. The object of love, "goodness," is both "immanent" and "transcendent." It is a nondiscursive essential "entity" (*EG*, 502).

The passage where these appear has a neo-Platonic quality, although Anthony's mystical perception of a perfect "simple entity" that is not an image and cannot be expressed in language is too abstractly conceived to be associated with any single philosophy. Later in the concluding chapter of *Eyeless in Gaza*, Huxley will add important qualifications to this concept. For now it is sufficient to note that Huxley has injected another crucial element into his philosophy of history: an entity that while properly transcendent is also immanent within the world of historicist process. However, Huxley rejects Hegelian notions of a progressive spirit unfolding itself within history and in fact congruent with the rational course of history. If "goodness" can be "embodied" in any "given situation," it is only "partially" present in an imperfect way and without any suggestion of a providential purposiveness generating broad historical movements towards some distant apocalyptic goal.

Yet the resolution of *Eyeless in Gaza* raises a number of critical problems that Huxley could not solve in a conceptually satisfying way. *Eyeless in Gaza* differs markedly from *Point Counter Point* and the novels of the twenties in three important respects. First, there is a discernible accentuation of political and historical themes to the extent that contemporary history intertwines itself with the lives of almost all of the characters, destroying some and deeply scarring others. Second, the novel contains the first protagonist to undergo a complete and positively conceived transformation. Third, Huxley has introduced for the first time a set of trans-historical values that inspire the exemplary reformation of Anthony Beavis and significantly alter Huxley's own philosophy of history. Not unexpectedly, the resolution of *Eyeless in Gaza* exhibits the strains and fissures that accompany such a burden of thematic and conceptual revision. In the first place, both in *Ends and Means* and *Eyeless in Gaza*, Huxley tends to betray a divided allegiance to both historical process and a trans-historical absolute. His rejection of historicism and conviction that the "historical" is not a source of value are partially offset by the persistent effort throughout *Ends and Means* to define rational political and economic goals on the historicist level—just as *Eyeless in Gaza* appears to hold out the hope that organized pacificism could alter the course of modern history. Nevertheless, both *Eyeless in Gaza* and *Ends and Means* conclude with an analysis of a quietistic doctrine of "non-attachment" validated by an apocalyptic mysticism. These are fundamentally unrelated impulses that Huxley attempts to bind together in the concluding chapters. Indeed, it can be argued that his desires to both reform the world and to wholly transcend it have created a line of cleavage that can be traced throughout the interrelated themes of the novel.

Anthony Beavis's new "total man" is not radically new; indeed, there is, I would argue, no feature of this exemplary ideal that cannot be found in the identical matrix of values that informs the actions of George Eliot's self-effacing heroines. Dorothea Brooke, for example, could easily see her own reflection in such an image of ascetic humility and non-attachment to material values and sensual experience. More important, the ideal of non-attachment dramatized in *Eyeless in Gaza* and discursively analyzed in *Ends and Means*, when coupled with Anthony's theory of self-renunciatory love, raises a distinct problem. Huxley's appropriation of Blake's theory of the states (discussed earlier) is necessary to undercut the notion of continuous identity based on a self or personality persisting through time, a basic historicist assumption. However, while denying both history and personality, Huxley cannot accept the moral unaccountability that results once the stable identity of the self is rejected. Caught on the horns of a dilemma, he is forced to insist on the function of memory in fabricating a moral self, despite his belief that we are nothing but a succession of unrelated discrete selves or states. On the other hand, as Huxley dramatizes them, the states demonstrate a stubborn continuity. For instance, Helen Amberley suffers through a series of marriages and affairs, first with the novel's representative capitalist Gerry Watchett, and then with Hugh Ledwidge, an impotent idealist whom she eventually marries. When her relationship with Hugh begins to deteriorate, she turns to Anthony, the detached scientist, and finally becomes involved with Ekki Giesebrecht, the communist ideologue. Helen's centrality in *Eyeless in Gaza* is obvious in that she allies herself with a series of men who individually symbolize the various contending philosophies of the novel; but her role is not confined to the level of symbolism. Her disastrous affairs reveal much about Helen, especially an emotional dependency on men and an habitual impulsiveness that together suggest a persisting combination of psychological features rather than a series of unrelated states. Similarly, our first glimpse of Hugh Led-widge, masturbating in his solitary cubicle at Bulstrode, is a scene that emblematically foreshadows his impotent isolation in his later marriage, where the mental voyeurism of the adolescent onanist has developed into the cerebral idealism of the author of *The Invisible Lover*. Huxley's characters tend to undermine the theory of the states, much as Huxley's tendency throughout *Eyeless in Gaza* to lay flat the surrounding social and cultural landscape, creating a bleak and loveless wasteland, weakens the reader's confidence in Anthony's theory of love.

Eyeless in Gaza achieves closure by juxtaposing two sharply con-trasted attitudes toward history. Both final scenes are carefully devel-oped to suggest a final apocalyptic vision. The first of the two scenes (chapter fifty-three) is a somber revelation of historicist process; the sec-ond (chapter fifty-four) is a presumably more enlightened perspective on a trans-historical absolute. The former is set in Basel, Switzerland, on the German border. Helen Amberley has accompanied Ekki Giesebrecht, who has journeyed to Basel for a clandestine meeting with Ludwig Mach, a leader of the communist opposition now outlawed in Hitler's Germany. Not permitted to attend the meeting, Helen wanders through the city and suddenly finds herself "beside the Rhine":

Leaning over the parapet, she watched the green water hurrying past, silent, but swift and purposive, like a living thing, like life itself, like the power behind the world, eternally, irresistibly flowing . . .

The Rhine has become for Helen a symbol of Hegelian history, the onrush of events in which can be discerned a "power" immanent within historical process, "behind the world" but purposively guiding it. She continues to meditate and grows more enthusiastic:

[She] watched it, until at last it was as though she herself were flowing along with the great river, were one with it, a partaker of its power. . . . And suddenly it seemed certain that they would win, that the revolution was only just around the corner—there, after that first bend in the river. Irresistibly the flood drove on towards it. (*EG*, 598)

Helen's river of history, invincibly undulating towards a revolution validated by an immanent power, is for Huxley an ideological illusion. And while her historicist faith in history and progress is strengthened during her meditation by singing choruses of "And Shall Trelawney Die," her dynamic current of revolutionary process will shortly be trans-formed into an impassable static barrier (the Audenesque frontier) after Ekki is drugged and carried across the Rhine into National Socialist Ger-many. Forcefully separated from Ekki, Helen's dream of a vaguely

Hegelian, spiritually sanctioned change is shattered by the realities of not only "the present situation in Germany" (EG, 594) but a dark tradition extending back into Germany's romantic, death-intoxicated past.

Before Helen learns of Ekki's abduction, she leaves the Rhine and enters a "picture gallery" where she contemplates two paintings that despite their comic aspects, are grotesque intimations of Ekki's future and the meaningless violence inevitably accompanying the twists and terms of Helen's river of history: "And here—unspeakable joy—was the *Toteninsel*. The funereal cypresses, the white tomb-like temples, the long-robed figures, the solitary boat on its way across the wine-dark sea . . ." (EG, 599). Huxley's use of paintings and architecture is always informed by specific thematic purposes. In this case the dark and feverish world of German romanticism is aptly invoked in terms of Boecklin's evocation of isolation and death by means of a boat journey to a distant island-temple. After Helen contemplates this "baroque-romantic" icon, she moves on to a second painting, "a picture of the martyrdom of St. Erasmus" and its grotesque depiction of the removal of the saint's intestines. Both paintings foreshadow Ekki's torture and martyrdom at the hands of the Nazis in "the ultimate slaughter-house" of Hitler's Germany (EG, 600), but they also hint at Huxley's wider view of German history, including his celebration of Erasmus in preference to the more romantic Luther.[12]

Helen's apocalypse of history, informed and energized by an immanent "power," becomes a nightmare which she must like Stephen Dedalus attempt to dispel. In chapter fifty-four, her Marxist idealism has yielded to a withering contempt for politics and ideology. Succumbing to her grief for Ekki, she renounces dialectical history, substituting for her earlier faith a self-lacerating pursuit of wealth and luxury. Sensing her self-contempt, Anthony attempts to convince her that her present despair is a consequence of pursuing the wrong "alternative," that the solution to her present impasse is simply "a matter of choosing" (EG, 604), and the right ethical choice is "to cultivate the difficult art of loving people" (EG, 606). Anthony briefly categorizes the various types of idealists, placing Ekki with those ideologues who "genuinely believe that the end justifies the means" and that "the means don't condition the end" (EG, 605). While Helen listens, Anthony's remarks begin to blend for him into a meditation on "unity" in which he is overwhelmed by a final revelation of truth.

Anthony's apocalypse differs from Helen's vision of history in that while it stresses the collective unity of mankind, it seems peculiarly private. Abjuring political ideologies, where individual responsibility is dissolved within a collective abstraction, Anthony meditates but absorbs the discrete personality within a more comprehensive level of being. Anthony's culminating act of self-sacrifice (his decision to attend the Battersea meeting) seems less an endorsement of a particular moral position within an active and widespread political movement than a private ceremony of purification. In *Ends and Means* Huxley argued that "virtue is the essential preliminary to the mystical experience" (*EM*, 299), a principle that while not a conscious motive in Anthony's decision to become a pacifist, explains the religious rather than political caste of the final chapter of *Eyeless in Gaza* with its stark omission of any references to the wider activities of the pacifist movement.

Anthony's growing sense of social unity based on an ethic of nonviolence is both reinforced and, to a degree, displaced by a deeply religious revelation, the implications of which are principally ontological rather than political—although specific political values would naturally flow from such a concept of universal concord. After a sustained meditation on the chemical and physical unity of all life-forms, he goes on to develop this idea not only in terms of the discrete existence of unique organisms, including individual minds, but of their deeper interconnection: "And minds—minds also are unique, but unique above a substratum of mental identity." This unitary sharing of an ontologically prior level of being guarantees the efficacy of Anthony's theory of love. What he refers to as "the mental pattern of love" can, as a consequence of such a universal affinity, "be transferred from one mind to another." Anthony does not relinquish the "equal reality of division" on the phenomenal level, but he insists that "an intuition coming at random, or sought for, step by step, in meditation" (*EG*, 614) reveals a more fundamental coherence. The attempt to come into contact with such a source of unity involves two important conclusions. First, separation and diversity are necessary conditions of human existence: "being must be organized in closed universes." Second, "the good man is merely a less completely closed universe" (*EG*, 615). Like F. H. Bradley's finite center,[13] each self exists at the hub of its own circumambient world, but such "separation is evil," the Marquis de Sade being Huxley's favorite example of the endorsement of such a position. The "paradox" that underlies this belief in both the necessary separation and the fundamental unity of human minds is candidly avowed by Anthony: "That which is demanded, that which men come finally to demand of themselves, is the realization of union between beings who would be nothing if they were not separate; is the actualization of goodness by creatures who, if they were not evil, would not exist" (*EG*, 615).

While necessarily separate, Mark Staithes hiding in his dingy house, Mary Amberley in her squalid Paris apartment, and John Beavis withdrawn into his domestic "burrow" have succumbed to an intensified social atomism, refusing to rise to the challenge of political reintegration, much less the mystical illumination of a deeper ontological "unity." As a result, they are pointedly associated with de Sade. But for Anthony "unity was the beginning and unity the end," a circular process of development in which the individual's history of painful segregation is an indispensable prelude to an apocalyptic recovery. *Eyeless in Gaza* begins with a child separated from his mother and alienated from his father whose lost world of innocence and love is only rediscovered in a higher form after a pilgrimage through a world of historicist illusion. Such a movement from a lesser to a higher unity is a basic postulate of Blake's myth of the fall of man into a divisive state followed by his painful struggle to recover a vanished harmony free of the historicist categories of space and time. Similarly, the dialectical tension between open and closed forms in Blake's system is present in Anthony's insistence on moving beyond the "closed" towards progressively more "open" universes. Blake's "caverned man,"[14] like Huxley's "man-in-a-burrow," is confined to the narrow horizons of his subjectively ordered world. Anthony's decision to break out of his "private box" and enter the more human realm of direct social interplay is only a provisional form of unity in which politics and history, of themselves, offer no final truths and no absolute solutions. On the level of historicist experience, failure is inevitable: "Even for the highest goodness the struggle is without end; for never in the nature of present things can the shut become the wholly open; goodness can never free itself completely from evil. . . . Lifetimes passed in the attempt to open up further and a little further the closed universe that perpetually tends to spring shut the moment that effort is relaxed" (*EG*, 617). This passage is fairly representative of Huxley's very circumspect approach to the possibility of moral and spiritual progress; indeed, it qualifies Anthony's fervent belief in the self-energizing power of love and marks an important distinction between Huxley's and Blake's view of man's necessary involvement in the world of space and time.

Where the ebullient Blake can joyfully accept the rigors of the world of experience even while insisting on the necessity to abandon it, Huxley's ideas are rooted in a more Christian *contemptus mundi*. He has clearly come a long way since his celebration of the Blakean "life-worshipper" in *Do What You Will*, and thus while Blake's ideas continue to play a central role in *Eyeless in Gaza*, Huxley can no longer share Blake's delight in the senses or the challenging complexities of Experience with its energetic interplay of contraries. Similarly, the final state of spiritual revelation and ontological transcendence envisioned by Anthony in the last chapter of *Eyeless in Gaza* is radically antithetical to Blake's Jerusalem conceived as a dynamic condition of "intellectual warfare." Blake can redeem his primary villain, the sadistic and egocentric Urizen, the poet's concept of evil being inseparable from his theory of the states. But despite Huxley's use of Blake's hypothesis of personality as a transient and insubstantial condition capable of being cast aside, Huxley's personification of evil, the Marquis de Sade, seems less amenable to change than Blake's Urizen. The result of this lingering darker view of human depravity can be seen in the overall pessimism of *Eyeless in Gaza* and the persistence of uneducable characters like Mark Staithes. Huxley will return to this theme in *After Many a Summer Dies the Swan;* in *Eyeless in Gaza* his adherence to Blake's theory of the states and all that implies regarding the insubstantial nature of both the egocentric self and evil (the two being synonymous) clashes with an almost Freudian theory of neurosis—of a deeply rooted and persisting condition of egocentric appetite and near-permanent psychological impairment.

Huxley attempts to mediate this problem through the dramatic appearance of the Audenesque healing hero, Dr. Miller, a *deus ex machina* whose philosophical patter is at best unconvincing and at worst intellectually shallow. Huxley of course did not know that Hitler was a vegetarian, and much of the nonsense regarding good posture and diet can be attributed to Huxley's own chronic health problems. But Dr. Miller is best seen as a catalyst who reinforces a process of spiritual growth already set in motion by Anthony himself. Moreover, it can be argued that Anthony's best teacher is Mark Staithes, whose example is more crucial than Miller's medical advice, while Anthony had formulated his theory of the new "total man" and adopted his Blakean theory of personality years before he met Miller. Equally important, Anthony's mysticism is not derived from Miller, who confines his activities to the more practical pacificist movement.

The final mystical revelation that brings the novel to closure is an apocalyptic vision in the traditional sense; that is, an unveiling of the final ontological truth that defines man's status as an historicist phenomenon of no particular significance and reveals the possibility of a final merging with a shifting and tenuous absolute.

As Anthony's meditation continues, his experience of an "unmediated" vision of reality involves two distinct metaphors, the sea and a mysterious light, integrated by a third metaphor of two cones connected at their tips. The first is an image of an ocean whose quiet depths are obscured by a surface of waves and stormy conflict, an image that has a distinctly Blakean resonance. This composite image of the stormy surface of an ocean across which are driven "separate waves" involves three

Blakean ideas: the wave is the discrete state or personality; the sea is Blake's ocean of materialism, the sea of space and time that recurs in the major epics; and finally the storm is Blake's war of contraries, the clash of opposing ideas and forces that characterizes life at the level of experience. Huxley describes the turbulent surface as governed by contrary "cravings and aversions," but unlike Blake he does not envision such an interplay as essentially creative. His real sympathies lie with the ocean depths:

The same peace for all, continuous between mind and mind. At the surface, the separate waves, the whirlpool, the spray; but below them the continuous and undifferentiated expanse of sea becoming calmer as it deepens, till at last there is an absolute stillness. Dark peace in the depths. A dark peace that is the same for all who can descend to it. Peace that by a strange paradox is the substance and source of the storm at the surface. (*EG*, 618)

The descent to a "dark void beyond all personal life" (*EG*, 619) is the final goal of Anthony's progress, not pacifism or politics. The final image of the "circle," like Anthony's circular movement from unity to unity noted above, is a traditional symbol of perfection. The curious image of the two cones involves two circles—the base of the uppermost cone forming the surface of storm and waves, while the base of the lower cone is beyond the realm of turbulent sea surface and peaceful sea depth. It is defined by Huxley as "the ultimate light that is the source and substance of all things" (*EG*, 620), simultaneously immanent and transcendant, like the One Spirit of Shelley's *Adonais*, a poem increasingly valued by Huxley.

Roused from his meditation by the clock, Anthony returns to the world of time and conflict strengthened in his resolve to attend the Battersea meeting despite the risk to his own life. His dispassionate lucidity of spirit emphasized in the concluding paragraph of the novel is the spiritual clarity of a man no longer eyeless in a modern Gaza. Anthony's final apocalyptic "illumination" contrasts vividly with its darker counterpart, the earlier "apocalyptic time" (*EG*, 22) in Paris with Helen Amberley that marked the beginning of a sinister causality culminating in Brian Foxe's suicide as well as the spiritual nadir of Anthony's progress. Anthony's return to the turmoil of history, and its necessary but repellant violence, is made possible by his confidence in a promised serenity, a freedom from personality and desire that overcomes his fear of death and almost completely displaces Dr. Miller's pacifism as a serious political alternative. Pacifism is the occasion for Anthony's act of heroic self-sacrifice but not its primary motivation. Helen Amberley's river of purposive history has been swamped by Anthony's ocean of random historicist violence, just as Ekki Giesebrecht's ideology has been displaced by a supra-historical revelation. Huxley, however, not content with this assault on the premises of ideological historicism and increasingly disturbed by the intensification of international violence in the years immediately following the publication of *Eyeless in Gaza*, will return to this subject in *After Many a Summer Dies the Swan*—an elaborate exercise in the grotesque and his most systematically conceived attack on what he saw as his contemporaries' drastically misplaced faith in the "historical"nature of man.

# CHAPTER FIVE

# *Conclusion:* After Many a Summer Dies the Swan

### 1. Huxley's "Most Serious Parable" and the "Spiral of Development"

In a letter to his brother Julian, written in the spring of 1938 shortly after Hitler's annexation of Austria, Huxley described himself as hard at work on a new novel, a primarily political work that in its opposition to "communist, fascist or merely plutocratic" political philosophies, would provide "a viable economic and social basis to philosophic anarchism."[1] By the end of the year, after the Munich crisis and the annexation of the Sudetenland, the scope of the novel had ambitiously expanded to embrace "an analysis of narratives in general . . . the nature of individuality" and "the relationship between words and things." In addition, he hopes to conclude with "some kind of general theory of the world."[2] By July of the following year, after the invasion of Czechoslovakia and the gradual weakening of Republican forces in Spain, the book had become "a kind of fantasy, at once comic and cautionary, farcical, bloodcurdling and reflective."[3] In its rapid oscillations between a defeated weariness and a skeptical energy, *After Many a Summer Dies the Swan* was very much a product of its time, mirroring the social and psychological ferment of a society on the brink of war and, in its effort to wed "a wild extravaganza" with "a most serious parable,"[4] productive of a correspondingly chaotic atmosphere of anxiety and hope —a confusion of aims not lost on the book's reviewers.

Huxley's contemporaries tended to see the novel as an unsuccessful union of "parable" and "fantasy," containing the wide-ranging erudition and satirical energy of his best work but compromised by traces of a spiritual exhaustion, difficult to define yet inescapably evident. The anonymous reviewer of the *Times Literary Supplement* who praised the novel's intellectual rigor also described it as "the perfected bloom of Huxleyan pessimism," in which he detected "a graveyard aroma of the flesh" enveloping the characters in an atmosphere of "corruption and decay" and undermining the "impulse of faith or religious experience" presumably at the core of the novel's vision. Dismissed by Edgar Johnson in the *Kenyon Review* as an indigestible "literary sandwich" and damned by Anthony West in the *New Statesman* as Huxley's "petition in moral bankruptcy,"[5] *After Many a Summer Dies the Swan* marks a transition point in Huxley's popularity.

Huxley's first California novel gathers all the themes and preoccupations of the novels and essays of the previous two decades. In this respect, *After Many a Summer Dies the Swan* belongs to the period of *Eyeless in Gaza* and *Point Counter Point*, synthesizing and clarifying the theory of romanticism gradually evolved from the essays of *On the Margin* and *Music at Night* and drawing on the structural conventions of *Crome Yellow* and *Those Barren Leaves*. Indeed, it is the latter novel and not *Antic Hay*, as Peter Bowering has suggested,[6] that lies behind the form and style of *After Many a Summer Dies the Swan*. And while it can be argued that its theme is "contrapuntal" to that of *Time Must Have a Stop* and the later novels,[7] its preoccupation with "the nature of individuality"—with the meaning of history, significance of language, and persistence of the baroque-romantic impulse in European culture—make it a synoptic index to the presiding concerns of the novels of the interwar period.

A great part of the dissatisfaction with *After Many a Summer Dies the Swan*, so pungently expressed by Huxley's early reviewers, lies with what Thomas Mann described as Huxley's "cold attitude toward everything that burns under our skin, the things we love and hate."[8] Obviously such a general indictment could easily be leveled against *Point Counter Point* or *Eyeless in Gaza*, but it is nevertheless particularly appropriate to *After Many a Summer Dies the Swan* and *Time Must Have a Stop*. By the end of the 1930s, Huxley's characteristic skepticism, exacerbated by events in Germany and Spain, had assumed increasingly misanthropic dimensions. His sense of living in a society corrupted by the irrational values of romantic idealism but still amenable to criticism had yielded to a feeling of isolation and helplessness in the face of a world gone mad. In a letter to Julian written shortly before the appearance of *After Many a Summer Dies the Swan*, he remarked on the intensification of his sense of radical detachment from the individuals around him, a disengagement that inevitably fostered his own melancholy feelings of isolation within a world coming more and more to resemble a madhouse:

. . . I find myself often a bit overwhelmed by the curious rigidity and opacity of most human beings. There's something dismally fixed, stony, sclerotic about most of them—a lack of sensibility and awareness and flexibility, which is most depressing. There seems to be nothing much to be done, beyond, of course, doing one's best to prevent the oncoming of mental sclerosis in oneself, to keep the mind open to the world and to that which transcends the world and gives it sense and value. Such seems to be the only genuine contribution that one can make to the betterment of the concern—making oneself into a little window through which at least some light can be admitted; keeping oneself alive and aware so that at least some point in the vast stony structure shall be in a position to grow and respond.[9]

Between the metaphors of universal ossification and spiritual optics lies the sinister image of an inherently psychotic world. Huxley seems to wander the halls and corridors of a vast asylum, greeted only by the blankly uncomprehending gaze of the chronic inmate. Human beings are reduced to the status of objects, arrested in postures of stony unresponsiveness and incapable of growth, while Huxley—one suspects swayed partly by his own Medusa vision—is compelled to withdraw like Candide to the dwindling light of his private spiritual garden. As he remarks in a letter of the same period to Eva Herrmann, "this hideous world" is in essence a vast "lunatic asylum"[10] in which the good man's sphere of influence is severely circumscribed.

The image of the world as an immense bedlam is closely associated with the castle built by Joseph Panton Stoyte in *After Many a Summer Dies the Swan* as well as the "vast stony structure" referred to in Huxley's letter to his brother. The novelist clearly envisages himself as an inhabitant of a Piranesian labyrinth, his despair at the passivity of his fellow inmates heightened by an alternating belief in their potentiality for growth and contempt for their spiritual inertia. Complicating this view of the world as both prison and asylum is Huxley's qualified acceptance of an entropic universe marked on the human-temporal level by mounting chaos and decreasing vitality. In the letter to Julian, the world is described in terms of increasing petrification, in which only isolated individuals survive to combat the "oncoming" plague of universal sclerosis and preserve "a point" of wan light in a progressively darkening world. In *Ends and Means*, published two years before *After Many a Summer Dies the Swan*, he described "the prevailing cosmology" of modern science as inherently entropic: "the universe is regarded as a great machine pointlessly grinding its way towards ultimate stagnation and death; men are tiny off-shoots of the universal machine, running down to their own private death" (*EM*, 123). While Huxley recognized that such a picture was a scientific abstraction from "an incalculably greater whole" (*EM*, 254), and thus probably false, it did accord with his own increasingly pessimistic view of life lived solely on the level of temporal experience where process had become synonymous with stagnation rather than growth.

The problem lay with the fact that in Huxley's view most of his European contemporaries endorsed such a "cosmology" and consequently wandered wistfully "through life hollow with pointlessness, trying to fill the void within them by external stimuli" (*EM*, 124). Such a declining world casts its own golden glow, symbolized in *After Many a Summer Dies the Swan* by Watteau's *Embarcation for Cythera*, a late baroque masterpiece contemplated by Jo Stoyte while undergoing a medical examination in his mistress's bedroom. What he sees is a painting that evokes the wistful self-absorption of an essentially romantic pilgrimage in which one "mournful paradise" is abandoned by its "inhabitants," who having surrendered to an undisciplined submergence in the realm of time and the merely human, prepare to set sail "for some other paradise, doubtless yet more heartbreaking" (*AMS*, 156). The delicate colors and graceful forms of the Watteau may seem at a far remove from the stony carapace that Huxley perceived as having obscured the human lineaments of twentieth-century European civilization. But as an image of a society migrating unpredictably between baroque-romantic idealism and a more cynically modern hedonism, it participates in the same hopeless cycle of "perpetual self-frustration and self-destruction"[11] that Huxley repeatedly refers to in the letters of the late thirties.

In *After Many a Summer Dies the Swan*, the dreamy idylls of Watteau's *fêtes galantes* are replaced by a more grotesque rendering of the modern European's obsessive quest for distraction, with the customary Huxleyan convention of the inverse romantic's decline into a state of cynical nihilism extended into a prolonged process of entropic stagnation. Gog's Court and the burrow motif are carried to their grimly logical conclusion in the Fifth Earl of Gonister's subterranean cave where he degenerates into absolute bestiality, while Lilian Aldwinkle's baroque palace of art, the Cybo Malaspina of *Those Barren Leaves*, is satirically inflated to the crazy dimensions of Stoyte's castle. The world is indeed a "lunatic asylum," and Huxley, convinced that "the behaviour of the insane is merely sane behaviour, a bit exaggerated and distorted" (*EM*, 270), has assembled his inmates with a curious blend of "realistic psychological elements" and tumultuous "phantasy."[12] By 1937 his contempt for a world that he had come to regard in terms of mass "neurasthenia" and "mania" (*EM*, 125) could only be adequately rendered in a style of "extravagant exaggeration" (*EM*, 289)—or put another way, in *After Many a Summer Dies the Swan*, Huxley had evolved his own peculiarly baroque idiom.

To return briefly to the letter to Julian quoted above, it is important to note that in the midst of his denunciation of an increasingly sclerotic culture, Huxley alludes to the theory of "double consciousness" he had previously explored in *Eyeless in Gaza* and *Ends and Means*. Acknowledging that there "seems to be nothing much to be done" about the present state of European culture, he nevertheless holds out the possibility of achieving a kind of double perspective, an ability both "to keep the mind open to the world" and—simultaneously—"to that which transcends the world." Anthony Beavis of *Eyeless in Gaza* labored to integrate, morally and psychologically, his sense of a negative yet nonetheless persisting identity and at the same time to turn away from self towards a higher level of mystical perception. In *Ends and Means* Huxley links these two essentially different, even potentially conflicting perspectives by arguing that "if we would transcend personality, we must first take the trouble to become persons" (*EM*, 325). Moral reformation, including an ethic of radical self-renunciation, is necessarily antecedent to the transcendence of a normally atomized and sclerotic personality.

In a letter to Gordon Sewell written shortly after the appearance of *After Many a Summer Dies the Swan*, Huxley attempted to discriminate among the various competing levels of human existence by means of a metaphor of "spiral development," an image of evolutionary spiritual growth on a continuous curve ascending "from unconscious animal, through conscious human up to what for lack of better words may be called superconscious spiritual, which last exhibits the characteristics of the animal plane, but transfigured and on a higher level."[13] As William Propter will argue in *After Many a Summer Dies the Swan*, the most dangerous of the three planes is the second, the "conscious human level" informed by what Huxley calls "human grace,"[14] a state based on the ethic of self-renunciation essential to Anthony Beavis's achievement in *Eyeless in Gaza*. As in the letter to Julian discussed above, the world is viewed as a sclerotic wasteland where the political activism of an Anthony Beavis is for the most part futile. In such a world, given over wholly to "large-scale lunacies,"[15] Huxley can only shape his own spirit into "a little window" onto the Absolute. No mention is made of active political engagement in either of these letters because "human grace is an *ersatz* for spiritual grace—an *ersatz* ultimately destructive." The entire humanist tradition of Western art, philosophy, religion, and politics has for Huxley become synonymous with something evasive and contrived, an improperly conceived substitution of "inspiration from and self-sacrifice to strictly human 'ideals,'" or "causes," for the "spiritual grace"[16] of the mystic.

This tension between two conflicting teleological perspectives also involves two related but separable views of the self or personality. In *Eyeless in Gaza* Huxley struggled to integrate "human" and "spiritual grace" in his portrait of Anthony Beavis as the "total man," whose moral life was modeled on the "ideal personality conceived by the Jesus of the Gospel" (*EG*, 107). But such an ethic had become obstructive by the time Huxley had completed that novel. Self-renunciation came to be conceived by him not as a social virtue—that is, a moral stance taken by the individual for the benefit of others—but a private spiritual discipline designed to subordinate the exigencies of self preparatory to the individual's ascent up the "spiral" of human development. Christian self-sacrifice, then, is not a humanistic end but a spiritual means, a necessary turning away from self—and humanity—towards a higher and essentially numinous level of being in which the virtue of "charity" celebrated in *Ends and Means* has lost much of its force. The conclusion of *Eyeless in Gaza* emphasizes neither Anthony's concern for the sufferings of humanity nor his approaching death in an act of self-sacrifice but rather his acquisition of Huxley's "little window" onto the "dark void beyond all personal life" (*EG*, 472). Similarly, in *After Many a Summer Dies the Swan*, William Propter's Jeffersonian sentiments will stand in uneasy alliance with his puritanical aversion for all aspects of human experience. As Huxley observed in *Ends and Means*, "in life ethics and metaphysics are interdependent" (*EM*, 329), an axiom operative, as we shall see, on all planes of the "spiral" of development.

*After Many a Summer Dies the Swan* opens with the arrival in California of Jeremy Pordage, an English historian of the romantic period hired by Jo Stoyte to catalogue the Hauberk papers. Jeremy's subservience to his mother is a typical example of Huxley's fascination with what he described in a letter to Leonard Huxley as "the Freudian 'complexes' for which family relationships are responsible."[17] Jeremy's background draws on Huxley's earlier study of a sexually crippled male, Francis Chelifer in *Those Barren Leaves*. As a delicate and insecure child, Chelifer regularly abandoned his "terrifying night nursery" in order to find and be reassured by his mother, while his "bearded father" looked on "like an outraged god" (*TBL*, 144). After the death of his father, Mrs. Chelifer—a genteel vegetarian, devoted to charity and morris dancing—lived on in an "old Oxford house" designed by Ruskin. Chelifer remembers it as "dark, spiky and tall," repeatedly associating it with death in the form of a "tomb" containing a "chamber" wherein lay the "mummy" of his smothered youth (*TBL*, 115). Pale and cultured, his mother seems a curiously sinister figure whose "dim gentle smile" (*TBL*, 115) reappears in the mysterious "smiling" of Barbara Waters (*TBL*,

139–40), However, when Barbara Waters rejects him for another man, intensely masculine with "black eyebrows" and "black stubbles" on "his jowl" (*TBL*, 149), Chelifer is denied the intensely desirable woman who reminds him of his mother and his childish dependency on her. Similarly, when he almost drowns on the Viareggio, Chelifer's last thoughts are about his mother, who as an inconvenient consequence of his death, would be forced to journey to Rome unaccompanied. Admittedly, the details are so sketchy that it is by no means clear just how we are to regard Mrs. Chelifer's influence on her son; but his effete passivity as a result of his sexual failure in the Barbara Waters affair and his morbidly regressive retreat into Gog's Court form a suggestively hazy pattern that involves something more than the conventional career of the Huxleyan inverse romantic. In *Point Counter Point*, as I have shown in chapter three, Huxley handled the theme of what Jeremy Pordage calls "the Oedipus business" with greater suppleness and self-assurance. There the dark and vagrant workings of Maurice Spandrell's mind were shaped into an etiology of psychological perversion that deepened and complicated Huxley's portrait of the unstable emotional basis of the inverse romantic's obsessive idealism. In both *Eyeless in Gaza* and *After Many a Summer Dies the Swan*, Huxley was to return to this theme with remorseless logic.

Jeremy Pordage has so consciously sacrificed his sexual independence on the matriarchal altar that his curiously frivolous chatter on the subject brings to mind the sardonic Cardan's complaint that "too much light conversation about the Oedipus complex and anal eroticism is taking the edge off love" (*TBL*, 38). Jeremy's sexual appetite—like Francis Chelifer's, who candidly admitted to his "lacking a native enthusiasm for love" (*TBL*, 323)—is so dulled by his early exposure to "excessive maternal love" (*AMS*, 218) that he can only conceive of women in situations that render them harmlessly passive. If Spandrell was led to pursue prostitutes, Jeremy prefers to encounter them safely within the covers of a pornographic novel; like Chelifer, he has experienced only one serious relationship which appears to have left a mark on his subsequent sexual behavior. Indeed, his resemblance to Chelifer is so remarkably similar as to suggest that Huxley had decided to make amends for his earlier reticence.

For example, Chelifer is associated with Oxford, as is Jeremy with Cambridge. Chelifer's genteelly cultivated mother lived in a house designed by Ruskin; the "cultured Mrs. Pordage," referred to as "Oscar Wilde's old friend," lived in "The Araucarias" (*AMS*, 7), a middle-class house of similar Victorian respectability. Both Chelifer and Jeremy are writers acutely self-conscious of the fundamental absurdity of their work. More important, they both display the characteristic traits of the Huxleyan inverse romantic, including a pronounced aversion for human emotions and passion that invariably expresses itself in acts of rejection, regression, or withdrawal at the expense of more natural impulses. Chelifer's preference for the security of "the hot dark hive" (*TBL*, 145) of Gog's Court, or what he refers to in terms of a regressively umbilical attachment for "the navel of reality" (*TBL*, 98), reappears in Jeremy Pordage's obsession with retreating into some kind of secure enclosure where he can realize his ideal of "infinite squalor in a little room." The "little room" is occupied by two prostitutes—either "Mae or Doris," it doesn't seem to matter—and located in "their flat in Maida Vale" (*AMS*, 120). While his actual relationship to these women is never directly described by Huxley, the infantile quality of Jeremy's quest for a womblike "closed universe of utter cosiness" (*AMS*, 196) leaves little doubt as to the nature of the goings-on in the Maida Vale. Emasculated by his "greedy possessive mother" (*AMS*, 218), who in one of Huxley's more pointed allusions "had come to be for him almost like an organ of his own body" (*AMS*, 220), he desires only "the security" of his "mother's shadow" and a "sexual life" that was "simultaneously infantile and corrupt" (*AMS*, 223).

*After Many a Summer Dies the Swan* continues and expands Huxley's exploration of the baroque-romantic impulse but with a uniquely intense emphasis on a corrupt eroticism. Jeremy Pordage's infantile sensuality, the senescent fumblings of Jo Stoyte, and the sadomasochistic energies of the Fifth Earl of Gonister combine with the sophomoric romanticism of Pete Boone, the clinically remote voyeurism of Dr. Obispo, and the mindless promiscuity of Virginia Maunciple to yield a bleak picture of human passion hardly comparable to one of Watteau's charming *fêtes galantes*. In order to discredit what William Propter contemptuously refers to as "the human level of time and craving" (*AMS*, 134), Huxley has attacked the very ground of the human experience of time—organic growth and sexual generation. In a manner reminiscent of Blake's Thel, the world of bisexuality and propagation has become for Huxley a yawning grave filled with strange voices. Unlike *Eyeless in Gaza*, a work similarly focused on sexual and emotional decadence, there is with the exception of Pete Boone an absence of love in *After Many a Summer Dies the Swan*. And by grossly cheapening love and generation, Huxley has caricatured time itself, a necessary strategy if the reader is to recoil from the capering licentiousness of the simian Earl into the colder antithetical embrace of Propter's misanthropic Puritanism and the latter's systematic denial of human identity and history.

## 2. History and the Castle-Museum

The formal dimensions of *After Many a Summer Dies the Swan* are closely allied to its moral design. The major themes of sexual degeneracy, baroque-romantic idealism, the inherent irrationality of history, and the relationship of personality and language to non-personal and supra-linguistic levels of experience are elaborated and defined within a symbolic landscape of subterranean enclosure and repressive confinement. Standing at the center of this symbolic matrix of prison and burrow is Stoyte's castle, a grotesquely conceived structure emblematic of the seige mentality of the confused and corrupted baroque-romantic, while all roads in this claustrophobic novel seem to lead from Stoyte's imposing fortress to the Stygian cellars of the Earl of Gonister's subterranean "catacomb." For example, Virginia Maunciple's world is conceived in terms of enclosure and confinement. She occupies a combination bedroom and soda fountain, the physical counterpart to the "narrow little universe" (*AMS*, 53) of childish tastes and pleasures that constitutes her personality, or in Propter's words, her "cage." This state of mental bondage is neatly emblematized in the small shrine containing an effigy of the Virgin Mary that she has installed in her bedroom. Her worship of the Virgin Mary is essentially a projection of her virgin illusions in which the tiny occupant of a "sacred doll's house" functions as a parodic reflection of her own status within Stoyte's castle (*AMS*, 201). Similarly, Jeremy Pordage pursues his goal of a "closed universe of utter cosiness" by descending into the dark vaults of Stoyte's castle, where "safely underground with the Hauberks" (*AMS*, 215), he spends his time eagerly fashioning a spiritual nest amid the mass of papers, accounts, letters, and books that for Huxley symbolize the chaotic and meaningless flux of history. Even the cynically materialistic Dr. Obispo desires only "nice cellars," insisting that "nobody can have enough privacy" (*AMS*, 289), while the old Earl of Gonister chooses as his final dwelling place a subterranean labyrinth of tunnels, vaults, and cellars. Huxley's characters suffer from a kind of spiritual agoraphobia, seeking their secure enclosures with a lemming-like inflexibility. The old Earl celebrates prisons with his cry of "long live the Bastille" (*AMS*, 247), while Jeremy Pordage identifies the romantic sensibility with the confining but iridescently colored interiors of "the Pavilion at Brighton" (*AMS*, 77). *After Many a Summer Dies the Swan* is a Piranesian meditation on human nature and history as a maze of "cages," "vaults," "cellars," "corridors," and prisons. If as Huxley argued in *Eyeless in Gaza*, the individual who aspires to a goal within the historicist sphere of "time and craving" is "a man in a burrow"

(EG, 355), either a self-deluded idealist or helpless cynic, then *After Many a Summer Dies the Swan* is Huxley's fullest and most elaborately conceived rendering of this bleak thesis.

The architectural motif of rigidly circumscribed and imprisoning enclosures is a symbolic extension of William Propter's definition of human nature as "the cage of flesh and memory" (*AMS*, 310) and his belief that "the life of personality" is a form of "bondage" (*AMS*, 111), the primary image of such a cage being the castle itself. At once a symbol of romantic isolation and baroque ambition, the castle is a monument, in Propter's words, to the "intensification of the ego within the world of time" (*AMS*, 131). Constructed in a "gothic, medieval, baronial" style out of ferroconcrete and chromium, it is both the modern Blenheim of a captain of industry and a Victor Frankenstein "nightmare on a hilltop," containing its own mad scientist and underground laboratory (*AMS*, 19). As a romantic edifice, it is associated with the castle of "Sir Leoline" in Coleridge's *Christabel* and on more than one occasion linked with Shelley's "tower in *Epipsychidion*" (*AMS*, 47), as well as the "magic casements" of Keats's "Ode to a Nightingale" and "the turrets of Brighton Pavilion." The castle, Brighton Pavilion, and "Percy Bysshe Shelley" (*AMS*, 77) form a baroque-romantic melange wherein Lilian Aldwinkle's Cybo Malaspina reappears in a monstrously enlarged form, not only as a palace of art but as a conflation of museum, warehouse, cemetery, and modern research laboratory. Associated with the dynamic tension of "concrete dams" and the imposing heights of the American "skyscraper" and yet imbued with the "Gothicity" of "the thirteenth century," the mad eclecticism of Stoyte's castle rises above "vulgar historical necessity" (*AMS*, 18). Indeed, all history is grist to Stoyte's mill as he collects not only art works and libraries but any object that his fancy seizes upon. The Beverly Pantheon and the Stoyte home for sick children are merely outworks of the castle, containing their grim assemblages of the sick, the dying, and the dead, just as the decorative ironwork from Spain arrives at the castle with a quantity of mummified nuns—like the sculpture and iron grills, refugees from the Spanish Civil War. All are gathered together to testify to Stoyte's power to reach out and manipulate the things of his world and thus to shore up his increasingly vulnerable sense of personal mortality.

However, Stoyte can only collect the detritus of history, and Pordage can only inventory it. Propter, on the other hand, insists that history must be wholly transcended, arguing that the evidence supplied by "history and contemporary life" (*AMS*, 283) endorses his pessimistic view that progress or "evolutionary growth" towards "some remote future" (*AMS*, 280) is an historicist illusion. The particular urgencies of contemporary history are dramatized by Pordage's brother Tom, who worked in the "Foreign Office." After "the row over Abyssinia," he avoided a "nervous breakdown" by converting to Catholicism. His wife conceived a child "on the very night that the Spanish Civil War began," while two days "after the sack of Nanking," he "published a volume of comic verses." His response to the irrational exigencies of modern history takes the form of helpless self-indulgence: "Meanwhile, he was steadily gaining weight; between the *Anschluss* and Munich he had put on eleven pounds. Another year or two of Farm Street and power politics, and Tom would turn the scale at fourteen stone and have written the libretto of a musical comedy" (*AMS*, 222). Jeremy concludes that it is better to live "aesthetically," to withdraw from the turbulence of contemporary history, "for this getting fat on *realpolitik*, this scribbling of comic verses on the margins of an engraving of the Crucifixion" is "too inelegant" (*AMS*, 223).

The relationship between "history and contemporary life" is further developed by means of the commentary of the cynical Dr. Obispo on the diaries of the Earl of Gonister. When the latter hypocritically pretends to "humanitarian" values, Obispo compares him to "Field-Marshal Goering" (*AMS*, 296), and when the old Earl carefully bargains with his children for his survival, Obispo approvingly remarks, "If only Chamberlain had understood them [the principles of diplomacy] a little better before he went to Munich!" But he sardonically adds, "Not that it would have made much difference in the long run . . . nationalism will always produce at least one war each generation. It has done in the past and I suppose we can rely on it to do the same in the future" (*AMS*, 297–98). All that "the past" can teach is the inevitability of war, or else it is ransacked for models of the "bogus antiquity" (*AMS*, 232) that in the form of statues, monuments, and miniaturized architecture decorates Stoyte's cemetery, the Beverly Pantheon. The detritus of history not only fills the rooms and galleries of the castle but forms its foundation as well. The cellars of the castle overflow with a chaotic assemblage of antiques, historical objects, and works of art. On his way to unpack the Hauberk papers, Jeremy must thread his way through basement rooms "crammed with totem poles and armour, with stuffed orangutans and marble groups by Thorwaldson, with gilded Bodhisattvas and early steam engines, with lingams and stage coaches and Peruvian pottery, with crucifixes and mineralogical specimens" (*AMS*, 65). In the midst of this mass of historicist fragments are the Hauberk papers, including the personal diaries of the manic Earl of Gonister. The old Earl is the voice of history, the final dramatization of the Sadean will to power that informs it. Indeed, he acknowledges as much when he defines "Man" as "systematically and continuously cruel" (*AMS*, 269). The psychopathic amorality of the old Earl subsumes all experience under the chronic pursuit of "Power" (*AMS*, 25), a pursuit that enhances his sense of self or personality, despite his insistence that the word "Man" is "the general Name applied to successions of inconsistent Conduct," a generalization that applies with equal force to both history and the events that occur within Stoyte's castle (*AMS*, 266).

The castle is more than—to use Huxley's phrase for the Mormon Temple in Salt Lake City—a "cyclopean gazebo"[18] designed to commemorate Stoyte's titanic personality. Its interior resembles a Louvre conceived by Salvador Dali and later remodeled by Franz Kafka. As an aggregation of historical objects, however, it functions as an anti-museum. A museum endeavors to order the past in terms of a shared collective vision based on what is assumed to be a dynamic process of traceable causal sequence. In Stoyte's castle-museum history is presented as a static assemblage of indecipherable fragments, a petrified collection haphazardly organized yet subtly endowed with its own sinister logic. It is no accident that Jeremy Pordage is an historian of the romantic period, "from the invention of Ossian to the death of Keats" (*AMS*, 33), who savors the castle with "a connoisseur's appreciation of romantic absurdity" (*AMS*, 27) and soon finds himself completely at home in the confusing medley of the castle's collections.

Entering the huge edifice, Jeremy discovers a disorderly conflux of historical objects whose conflicting styles suggest a fundamental anarchy that transcends the more innocent jumble of architectural schools he observed in the suburbs on his drive to the castle. He approaches the interior by stages, passing through a "Gothic portal," crossing "a pillared Romanesque lobby," and entering the castle's sanctum, "the cathedral twilight of the great hall" (*AMS*, 43). In the fading light of this temple of art, Jeremy stands, resembling Tennyson's narrator in "The Palace of Art," within a paradigmatic enclosure—dim, secure, and yet despite the beauty of its treasures, not finally satisfying. Its design is suggestive of further implications and disturbing questions that, contrary to Dr. Mulge's confident conflation of "art" with "the Religious Spirit," stubbornly manage to insinuate themselves (again reminiscent of Tennyson's "The Palace of Art") by means of allegorical paintings:

A hundred feet overhead, the sound of the two men's footsteps echoed in the vaulting. Like iron ghosts, the suits of armour stood immobile round the walls. Above them, sumptuously dim, the fifteenth-century tapestries opened windows upon a leafy world of phantasy. At one end of the cavernous room, lit by a hidden searchlight, El Greco's *Crucifixion of St. Peter* blazed out in the darkness like the beautiful revelation of something incomprehensible and profoundly sinister. At the other, no less brilliantly illuminated, hung a full portrait of Helene Fourment, dressed only in a bearskin cape. Jeremy looked from one to the other—from the ectoplasm of the inverted saint to the unequivocal skin and fat and muscle which Rubens had so loved to see and touch; from unearthly flesh tints of green-white ochre and carmine, shadowed with transparent black, to the creams and warm pinks, the nacreous blues and greens of Flemish nudity. Two shining symbols, incomparably powerful and expressive—but of what , of what? That, of course, was the question. (*AMS*, 43–44)

Like T. S. Eliot's Prufrock, Pordage is confronted with an over-whelming question, one compounded equally of both nonhuman "reve-lation" and human sexuality. And like Prufrock, Pordage will exhibit the same fastidious hyper-refinement and indecisiveness. The great hall is at once a museum gallery filled with art objects and something more, a dimly lit church whose religion of art contains its own promise of paradise in the form of Keatsian "windows" that open upon a "leafy" romance "world of phantasy." But the possibility of such a romantic escape is quickly overshadowed by the two illuminated canvases.

Huxley's choice of paintings is typically circumspect, particularly with regard to the apparent antithetical relationship between the two figures of St. Peter and Helene Fourment. To begin with, he considered both El Greco and Rubens as baroque artists. To classify Rubens as a baroque painter was and is a commonplace, but El Greco with his distended figures, curiously lustrous colors, and mannerist style has been tradition-ally a difficult painter to categorize. Huxley, however, did not hesitate to place him with the baroque, writing in *Music at Night* that of El Greco, "the most one can say, by way of classification, is that, like most of the great artists of the baroque, he believed in the validity of ecstasy, of the non-rational, 'numinous' experiences out of which, as a raw material, the reason fashions the gods or the various attributes of God" (*MN*, 62). Yet according to Huxley he was not a typical baroque artist of "facile ecstasies and the orthodox Counter-Reformation theology" (*MN*, 63) but rather the creator of a "disquieting world" of spiritual claustrophobia, whose subjects "are shut up in a world where there is perhaps just room enough to swing a cat." El Greco's saints and aristocrats are confined within a "prison" (*AMS*, 59), an enclosed world redolent not of spiritual ecstasy but of the constructing atmosphere of a purely "physiological state" (*AMS*, 66).

The problem posed by the juxtaposition of the El Greco crucifixion and the Rubens portrait is not, as Peter Bowering would have it, "the eternal tug-of-war between the flesh and the spirit."[19] The El Greco is ex-plicitly characterized as "sinister," its significance lying with its histrionic emotionalism, a theatrical heightening that Huxley consistently associ-ated with the baroque style. Its ostensible spirituality is tainted by an all-

too-human projection of egoistic aspiration within the context of an an-
thropomorphic Christianity. Huxley, in denying *personal* survival after
death as well as a *personalized* deity, also rejected what Anthony Beavis
dismissed as "the fundamental Christian man of our history." In this
respect, the crucified St. Peter with its "disquieting" atmosphere of
visceral enclosure is "profoundly sinister" (*AMS*, 434) because it en-
shrines a wholly personalized ideal, or what William Propter calls "the
projection, on an enormously enlarged scale, of some aspect of personality" (*AMS*, 124). Accordingly, like Virginia Maunciple's statue of
the Virgin Mary, the painting of St. Paul mirrors a facile egocentricity.
Equally important, the main hall of Stoyte's castle is a typical Huxleyan
set piece, a detailed evocation of a baroque apocalypse. It resembles
Lilian Aldwinkle's temple crowning a sequence of ascending architectural
patterns at the Cybo Malaspina in that the main hall displays the characteristic baroque attempt to control total space by means of enormous
scale reinforced by the dramatic contrast of light and darkness. The two
large convases hang in a vast chamber one hundred feet high, carved out
of the circumambient darkness by two hidden searchlights. These the-
atrically highlighted images, like the Etruscan faces illuminated within
their dark tombs by the guide's torchlight in *Those Barren Leaves*, or the
oaken drainpipes suddenly revealed by Wimbush's flashlight at the conclusion of *Crome Yellow*, are either spurious or enigmatic revelations. In
the present case, the El Greco and the Rubens blaze with an apocalyptic
radiance designed to organize architectural space rather than illuminate
the mind of the observer.

El Greco's St. Peter, then, symbolizes a baroque and thus for Huxley a
psychologically deformative impulse in which the crucified saint is an
emblem of a false metaphysic, the misplaced emphasis of which involves
bondage to a purely physiological ecstasy. It is not surprising that Huxley has chosen an "inverted" saint who in his agony points downward,
nor is it at all accidental that Huxley's baroque El Greco, who "im-
prisons" his subjects in "Black Holes" (*AMS*, 67 and 68), should occupy a
central position in a novel governed by a symbolic matrix of prison, cage,
and subterranean labyrinth. However, more important is the meaning
Huxley attached to the adjective "physiological" within the wider context
of baroque art. In the earliest of his two essays on El Greco, he repeatedly cited this emphasis on "the primary physiological fact of religious
experience" as evidence of El Greco's curiously "visceral consciousness"
(*MN*, 65), a peculiar failure of vision that fascinated Huxley and he associated with an ambience of imprisoning spaces reminiscent of Piranesi.
But in the essay "Variations on a Baroque Tomb," he clarified this

perplexing concept in a way that illuminates the symbolic interrelation-
ship of the El Greco and the Rubens in the great hall of Stoyte's castle:

In Baroque art the mystic is represented either as a psychic with supernormal
powers, or as an ecstatic, who passes out of history in order to be alone, *not with
God*, but with his or her *physiology* in a state hardly distinguishable from that of
sexual enjoyment. (*CE*, 205)

The intestinal smothering that Huxley sensed everywhere in El Greco's
work is for the most part synonymous with "sexual enjoyment," a
strangely sensual embrace that despite its apparent spirituality reflects
the more explicitly sexual theme of the Rubens. In "Variations on El
Greco" Huxley traced the "strangely oppressive" atmosphere of El
Greco's work to a pervasive stylistic feature, an emphasis on enclosed
space: "his compositions are centripetal, turned inwards on themselves.
He is the painter of movement in a narrow room, of agitation in prison"
(*TV*, 190). Equally important, his judgement of El Greco's failure to
achieve an authentically spiritual vision is unequivocal: "the agitation of
quasi-visceral forms in an overcrowded and almost spaceless world,
from which nonhuman Nature has been banished, cannot, in the very
nature of things, express man's union with the Spirit who must be worshipped in spirit" (*TV*, 195–96). Huxley's analysis of El Greco's treatment
of space is highly speculative and on occasion genuinely ambiguous; but
he consistently maintains that El Greco's "conscious aspiration" towards
incarnating in his painting a vision of "the divine Spirit is overridden by
a subconscious longing for the consolations of some ineffable uterine
state" (*TV*, 200). Such an unstable conflation of spiritual aspiration and
psychological regression coincides both with the major themes of *After
Many a Summer Dies the Swan* and the incrementally developed motif of
enclosure, confinement, and repression. In this respect, the El Greco is a
fitting addition to Stoyte's collection and, enshrined in the main hall,
symbolizes the corruption of spirit endemic in Stoyte's world.

The choice of Rubens's portrait of Helene Fourment was doubtless inspired by the full-length portrait in the Kunsthistorisches Museum at
Vienna entitled *Helen Fourment in a Fur-Coat*. With her body pivoting
slightly on her left leg and the heavy opulent fur draped over her left
shoulder leaving her breasts exposed, she stands facing the viewer
holding the edges of the coat together in order to conceal her midsection,
gazing slightly to the viewer's left with a self-assurance born of a harmoniously normative sexuality. But her significance for Huxley is not
limited to the self-confidence of a frankly sensual young woman. Helene
Fourment was the youngest sister of Suzanne Fourment, Rubens's mis-

Rubens' dramatic full-length portrait of his young wife, *Helene Fourment in a Fur Coat*, is carefully evoked by Huxley as a spirited assertion of sensuality, the human figure dominating the canvas in a manner antithetical to the cool reserve and emotional detachment of Vermeer's young woman. (Photograph printed with permission of Kunsthistorisches Museum, Vienna.)

tress. When Suzanne Fourment died, Rubens at the age of fifty-three fell in love with Helene, who at sixteen (precisely the age of his eldest son) became his wife. Described by one of Rubens's biographers as "a pretty, immature blonde with blue eyes" and "a generously endowed figure" who relished her life in Rubens's "art-filled palace" and became the subject of his "most lavishly baroque"[20] portraits, Helene is not difficult to equate with the twenty-two year-old Virginia Maunciple, Jo Stoyte's "daughter-mistress" and "concubine-child" (*AMS*, 241). Like Helene, Virginia is the sexual partner of a much older man, and with her plump figure, "auburn hair," and "blue eyes," she physically resembles Rubens's young wife. And while not married to Stoyte, she is a walking emblem of immature promiscuity.

The paintings of St. Peter and Helen Fourment face each other like two mirrors, endlessly repeating the ungovernably passionate impulses of humanity in an infinite series of images that in turn reflect the "infinity-track" of the complex maze of the castle itself (*AMS*, 174). Thus Jeremy in the great hall of Stoyte's castle is confronted not by a simple juxtaposition of the spiritual and sensual but by a choice of similar forms of bondage specifically conceived by and peculiar to the mind of Joseph Panton Stoyte. This does not, however, restrict their scope so much as it deepens and complicates their meaning. The two paintings are not antithetical extremes, each demanding that it be selected in preference to the other. Rather, they symbolize an illusory choice between two subtly related forms of enslavement to the desires and fears Huxley associated with the solely human level of "time and craving." Both are images of escapist desire, of the baroque-romantic impulse that in his view had impaled itself on the twin horns of a passionate but misguided yearning for revelation and transcendence, and an equally passionate sensuality. But in Stoyte's castle the Virgin Mary and Virginia Maunciple occupy one room. Accordingly, it is only by ignoring the third painting that Huxley's critics have been able to interpret the Rubens and El Greco as two clearly defined antitheses symbolizing a fundamental opposition of body and soul, or sensuality and spirituality.

On leaving the great hall, Pordage is suddenly arrested by the dramatic appearance of a painting by Vermeer, one that closely resembles Vermeer's *A Young Lady Seated at the Spinet* (now in the National Gallery in London). It is hidden in an elevator—another image of enclosure; as the doors of the elevator open abruptly, the Vermeer is juxtaposed with the two baroque canvases that Pordage had been recently contemplating:

The door of the elevator was in an embrasure between pillars. Mr. Stoyte opened it, and the light came on revealing a Dutch lady in blue satin sitting at a harpsi-

In this painting, Vermeer's *A Young Lady Seated at the Spinet,* and in his *A Young Lady before a Spinet,* Huxley found the compositional values that he admired most: geometrical balance, hard-edged symmetries of line and picture plane, serenity and detachment of subject matter. He would have found both paintings together in the National Gallery. His fictional version is a conflation of elements from both, but stressing the former. (Painting reproduced by courtesy of the Trustees, The National Gallery, London.)

Vermeer's *A Young Lady before a Spinet*. (Painting reproduced by courtesy of the Trustees, the National Gallery, London.)

chord—sitting, Jeremy reflected, at the very heart of an equation, in a world where beauty and logic, painting and analytical geometry, had become one. With what intention? To express, symbolically, what truths about the nature of things? (*AMS*, 44)

Although Huxley felt a great aversion for baroque aesthetics, he nevertheless singled out three Baroque artists as exemplary figures: Vermeer, Rembrandt, and Sir Christopher Wren. Like his favorite Piero della Francesca, he saw them as proponents of a formal aesthetic that placed at the center of its vision a resolutely sustained emphasis on rational order and mathematical proportion, as well as the prime Huxleyan values of "solidity" and "mass." The explicit sensuality and atectonic deformity of the baroque style present in El Greco, Rubens, and Bernini was entirely foreign to the work of Wren and Vermeer. The latter in particular was praised not only for the aesthetic values embodied in his work (in terms that compare favorably with those Huxley used for Piero della Francesca) but also for his ability to subordinate the personalities of his subjects to something far more important, the manifestation of "their divine essential Not-self." Vermeer, whom Huxley somewhat paradoxically associated with William Blake, was a visionary artist—not the prophet of a baroquely conceived flaming New Jerusalem but a disciplined craftsman who perceived "the essential Not-self . . . very clearly in things and in living creatures on the hither side of good and evil. In human beings it was visible only when they were in repose, their minds untroubled, their bodies motionless. In these circumstances Vermeer could see Suchness in all its heavenly beauty—could see and, in some small measure, render it in a subtle and sumptuous still life" (*CE*, 334). The painting in Stoyte's elevator embodies not an orthodoxly religious concept but an ontological truth, profounder and more authentic than El Greco's conventionally Christian and flamboyantly emotional representation of St. Peter.

It is entirely fitting, then, that Vermeer's painting should not be given a prominent place in the great hall of Stoyte's castle, just as its values have not been given the attention they deserve throughout the all-too-human history that the castle-museum is intended to allegorize. Vermeer's painting—unlike the El Greco imbued with the emotional passion of St. Peter's crucifixion, or the Rubens with its forthright sensuality—is a denial of personality and the egoistic rhetoric of the high baroque. His female subjects, unlike Rubens's Helene Fourment, "never say their prayers or pine for absent sweethearts, never gossip, never gaze enviously at other women's babies, never flirt, never love or hate or work" (*CE*, 334). In short, they do not exist as identifiably human personalities.

Pordage, then, *is* faced with a choice; but it is a choice rather obliquely presented to the reader, who initially assumes that given their central but opposing positions within a carefully contrived symbolic setting, the two paintings in the great hall pose the chief question of the novel. The unexpectedly comic appearance of the Vermeer introduces a third term that significantly alters the reader's perception of the role of the El Greco and the Rubens.

The choice confronting Pordage is not between spirituality and sensuality but between the subordination and the intensification of the ego. Both the El Greco and the Rubens are, like the castle itself, "merely the projection . . . of some aspect of personality" (*AMS*, 124), and as such they are designed to celebrate and promote "the intensification of the ego within the world of time and craving," rather than open a perspective onto the "non-personal experience of timeless peace" (*AMS*, 131). But the Vermeer with its mathematical cohesion, purity of mood, and luminous yet serene atmosphere is endowed with precisely this quality of transcending the exigencies of self with an ontological rather than theological intensity. Moreover, it is the Vermeer that reappears at the novel's conclusion when the passionately egoistic Jo Stoyte, overcome with jealousy, ascends in the elevator accompanied by the Vermeer and impatiently clutching an automatic pistol. Bursting out of the elevator, he brutally murders Pete Boone in a paroxysm of rage while "the young lady in satin still occupied her position of equilibrium in a perfectly calculated universe" (*AMS*, 306).

If the significance of the castle-museum is partially defined in terms of its collection of baroque and rococo paintings, its role is further clarified by a series of references to romantic poetry. Moreover, the references are primarily to quest-romances like Coleridge's *Christabel* and *The Ancient Mariner*, Browning's "Childe Roland," Tennyson's "The Palace of Art," and Shelley's *Epipsychidion*, which closes with the promise of a journey to a combined "tower" and "pleasure-house" filled with the treasures of art, literature, and music as a prelude to a further life "in the world divine." Huxley was fascinated by this work, using it in *Crome Yellow*, *Those Barren Leaves*, and *Eyeless in Gaza* as a typically baroque-romantic document that with its emotional intensity and Platonic idealism was as intellectually irrational and emotionally unbalanced as the El Greco in the great hall of Stoyte's castle. In *Crome Yellow* Mr. Scogan compares the tower in *Epipsychidion* unfavorably with the towers of Crome, while Helen Amberley in *Eyeless in Gaza* studies Shelley's poem in a despondent effort to buttress her dwindling faith in romantic love. In *After Many a Summer Dies the Swan*, Huxley again draws on Shelley's romance, transforming its idealistically conceived tower of art and culture and its feverish eroticism covertly present in the "pleasure-house" into Jo Stoyte's grotesque edifice, a palace filled like Shelley's with the various instruments of human culture but whose occupants are obsessed with solely erotic pursuits.

The journey of Watteau's pilgrims to and from the island of Venus, appropriately hung in Virginia Maunciple's boudoir, is as meaningless as the desperate quest of Browning's knight in search of the dark tower. Indeed, like Childe Roland, Jeremy must first pass through a surrealistic wasteland before arriving at the castle, and as in Browning's romance the castle is associated with human mortality. And like Sir Leoline's Gothic castle, it is redolent of sexual guilt. Sir Leoline, whose first wife is dead, as is Jo Stoyte's, finds himself welcoming a young woman identified with both sexual sin as well as his own daughter. It is impossible to decide how aware Huxley was of the incest theme in *Christabel*, but Jo Stoyte's pleasure in Virginia's child-daughter status is repeatedly underscored throughout the novel. Similarly, Jeremy Pordage has assumed the role of the occupant of Tennyson's "Palace of Art," but unlike Tennyson's narrator he remains untroubled by social values and steadfastly refuses to abandon the castle-museum. All of these allusions to romantic poems or the essentially romantic postures of Victorian poets culminate early in the novel in Jeremy's entrance into one of the castle's elaborately decorated dining rooms:

In the small dining-room, most of the furnishings came from the Pavilion at Brighton. Four gilded dragons supported the red lacquered table and two more served as caryatids on either side of a chimney piece in the same material. It was the regency's dream of the Gorgeous East. The kind of thing Jeremy reflected, as he sat down on his scarlet and gold chair, the kind of thing that the word "Cathay" would have conjured up in Keats's mind, for example, or Shelley's, or Lord Byron's—just as that charming Leda by Etty, over there, next to the Fra Angelico Annunciation, was an accurate embodiment of their fancies on the subject of pagan mythology; was an authentic illustration (he chuckled inwardly at the thought) to the Odes to Psyche and the Grecian Urn, to "Endymion" and "Prometheus Unbound." An age's habits of thought and feeling and imagination are shared by all who live and work within that age—by all, from the journeyman up to the genius. Regency is always Regency, whether you take your sample from the top of the basket or from the bottom. In 1820, the man who shut his eyes and tried to visualize magic casements opening on the foam of faery seas would see—what? The turrets of Brighton Pavilion. (*AMS*, 77)

This is an important passage that, coming as it does shortly after Pordage's initiation into the metaphysical mysteries of the castle's great hall, marks another stage in his progress—in this case, in relation to the castle's significance as a symbol of human existence on the plane of history. Pordage, however, is an accomplice in this gradually unfolding symbolic masque of cultural degeneration and finds himself increasingly at home in the teeming conflux of historical objects that Stoyte has greedily amassed. The virtual absence of order in the arrangement of Stoyte's collection is an additional attraction to Jeremy, guaranteeing him an irresponsible freedom for indulging his essentially anarchic impulses. As an aspect of Stoyte's castle, the Brighton Pavilion only serves to titillate Pordage's sardonic but frivolous sense of humor. Just as baroque art dominated the great hall, the dining room is a vivid re-creation of the purely romantic setting of the Pavilion and, for Jeremy at least, suggestive of the art of Keats, Shelley, and Byron. But its primary function is to introduce another form of bondage, namely the imprisoning ethos of the historical moment that narrowly circumscribes the intellectual, aesthetic, and even emotional horizons of all who share "an age's habits of thought and feeling and imagination." Each age is, like the personalities who compose it, a "spatiotemporal cage" locking its generation into a characteristic set of "habits," while the movement of history from age to age is as chaotic and meaningless as the collections scattered throughout the castle-museum.

William Propter, who occupies the moral center of *After Many a Summer Dies the Swan*, is a historian of the baroque period whose collected essays, "Short Studies in the Counter-Reformation," is regarded by the romantic historian Jeremy Pordage as one of his "favourite books—a model, he had always thought, of their kind" (*AMS*, 22). But Propter has repudiated both history and language, while the historicist Pordage, an uninspired cataloguer of relics, remains passively dependent on words and the written text, devoted to history for a pastime as a minor offshoot of literature. In the passage quoted above describing the small dining room and its romantic-Regency decor, Huxley has attacked the distorting lens of the romantic sensibility by means of a reductive conflation of the collective vision of Keats, Shelley, and Byron with the exuberant architectural fantasia of the Brighton Pavilion. Just as the Regency transformed the reality of China into the phantasmagoria of "Cathay," the romantic sensibility finds itself mirrored in a prison of its own fashioning, unable to break out of its own peculiar way of apprehending the world and bound by the conventions of its own conceptual processes.

The implications of such a position are carried a stage further by Huxley's inclusion of two paintings hanging in the dining room. The first is a romantic interpretation of Leda by Etty, and the second an annunciation by Fra Angelico. While it is difficult to imagine the delicately pale tints of a Fra Angelico amid the vividly lacquered reds and golds of the Pavilion, the symbolic significance of these paintings is easier to grasp. The classical "Leda" and the Christian "Annunciation" celebrate the birth of two children, Helen and Christ, both of whom altered the course of history and who as allegorical figures reintroduce the illusory oppositions of Rubens's Helene Fourment and El Greco's St. Peter. Collectively the two children suggest the Greco-Roman and Judaeo-Christian basis of Western history, and separately they serve as subtle reminders of the false antithetical vision enshrined in the great hall. The small dining room is an emblem of historicist subjectivity, the attempt to confer meaning upon history by means of a myth that celebrates the penetration of mundane time by a divine or supernatural agency. The two incarnational moments depicted in the Etty and the Fra Angelico are for Huxley further evidence of opposing ways of conceiving the same thing, peculiar visions of different cultures that collectively add up to nothing. The emphasis on the inherent blindness and isolation of each successive historical period, when linked to the allusions to Helen, Christ, Prometheus, and Endymion interspersed throughout this passage, creates the enlarged context required for William Propter's absolute repudiation of history based on its fundamental disjunctiveness and the irrationally obsessive idealism of its Promethean heroes. The single constant factor in history, at work in all periods but in superficially different ways, is baroque-romantic egoism:

"Reactionary or revolutionary, they're all humanists, all romantics. They live in a world of illusion, a world that's a mere projection of their own human personalities. They act in ways which would be appropriate if such a world as they think they live in really existed. But unfortunately it doesn't exist except in their imaginations. Hence nothing that they do is appropriate to the real world." (*AMS*, 167)

He adds, in two sentences that encapsulate the symbolic meaning of Stoyte's castle as a monument to the baroque-romantic impulse, "All their actions are the actions of lunatics, and all, as history is there to demonstrate, are more or less completely disastrous. So much for the romantic" (*AMS*, 167).

The connection between romanticism, history, and the burrow motif is further reinforced by Jeremy Pordage's project of cataloguing the Hauberk papers while safely enclosed and insulated within a "sub-terranean storeroom" (*AMS*, 59). Jeremy conceives of history in both romantic as well as erotic terms as he attempts to express the significance of the papers through an allusion to Keats: "Tied up in innumerable brown paper parcels, the Hauberk Papers awaited their first reader. Twenty-seven crates of still unravished brides of quietness. He smiled to himself at the thought that he was to be their Bluebeard" (*AMS*, 59). The disintegration of history into an arbitrary assemblage of brown paper parcels and twenty-seven crates ironically conflicts with the attempt to draw a parallel between the crates and Keats's urn as somehow affording a vision that stands above the tempo of events, virginally intact and endowed with meaning. But the crates are not as eloquent as Keats's urn nor as pure. Pordage's metaphor of unravished Keatsian brides gives way to the actuality of "two old spinster ladies," the sterile muses of the Hauberk papers, who as the last surviving members of the family, guard a bleaker secret than any hidden in Keats's urn, while the "delicious fragments of English history" are little more than a medley of unrelated chapters in "a tale told by an idiot." The chaotic records of the Hauberk family confirm William Propter's denial of the very basis of historical inquiry, the possibility of discerning an underlying coherence within a sequence of events and, more hopefully, the possibility of revealing a morally significant and progressively continuous transformation of humanity from one century to the next. As they plunge and bob meaninglessly in the stream of history, the Hauberks offer only a Spenglerian spectacle of the irresistible drive toward power, aggression, and cruelty:

A tale of cutthroats and conspirators, of patrons of learning and shady speculators, of bishops and kings' catamites and minor poets, of admirals and pimps, of saints and heroines and nymphomaniacs, of imbeciles and prime ministers, of art collectors and sadists. And here was all that remained of them, in twenty-seven crates, higgledy-piggledy, never catalogued, never even looked at, utterly virgin. (*AMS*, 60)

Many of the categories listed above can be applied to Jo Stoyte, who as patron of learning, shady speculator (the real-estate deal), art collector, and cutthroat (as the murderer of Pete Boone) has gathered around him a collection of sadists (Obispo), saints (the mummified nuns), nymphomaniacs (Virginia Maunciple), and minor writers (Jeremy Pordage).

If as Jacques Barzun has observed, history is essentially the play of imagination and judgement upon the surviving documents of the past, then Pordage's infantile prurience is a parody of the historian's craft: "Dipping blindly" into the "rich confusion" of the Hauberk papers—viewed alternately as appealing virgins and "a bran pie"—and sifting through letters, sickroom recipes, household accounts, and travel memoirs only to grasp "like a child" the pornography of the Marquis de Sade (*AMS*,

60), Jeremy Pordage, the author of "little essays" containing "twenty pages of erudition and absurdity—of sacrilege in lavender" (*AMS*, 71), is a miniaturist faced by a project of mural dimensions.

As one more subjective egoist in a world of solipsists, Jeremy and the effort to substitute his own "Cathay" for the Hauberk "China" are hardly surprising. But his acute awareness of his mother's influence in perverting his sexual appetites and his obsession with voyeurism introduce an additional perspective on Jeremy's role in relation to the wider context of Huxley's assessment of history. In *After Many a Summer Dies the Swan*, Clio is not alone in her confinement within Stoyte's castle. Most of its occupants border on the psychotic in their behavior, while the muse of history presides over a chronicle of collective "neurasthenia." The castle-museum is an asylum that reflects the substance of the Hauberk papers. After wandering through the castle, Jeremy dazedly observes that "It's as though one were walking into the mind of a lunatic," but he adds pointedly, "the mind of an idiot of genius. Positively stuffed with the best that has been thought and said" except that "every item is perfectly irrelevant to every other item" (*AMS*, 174).

## 3. Sadomasochism, Death, and History
## in the Beverly Pantheon

The theme of insanity and sexual degeneracy informs Huxley's handling both of the castle and history, beginning with the most impressive of the castle's outworks, the Beverly Pantheon. In the essay "Variations on a Baroque Tomb," Huxley carefully probed the preoccupation with death characteristic of the baroque period in an effort to illuminate both the connection between its flamboyant mortuary art and its philosophy of history, as well as the lapidary eroticism of the modern cemetery and its relationship to pornography. As we have seen, Huxley regarded the baroque aesthetic as animated by a steadfast commitment to the grotesque and the freakish. Its art was informed by a "systematic exploitation of the inordinate" (*CE*, 204) that betrayed itself in the "epileptic behavior" of the "gesticulating or swooning personages" that swarmed through its *trompe l'oeil* frescoes or ascended through the ceilings of its churches. Its mortuary art focused obsessively on physical corruption and death in a style that shattered the foundation of aesthetic rationalism laid down by Renaissance masters like Huxley's much-admired Piero della Francesca:

By an aesthetic necessity, because it is impossible for self-conscious artists to go on doing what has been supremely well done by their predecessors, the symmetrical gives place to the disbalanced, the static to the dynamic, the formalized to the realistic. Statues are caught in the act of changing their positions; pictorial compositions try to break out of their frames. Where there was understatement, there is now emphasis; where there was measure and humanity, there is now the enormous, the astounding, the demigod and the epileptic sub-man. (*CE*, 198)

The baroque taste for "the enormous, the astounding" reappears in the Beverly Pantheon but modified by a fundamental alteration of emphasis. "Baroque mortuary sculpture," Huxley argues, had as its "basic subject matter" the tension between "the historical and the existential," an unresolvable conflict between on the one hand the public status of the "representatives of great historical forces and even makers of history" (*CE*, 202) who symbolize man's unreconcilable yearning for the achievement of something tangible and enduring within history, and on the other hand the "falling out of history" represented by the essentially private drama of death and personal dissolution. Bernini's tombs of Urban VII and Alexander VII are carefully analyzed as baroque masques dramatizing the finality of death within the context of history. The formal elements of these elaborate monuments, including the grotesque skulls and gesticulating skeletons that surround the effigies of the seventeenth-century popes and monarchs whose achievements the tombs were ostensibly designed to commemorate, Huxley saw as the stark emblems of a belief in the ultimate absurdity of human pretensions—especially the idea of history.

Alert to the pitfalls of "historical generalizations," Huxley argues nevertheless that baroque mortuary fashions tend to bear out his theory that a widespread belief in the presence of a meaningful pattern within human history—including the assumption of a continuous development conceived in exclusively human terms—is incompatible with an obsession with death or even a significantly meaningful acknowledgement of its presence:

. . . at the risk of distorting the facts to fit a theory, I would suggest that, at any given period, preoccupation with death is in inverse ratio to the prevalence of a belief in man's perfectibility through and in a properly organized society. In the art and literature of the age of Condorcet, of the age of Herbert Spencer and Karl Marx, of the age of Lenin and the Webbs there are few skeletons. Why? Because it was during the eighteenth and nineteenth centuries that men came to believe in progress, in the march of history toward an even bigger and better future, in salvation, not for the individual but for society. The emphasis is on history and environment, which are regarded as the primary determinants of individual destiny. (*CE*, 202)

Despite his abhorrence for the theatrical exaggeration of the baroque style, Huxley evidently felt a degree of admiration for what he regarded as the seventeenth century's refusal to hide the spectre of death behind the banner of progress. Equally important, however, was the relationship between the optimistic rationalism of the postbaroque period and the degenerate sexuality observable in modern mortuary fashions—a relationship directly bearing on the major themes of *After Many a Summer Dies the Swan.*

Huxley argued that in their endeavor to gloss over "the essentially unrationalizable facts of private existence," the mortuary sculptors of the nineteenth and twentieth centuries "harp only on the sentiments surrounding death—sentiments ranging from the noble to the tender and even the voluptuous," the latter tendency most perfectly embodied in the "delicious buttocks" of "Canova's monument to the last of the Stuarts" (*CE,* 203). According to Huxley, the appearance of an imaginatively intensified and ubiquitous pornography, especially in mortuary art, coincided with the rise of an inherently progressivist and thus escapist philosophy of history, the minor symptom of an age increasingly dedicated to a facile optimism and self-indulgent fantasy: "And here let me add a parenthetical note on the pornography of the age which witnessed the rise of the ideas of progress and social salvation. Most of it is merely pretty, an affair of wish-fulfillments—Boucher carried to his logical conclusion. The most celebrated pornographer of the time, the Marquis de Sade, is a mixture of escapist maniac and *philosophe.* He lives in a world where insane phantasy alternates with post-Voltairean ratiocination; where impossible orgies are interrupted in order that the participants may talk, sometimes shrewdly, but more often in the shallowest eighteenth-century way, about morals, politics and metaphysics" (*CE,* 203). While Huxley's assessment of eighteenth-century culture is patently biased, the role of the Marquis de Sade as a perverse apostle of a superficial enlightenment ideology is a central issue in *After Many a Summer Dies the Swan.* So also the Beverly Pantheon is a monument to the modern endeavor to rationalize the irrational, a systematic evasion of death informed by a persistently pornographic impulse.

Within the metaphoric landscape of prison and subterranean enclosure of *After Many a Summer Dies the Swan,* the Beverly Pantheon is the ultimate burrow. Purged of any reference to "grief or age, any symbol of mortality, any image of the suffering of Jesus" (*AMS,* 230), it functions as the emblem of a society that refuses to accept the cessation of progress and to subordinate the matter of history to the demands of theology. In one of the main buildings of the Pantheon complex is a "circular marble room, with Rodin's image of desire at the centre" (*AMS,* 241). Like the El Greco and the Rubens in the great hall, the Rodin sculpture is a modern totem, a symbol of unyielding aspiration that even in the midst of death continues to celebrate energies of "desire," or what William Propter dismisses as life lived on the "level of time and craving." The Rodin sculpture has displaced the baroque skeleton in such a way as to introduce not only the characteristically modern refusal to acknowledge the finality of death but also an attendant eroticism—an eroticism, it should be added, conceived under the auspices of the Marquis de Sade. Charles Habakkuk, employed by Stoyte as the *genius loci* of the Beverly Pantheon, has single-mindedly pursued a policy of "injecting sex appeal into death" (*AMS*, 230). His finest inspiration, however, consisted of a plan to create a subterranean world of orgiastic displays centered around a large cavern containing a giant nude statue of a woman illuminated by concealed pink lighting. The imagery of prison and bondage converge at this point as Habakkuk envisions "a nice plaster group of some girls with no clothes on, just going to be eaten by a lion" (*AMS*, 233). The transformation of the cemetery into an eroticized landscape is further intensified by the sadomasochism that informs most of Habakkuk's projects, especially the planned tableau revolving around an "early Christian Virgin with her hands tied behind her back—because people got such a kick out of anything to do with ropes or handcuffs" (*AMS*, 234). In this respect, the presiding spirit of the Beverly Pantheon is the Marquis de Sade, the baroque-romantic idealogue of the Age of Progress and the proponent of what Huxley regarded as an Enlightenment philosophy of superficial rationalism masking a darker preoccupation with eroticism and violence.

The grounds of the Pantheon swarm with sculptured "nudes, all female, all exuberantly nubile" but always assuming poses that suggest something sadistically perverse involving both pain and bondage. The "statues of young ladies in nothing but a very tight belt imbedded, with Bernini-like realism, in the Parian flesh" (*AMS*, 16) are paler reflections of the bound slave-girl envisioned by Habakkuk and foreshadow the Fifth Earl of Gonister's masochistic slave, the "young mulatto girl" (*AMS*, 292) who satisfies his "latent Desire for Humiliation and even Pain," as a consequence of which "a man may enjoy the privilege of using the Birch, the Manacles, the Cage and any such other Emblems of absolute Power as the Fancy of the Conqueror may suggest" (*AMS*, 285). In *After Many a Summer Dies the Swan*, personality, history, and sexuality are defined as forms of bondage in which the endeavor to live for exclusively human ends as a historical personality leads only to the inevitable capitulation to irrational energies and cruelties. Accordingly, the prevalence of sexuality in the cemetery and absence of any forthright admission of the presence of death are for Huxley symptomatic of a deeply rooted addiction to the concept of historical progress, so compelling as to introduce elements of sexual propagation into the midst of death in an effort to evade the reality of "falling out of history." But if the modern cemetery is like the Beverly Pantheon converted into an escapist fantasy celebrating the very essence of the human experience of time—that is, sexual generation—a price is exacted in the form of a crippling perversion of precisely those aspects of sexuality interposed to shield man from death by perpetuating desire. The repressed knowledge of decay and dissolution subtly returns in the form of a corrupted eroticism. Huxley seems to be arguing that when the necessary wedding of sexual experience to the world of progress and change has been denied (i.e., the recognition and acceptance of dissolution as necessary to temporal process and fruition), it is replaced by an erotic impulse dedicated to death, pain, degradation, and bondage that turns the generative impulse against itself. In the Beverly Pantheon the denial of the natural cycle engenders an unnatural preoccupation with suppressed anxieties and erotic substitutes for death in which dying becomes "more strictly carnal even than the act of love" (*AMS*, 165). The very juxtaposition of the nubile bodies of sculptured nymphs with the grave is productive of an artificially heightened eroticism, more violent and far more dishonest than any baroque composition of skull and skeleton.

Huxley's interpretation of baroque mortuary art and its twentieth-century counterpart, the Beverly Pantheon, is confirmed in various ways by the recent writing of Philippe Aries and David E. Stannard. In *The Puritan Way of Death*, Stannard argues that the "death avoidance and denial"[21] characteristic of modern society and emblematized in modern cemetery sculpture and mortuary practices is traceable to the rise of romanticism in the nineteenth century. The sentimentalization of death, in which the gentler symbols of urn and weeping willow displaced "the grim skulls"[22] of Puritan funerary art, resulted in the banishment of death in favor of more engrossing fantasies focusing on the besetting self-consciousness (with its refusal to accept personal dissolution) of Huxley's romantic egoists. Huxley also noted the disappearance of mortuary motifs connected with physical corruption, including the death's head. His general observation is similar to Stannard's: "With the nineteenth century we enter an age of stylistic revivals; but there is never a return to the mortuary fashions of the Baroque. From the time of Mazzuoli [early eighteenth century] until the present day no monument to any important European has been adorned with death's heads or skeletons" (*CE*, 201). In the Beverly Pantheon, however, the cynical shrewdness of Charlie Habakkuk and the doomed compulsions of Jo Stoyte have combined to create a surreal landscape of erotic violence and voyeuristic self-indulgence. What Stannard has described as "the response of bewilderment and fear before the prospect of emptiness"[23] is implicit throughout the Pantheon, except on a scale corresponding to the manic intensity of Stoyte's fear of "falling out of history" and finally relinquishing his sense of enduring personal identity.

The Fifth Earl's increasingly virulent sadomasochism is a paradigmatic case study that finds itself mirrored not only in the funerary art of the Beverly Pantheon but also in Virginia Maunciple's lesbianism and Jeremy Pordage's voyeuristic fascination with the Marquis de Sade's pornographic novels appropriately discovered scattered throughout the Hauberk papers. Virginia Maunciple is the resident Venus of the castle, an ex-showgirl and promiscuous nymphet who attracts Jo Stoyte as a consequence of the erotically potent combination of virginal child and sensual prostitute in her bearing and features. This "curiously perverse contrast between the appearance of innocence and the fact of experience" has correspondingly aroused in Stoyte the "purest father-love and the most violent eroticism" (*AMS*, 50). For Stoyte the child can be dominated and the woman enjoyed only in a sadomasochistic orgy of "cannibalistic sentimentality" (*AMS*, 51) in which Virginia assumes the dual role of masochistic "concubine-child" and incestuous "daughter-mistress" (*AMS*, 241). *After Many a Summer Dies the Swan* is populated by symbolic reflections of Virginia Maunciple. She moves through the novel followed by a procession of avatars, from the nude sculptures of the Beverly Pantheon to the grotesquely simian female housekeeper in the underground labyrinth of the house at Farnham. She appears and re-appears in Rubens's Helene Fourment, the "half length Mary Magdalen by Titian" (*AMS*, 91), Giambologna's bronze nymph, Nerciat's Felicia, and even "the Queen of Heaven" whom Virginia worships in her boudoir. True to William Propter's axiom that "an ideal is merely the projection, on an enormously enlarged scale, of some aspect of personality" (*AMS*, 124), Virginia worships at the shrine of her own ego. As the occupant of a "sacred doll's house" and the heroine of a tiny costume drama, the Virgin Mary reflects Virginia's own status within Stoyte's castle; placed in a setting of velvet, silk, and brocade, she mirrors the silken eroticism of Watteau's *Embarcation for Cythera* that also occupies a symbolic niche in Virginia's bedroom. Repeating the motif of the illusory opposition of the El Greco and Rubens in the great hall, the pointedly orchestrated juxtaposition of the Christian "Queen of Heaven" and the Venus of Cythera in Virginia's boudoir represents less of an antithetical tension within her psyche than a fundamental perversion that underlies much of the sexual activity at Stoyte's castle.

The recurring juxtaposition of the religious and the erotic throughout *After Many a Summer Dies the Swan* is an integral element within Huxley's carefully coordinated assault on the baroque-romantic impulse and its unstable blending of an intense but essentially spectral idealism with a passionate sensuality. Obispo, for example, is amused by Virginia's vacillations "between Priapus and the Sacred Grotto" (*AMS*, 338), yet Obispo himself enjoys quoting from Dante's description of the love of Paolo and Francesca while contemplating the pornographic illustrations to de Sade's *Cent-Vingt Jours* (*AMS*, 207). Jeremy Pordage is delighted when opening "the ecclesiastical cover" of a copy of *The Book of Common Prayer* expecting to find "the Anglican ritual," he discovers instead the "coldly elegant prose of the Marquis de Sade" (*AMS*, 89). In a similar fashion, Jo Stoyte's eroticism is aroused by Virginia's peculiar blend of spirituality and sensuality, the face of a "child" in an "illustrated Bible" joined to the maturely developed body of a "showgirl,"while Virginia's sexual activities are placed on the same level as her "attending Mass" (*AMS*, 51). In a more general way, the merging of the Virgin Mary with the Venus of Cythera reappears throughout the Beverly Pantheon, where Charlie Habakkuk plans to intensify this perversely cerebral form of eroticism by means of a display of Christian virgins in various states of nudity and sadomasochistic bondage.

In *After Many a Summer Dies the Swan*, women are rigidly confined to the three roles of either saint, prostitute, or a prurient conflation of both, while the men are arrested in passively voyeuristic postures that both engender and depend upon this peculiar blending of saint and whore. Even the visitors who wander through the Beverly Pantheon soon find themselves in a landscape of nudes designed to encourage only a regressively passive attitude towards sexuality combined with undertones of sadism. Like Maurice Spandrell, Dr. Obispo is a voyeur, one who prefers to observe Virginia's moral and spiritual degeneration as "the enjoying, but always detached, always ironically amused, spectator" (*AMS*, 161). Similarly, Jeremy Pordage's obsessive fascination with pornography reaches its voyeuristically logical conclusion when he confesses, "Let Mr. Stoyte have all the girls he wanted; a well-written piece of eighteenth-century pornography was better than any Maunciple" (*AMS*, 90). Idolizing his mother and confining his sexual activities to the prostitutes hidden away in Maida Vale or between the covers of *Felicia*, Jeremy resembles Jo Stoyte, who perceives women as dualistically governed by what Wilhelm Stekel has described as the contending images of "the female animal" and "the ideal figure of the woman." Stekel argues that the inability to reconcile the romantically idealized image of woman with the less exalted reality of bodily functions, including sexuality, often results in a morbid attempt to separate the two that finally collapses into a neurotically unstable conjunction; in it "the sacred and the vulgar always appear condensed to a single symbol" of woman as "at the same time the saint and the prostitute."[24] Virginia is both Madonna and Magdalen in the eyes of Jo Stoyte, a showgirl with a seamy past whose "child-like innocence" gave her "an air of not having reached the age of consent" (*AMS*, 51). Stoyte, then, desires a virgin who is also a prostitute, a fiction he is eager to sustain, while Obispo wants to both observe with a voyeur's clinical detachment the virgin's dawning awareness of her own promiscuity and then to destroy the fiction of her innocence by forcing her to acknowledge her status as little more than a "tart on Main Street." Meanwhile, Jeremy turns completely to fiction, rejecting the physical Virginia for a volume of sadomasochistic pornography "better than any Maunciple."

This emphasis on endowing Virginia Maunciple with essentially fictive qualities as a consequence of the voyeur's preference for an essentially verbal world introduces the theme of language and its relationship with not only sexual abnormality but a wide range of conceptual and psychological distortion. William Propter identifies self-consciousness with language, holding the linguistically based ego responsible for a widespread inability to come to terms with the kind of instinctive sexuality he apparently admires: "Even when men thought they were being most exclusively animal in their sexuality, they were still on the human level. Which meant that they were still self-conscious, still dominated by words —and where there were words" (*AMS*, 261), he argues, man is governed by the kind of "accursed antitheses" that in "After the Fireworks" Huxley had attempted to replace with values implicit in the serene composure of the Etruscan Apollo of Veii. But the synthesis of contending impulses sought by Mark Rampion in *Point Counter Point*, and briefly embodied in the Etruscan Apollo of *Brief Candles*, has yielded to Huxley's increasingly pessimistic assessment of man's linguistic bondage to dualistic thinking. The Huxley who had earlier rejected philosophical monism in favor of an epistemology of pluralistic diversity has come to regard both antithetical thinking and the empirical level in which it is rooted as fundamentally erroneous. Propter argues that only on such a level of fractured experience could be found the aimlessly warring antitheses of "the past and the future, the actual and the fantastic; regret and anticipation; good and evil, the creditable and the discreditable; the beautiful and the ugly" (*AMS*, 261). Ethics, aesthetics, epistemology, and history are all repudiated as forms of inquiry hopelessly enmired in language. Concepts and ideas are the products of an anarchic snarl of words that tempt man with the illusion of universal truths, of ideas marked by a stable and determinate meaning, including our concept of an enduring personality.

In *After Many a Summer Dies the Swan*, no heroic heightening of the

Western philosophical tradition is permitted, while the corrupting power of language is extended even into the ostensibly physical realm of human sexuality:

> Among men and women, even the most apparently bestial acts of eroticism were associated with some or all of these non-animal factors—factors [words, concepts] which were injected into every human situation by the existence of language. This meant that there was no one type of human sexuality that could be called "normal" in the sense in which one could say that there was a normality of vision or digestion. In *that* sense, all kinds of human sexuality were strictly abnormal. The different kinds of sexual behaviour could not be judged by referring them to an absolute natural norm. (*AMS*, 261)

All of the occupants of Stoyte's castle are animated by prurient impulses that in turn are given psychological momentum by words in the form of pornographic fictions. Jeremy Pordage, who "had the scholar's taste for words" (*AMS*, 6), is governed by a dependency on linguistic formulations that transcends in intensity and scope mere academic pedantry. While he lovingly repeats inkhorn terms like "zoomorph" or "discalced Carmelites" for animal-shaped restaurants or mummified nuns, his appetite for language has grown to the proportions of an inhibiting obsession. He wanders through Stoyte's castle in a state of affable incoherence, quoting Coleridge, reciting Shelley, reading Wordsworth, paraphrasing Keats, and composing brief historical essays. Everything that Jeremy encounters is filtered through a screen of words and literary categories and thereby robbed of its power to disturb, stimulate, or challenge his comfortable assumptions about who he is and what he is doing. Jeremy in fact is an inherently linguistic entity who loathes "direct, unmediated experience." Preferring the safer haven of his own verbal conventions, he operates on the postulate that "things assumed meaning, only when they had been translated into words and confined between the covers of a book" (*AMS*, 27). Such a process of translation in which the complications of life are rendered into the safer legibilities of a text is represented by Pordage's devotion to his project of cataloguing the Hauberk papers, as well as writing letters to his mother and, above all, reading pornographic novels as a substitute for an active engagement with human sexuality. In short, Pordage has created a private linguistic world buttressed by novels, poems, manuscripts, diaries, letters, and papers of all kinds.

Even Jo Stoyte tends to perceive things through a haze of formulaic conventions, softening the harsh reality of his showgirl mistress by endowing her with the delicate qualities of "something in the works of Tennyson" (*AMS*, 69). Moreover, Stoyte is obsessively driven by his deeply troubled and alienated past, especially the memory of his puritanical wife, who before her death had poisoned his mind with her religious fanaticism, the vestiges of which survive not unexpectedly in the form of verbal formulations. Endlessly repeating the neurotic litany of "God is love" and "There is no death," he has only imperfectly assimilated Prudence McGladdery Stoyte's censorious moralities, and after her death his perceptions of love and sexuality are deeply divided as he seeks in Virginia a neurotically conceived conflation of saint and prostitute. I have described how having idealized his mother, Jeremy Pordage is similarly divided in his responses to women, reserving his emotional energy for his mother and his sexual energy for either prostitutes or pornography. Both men have been corrupted by falsely antithetical oppositions between good and evil, or the ideal and the real. As a consequence of these corrupting formulae, they seek satisfactions or pleasures totally dominated by verbal conventions in which the real woman is displaced by linguistically conceived substitutes answering to linguistically engendered needs. Reacting to Prudence's puritanism, Stoyte seeks out a prostitute; Jeremy, overcome by his mother's influence, riots quietly between the pages of a book. Even Dr. Obispo appears to be conscious of the overpowering need to compensate for a less than satisfactory world through the creation of self-deluding fictions; and while he scornfully rejects such a "beautiful verbal world" in which personal failures and inadequacies find a setting in which they become "right and reasonable" (*AMS*, 286), his own fascination with de Sade's pornography and his voyeuristic enjoyment of Virginia's moral degeneration bind him firmly to Pordage's verbal universe. Similarly, the Earl of Gonister dismisses Milton's religion as something that depends "upon the picturesque use of intemperate language" and restricts his approval to the Marquis de Sade, whom he regards as "a man of powerful genius," however "unhappily deranged" (*AMS*, 293).

Propter's insistence that "all history" (*AMS*, 134) confirms the innate destructiveness of humanity is dramatized in the form of the Fifth Earl of Gonister's "vellum-bound note-book." This historical document discovered by Pordage among the Hauberk papers records the human degeneration and simian recovery of an eighteenth-century English aristocrat. The earliest of the "miscellaneous jottings" that comprise the notebook reveals the Fifth Earl's sadomasochistic bent, or what he terms the "Art of coolly outraging a devoted female, and of abusing her Person" (*AMS*, 214). The works of the Marquis de Sade scattered among the Hauberk papers belong to the Fifth Earl, who like Spandrell in *Point Counter*

*Point* "had a tendency to take his pleasures rather homicidally" (*AMS*, 264). In *Ends and Means* Huxley had described the Marquis de Sade as "the most uncompromisingly consistent" of those who "have denied the value of non-attachment" (*EM*, 6). Bound to history and the human personality, the sadistic Fifth Earl fears death and clings to his increasingly enfeebled sense of self, despite his recognition that the self is condemned to "solitude." His preoccupation with personal annihilation is inseparable from his sadistic eroticism: "Dying is almost the least spiritual of our acts, more strictly carnal even than the act of love" (*AMS*, 244). The entries in the vellum notebook are a running commentary on the chief ideas of *Ends and Means* but from the perspective of an inverse romantic who refuses to draw the right conclusions. Conscious mainly of his need to dominate others, the Earl of Gonister's sense of personal identity battens on the infliction of pain and the awareness of "another's vicarious suffering" (*AMS*, 248). After seriously wounding one of his maids during an orgy of sadistic lovemaking, he retreats into an underground labyrinth in order to avoid legal prosecution and incarceration in a "private asylum." Sustaining life by means of a diet of raw carp intestines, he survives only to degenerate into a grotesque ape. Ironically, the Earl of Gonister has always been an occupant of a private asylum, his own tortured psyche. Furthermore, his biography dramatizes Huxley's final condemnation of history, in particular nineteenth-century theories of history as inevitably progressive, in that the Earl's gradual degeneration to a simian state is a satirical inversion of progressive theories of history.

In the final chapters of *After Many a Summer Dies the Swan*, a number of historians are mentioned. For example, Jeremy Pordage rejects the scholarly values of modern academic historians like "Coulton and Tawney and the Hammonds" (*AMS*, 293), while Propter dismisses "Marx" and "Spengler" (*AMS*, 323). Pete Boone, however, conceives of history as inherently cyclic, an alteration of "manic" violence and "depressive" inertia that he describes as "cyclic insanity." For Boone cultures and nations are "falling even at such times as they seemed to be rising; destroying what they built in the very act of building" (*AMS*, 312). The diary of the Earl of Gonister, like Henry Wimbush's *History of Crome*, is a chronicle of psychological aberration culminating in Huxley's final version of the burrow, a subterranean hovel far more grotesquely conceived than Francis Chelifer's Gog's Court. As a symbol of enclosure, of the world reduced to the subjective proportions of the inverse romantic, it can be traced back to Sir Hercules Lapith's dwarfish estate in *Crome Yellow*. Yet Sir Hercules was the author of a poem celebrating human history as an evolutionary progress toward higher, more ideal levels of being, while the Earl of Gonister has acted out a devolutionary process of intellectual degeneration and physical debasement.

*After Many a Summer Dies the Swan* reaches narrative closure as a result of two culminating events, both of which are intended to further develop and reinforce the role of Jo Stoyte as an avatar of the Earl of Gonister. Both men are manic egoists who refuse to accept personal dissolution. Wholly dedicated both to life as lived on Propter's "level of time and craving" and the mindless pursuit of perverse sexual satisfaction, they each commit a violent crime connected with irrational sexual possessiveness. The Fifth Earl avoids the resulting scandal as well as criminal prosecution for having sadistically abused the maid by faking his death and hiding himself away in a "subterranean Retreat" while his nephew takes over the estate at Gonister. Similarly, Jo Stoyte murders Pete Boone in a paroxysm of sexual jealousy, and he too avoids criminal prosecution when Dr. Obispo signs a false death certificate. Stoyte reinforces this connection when accompanied by Obispo and Virginia he journeys to England, where he enters Selford, the house near Farnham purchased by the Fifth Earl, who has survived into the twentieth century confined within a "veritable Catacomb."

The confrontation of Jo Stoyte and the Fifth Earl of Gonister takes place in a symbolic setting that consolidates all of the principal themes and satirical conventions of Huxley's interwar satire. Like Crome and the Cybo Malaspina, Selford is an architectural conflation of different historical styles, "Jacobean at one end, with strange accretion of nineteenth-century Gothic at the other." Furthermore, the estate is overwhelmed by the effects of time, screened by a grotesque mass of "great funguses," rotting trees, jungles of brambles, decayed formal gardens and a dilapidated "Grecian gazebo" (*AMS,* 339). The interior of Selford is also marked by the passage of time, in this case mutely recording a shadowy Victorian world redolent of dust, dry rot, and moth balls. Through the dwindling light the visitors are able to distinguish a Victorian melange of objects that form a still life, a composition most of whose elements are associated with time and history. This silent but expressive assemblage consists of "a mantelpiece with a gilt clock, a bookshelf, containing the Waverley novels in crimson leather, and the eighth edition of the Encyclopaedia Britannica, a large brown painting representing the baptism of the future Edward VII, the heads of five or six stags. Hanging on the wall near the door was a map of the Crimea; little flags on pins marked the position of Sebastopol and the Alma" (*AMS,* 342). Like Stoyte's castle, Selford contains only the fragments of the elusive past, what Propter dismisses as "the chance occurrences of earlier history" (*AMS*, 311) that individually and collectively resist any attempt to order their indifferent contingency. The Crimean War, mutely commemorated in the wall map at Selford, has given way to the Spanish Civil War, the detritus of which has made its way to Stoyte's castle, while the young girl who leads Stoyte and his companions to the secret passageway carries a gas mask filled with flowers, a grim emblem of the approaching world war. The presence of the Waverley novels is not a matter of minor detail or simply period atmosphere. In *Music at Night* Huxley noted that "from age to age the past is recreated. A new set of Waverley Novels is founded on a new selection of the facts." If each age "has its private history" (*MN*, 139), the conjunction of Crimean War and the approaching blitz of London suggests a meaningless repetition of international violence, not a continuity comprehensible in terms of a systematically conceived theory of historical development. In *The Varieties of History*, Fritz Stern also cites the Waverley novels as symptomatic of a shift in historical consciousness: "at the very beginning of modern historiography, in those upper reaches of history where it touches philosophy and religion, the influence of the entire pre-Romantic and Romantic movement was decisive." According to Stern, the single most important factor lay with "the great interest in the unique, the particular, and the local—characteristic of Scott and the Romantics."25 But such a program, reminiscent of George Wimbush's historicist antiquarianism satirized by Huxley in *Crome Yellow*, and however necessary to the practice of history, remains a romantic form of cultural nostalgia exhibiting no significance beyond itself. The Waverley novels are evidence of the compartmentalization of history, its essential discontinuity and subjectivity.

Before they descend into the subterranean labyrinth, Obispo spies "the Complete Works, in seventy-seven volumes, of Donatien Alphonse François, Marquis de Sade" (*AMS*, 349). However, the books are part of a false front of wood and leather designed to hide the hidden passageway to the maze beneath the house. In the catacombs the visitors wander aimlessly, baffled by the various passageways that form an architectural pattern repeatedly described by Stoyte as "downright crazy" (*AMS*, 351) and intended to echo Stoyte's own castle, compared by Jeremy Pordage to the mind of a lunatic.

The descent into the darkness of Selford's subterranean maze culminates in another satiric version of the baroque-romantic apocalypse, in this case the most grotesquely conceived of Huxley's interwar period: "beyond the bars, the light of the lanterns had scooped out of the darkness a narrow world of forms and colours." Sitting "at the centre of this world" is Huxley's climactic symbol of history and process, described by Obispo as a "foetal ape that's had time to grow up" (*AMS*, 353). The "narrow universe of lantern light" surrounded by "the foetid darkness" of the "prison" (*AMS*, 352) in which the Fifth Earl has incarcerated himself combines the symbol of subjective withdrawal, the "burrow," with the equally pervasive motif of apocalyptic vision. The feral state into which the Earl has gradually degenerated is Huxley's bleakest dramatization of the illusory values and premises underlying both romanticism and historicism and the culminating apocalypse of his interwar period.

The climactic revelations so common in romantic poetry customarily involve either the ascent of a sacred eminence or a descent into a hallowed cave. Wordsworth's *Prelude*, Shelley's *Prometheus Unbound*, and Byron's *Childe Harold's Pilgrimage* contain typical instances of this convention. Wordsworth ascends Mount Snowdon to confront an apocalyptic panorama at the conclusion of his epic; Childe Harold's journey is repeatedly associated with mountains and temples, culminating in an apocalyptic revelation in St. Peter's cathedral; while in *Prometheus Unbound* Asia undertakes a journey downwards to the oracular cave of Demogorgon. There are other examples, but Huxley tended to draw upon these works, particularly *The Prelude* and *Prometheus Unbound*. References to Wordsworth and Shelley abound in his novels and essays, and as I have shown in chapter one, his assessment of modern history and English society is closely linked to his analysis of romanticism and the detection of romantic values and aspirations in the behavior of his contemporaries. The romantic conventions of ascending or descending movement towards an intensified and augmented vision pervades Huxley's satirical novels, finding their counterpart in the opposition of tower and "tube" in *Crome Yellow* and the prophetic visions satirized in *Those Barren Leaves*. In the novels of this period, Huxley's favorite satirical convention for exposing what he regarded as the baroque-romantic illusion of apocalyptic experience involved the attempt by one of his characters to pick out and illuminate a special feature of a darkened area (either an interior or landscape) by means of a flashlight or torch. The light cast by the torch typically illuminates what can only be described as a parody of prophetic vision, be it the drainpipes of *Crome Yellow*, the murals in the Etruscan tombs in *Those Barren Leaves*, or the vision of the capering Earl of Gonister in *After Many a Summer Dies the Swan*.

The latter, while under few illusions regarding the meaning of history, is incapable of transcending the exigencies of personality. Despite the Earl's concession that the self is merely a proper noun "applied to particular successions of inconsistent Conduct" (*AMS*, 266), he cannot surrender the Sadean will to power, an irrational attempt to shore up his sense of self by dominating others. Like Mark Staithes of *Eyeless in Gaza*, who felt most himself when experiencing pain, the Fifth Earl becomes egoistically secure only when inflicting it. Insisting that "we are kind for the same reason we are cruel, in order that we may enhance the sense of our own Power," he concludes that "a man's sense of Solitude is proportionate to the sense and fact of his Power" (*AMS*, 245). And if the sadomasochistic Maurice Spandrell was a distillation of the prevailing values—or the "tics and tropisms"—of British society in the late twenties, the sadistic Earl of Gonister is a satiric emblem of a constant factor at work throughout the whole extent of human history. In this respect, the characters of *After Many a Summer Dies the Swan*, and the Fifth Earl in particular, represent a shift towards symbolic allegory in which "the novel of social history" is displaced by symbolic "parable." The Earl of Gonister represents for Huxley the psychological reality of history, a "cyclic insanity" informing "a continual process of gradual or catastrophic falling" (*AMS*, 308).

Such a process of chronic decadence is represented in *After Many a Summer Dies the Swan* by the fall of Barcelona, where the violence of the Spanish Civil War is evoked in terms that apply with equal force to Stoyte's castle and the Earl of Gonister: "Like every other community, Barcelona was part machine, part sub-human organism, part nightmare —huge projection and embodiment of men's passions and insanities— their avarice, their pride, their lust for power, their obsession with meaningless words, their worship of lunatic ideals" (*AMS*, 308). This Spenglerian pessimism is balanced in *After Many a Summer Dies the Swan* by the promise of a "teleologically" defined choice, in which the fettered will of the Sadean Earl is simply abandoned for a mystical, transhistorical level of experience. Turning from history, realpolitik, and the enslaving conceptions of historicism—including the habit of "regarding the ego or its social projections as real entities" (*AMS*, 312)—Propter insists that the only reasonable "philosophy of history" is that of "the religious psychologist" (*AMS*, 324). According to Propter, the actual conditions of the historical past are beyond recovery, and "the historian" can offer only vague generalizations that carry no great weight of truth: "that's all the historian can say insofar as he's a historian. Insofar as he's a theologian, of course, or a metaphysician, he can maunder on indefinitely, like Marx or St. Augustine or Spengler" (*AMS*, 323). What Propter nominates as "the intellectual key to history" is the recognition, prompted by the "direct experience" of enlightened liberation (*AMS*, 324), that time, history, and personality are phenomena belonging to a realm of illusion. Accordingly, the hectic piling-up of historical artifacts by Joseph Stoyte and their cataloguing by Jeremy Pordage are essentially meaningless activities, as compulsively anxious and evasive as the lapidary excesses of the Beverly Pantheon.

Stoyte, nonplussed by the Simian Earl, persists in his quest for a means of evading death and personal extinction and unflinchingly meets the blankly uncomprehending gaze of the human ape with a neurotic empathy. Driven by his fear of death, he observes that the Earl has at least survived, and ruled despotically by his time-bound personality, Stoyte accepts the grotesque apocalypse in the subterranean labyrinth of Selford—an estate, as its name suggests, given over to the preservation of self regardless of the human cost. Sunk in the "burrow" of selfhood and committed to the rigidly channeled values of a secular, historicist culture, Stoyte is Huxley's bleakest rendering of the psychotically "attached man." Clinging to temporal experience and eager to embrace what Huxley had come to regard as the enslaving conceptions of historicism, his choice of the feral nightmare before him can be attributed as much to Huxley's well founded assessment of European realities in 1939 as to the thematic and narrative logic of *After Many a Summer Dies the Swan.* The wayward lucubrations of Huxley's Sadean romantics and the symbolic topographies through which they erratically pursue their predatory dreams of power and personal survival have ended in the basement labyrinth of Selford. The single solution to this darkened maze lies with the emancipating release envisaged by Anthony Beavis and William Propter, a choice perennially present yet barely discernible on "the descending road of modern history."

In the fiction of the twenties and thirties Huxley was preoccupied with charting the excesses and anxieties of a world that he judged as "manifestly in regression" (*EM*, 8), and at least until *Eyeless in Gaza* in 1936 the possibility of influencing, reversing, or transcending such a process was only implicitly hinted at in the final chapter of *Those Barren Leaves.* As a satirical "philosopher of history" (*AMS*, 324), Huxley turned in this period increasingly to Pyrrhonist polemic, attacking either the Panglossian optimism of his liberal contemporaries or the hubristic menace of fascism and ideological historicism. Believing that "Marxian theories of history" (*TV*, 203) were merely symptomatic of the obstinate craving to rationalize nationalism according to Hegelian ideas, he would never accept Isaac Deutscher's contention that Stalin drove barbarism out of Russia by barbaric means. But if Huxley, unlike many of his contemporaries (including a large number of fellow novelists and poets) in both England and the United States, never experienced the allure of either communism or fascism, he also rejected the nineteenth-century liberal tradition—despite the liberal rationalism that occasionally surfaces in the essays of *Proper Studies* and *Ends and Means.* Huxley contended that the early decades of the twentieth century had "already witnessed the rise and fall of the liberal man" (*EM*, 2), a conviction that accounts for the absence of a liberal perspective in the novels. As a "philosopher of history," Huxley remained a consistent "Pyrrhonist," a term employed in both his letters and essays and the perspective by which he judged so many of his characters, especially his fictional historians from Henry Wimbush to Jeremy Pordage.

Aldous Huxley never surrendered the hope of a rational and stable society, and in the novels and essays of the 1940s and 1950s, he continued to explore such a possibility. But the terms for this inquiry were laid down in the satires of the interwar period, the novels of the 1920s representing perhaps his finest work. His satirical fiction, like that of Evelyn Waugh or George Orwell, is an important part of the cultural as well as the literary history of England during the two decades following World War I. In this respect, his satires reflect the collective aberrations of Auden's "low dishonest decade" and record the historical futilities of Eliot's wasteland. By 1939 history had become for Huxley a juggernaut beyond either control or comprehension. In the essay on Maine de Biran, he argued that "between the individual and the social, the personal and the historical, there is a difference amounting to incommensurability," but he also claimed that "certain regularities can be detected and certain sociological laws can be formulated" (*CE*, 218). The "novel of social history" defined in the 1934 letter to Russell Green was based on such a tentative endorsement and reached its most successful expression in *Point Counter Point* and *Eyeless in Gaza*. *After Many a Summer Dies the Swan* is a more grotesquely conceived rendering of "social history," but it is nevertheless a response both to the "dark historic page" that Sir Hercules had hoped to erase as well as the "degenerate" values espoused by Mercaptan in *Antic Hay* and Spandrell in *Point Counter Point*—a sadomasochistic decadence beyond redemption in a world where historical time had become profane time, and where if what is past is prologue, the healing vision of the Wellsian progressivist had become merely an exercise in the grotesque.

*Notes*
*Bibliography*
*Index*

# Notes

## Chapter One: The Dark Historic Page

1   R. G. Collingwood, *An Autobiography* (London: Oxford University Press, 1939), pp. 87–88.
2   Aldous Huxley, *Letters of Aldous Huxley*, ed. Grover Smith (London: Chatto & Windus, 1969), p. 377.
3   The various meanings attached to the word "historicism" or "historism" are examined by Maurice Mandelbaum in a brief but useful article in volume four of *The Encyclopedia of Philosophy* (New York: Macmillan and The Free Press, 1967). Mandelbaum defines historicism as "the belief that an adequate understanding of the nature of anything and an adequate assessment of its value are to be gained by considering it in terms of the place it occupied and the role it played within a process of development." Such a methodological principle links evaluation with genetic explanation and can be expanded, as Mandelbaum notes, to include an emphasis on "some larger developmental process" (*Philosophy*, p. 24).

Karl Popper's well-known *The Poverty of Historicism* (London: Routledge and Paul, 1957) and *The Open Society and Its Enemies* (5th ed. rev. [Princeton: Princeton University Press, 1966]) attack the notion of larger patterns, rhythms, laws, or trends within the historical process. An interesting discussion of Popper's ideas can be found in part one of chapter two of Gordon Leff's *Tyranny of Concepts: A Critique of Marxism* (University: University of Alabama Press, 1969). A very succinct and valuable essay on what has been called the crisis of historicism is "The Decline of the West" in Franklin L. Baumer's *Modern European Thought: Continuity and Change in Ideas, 1800–1950* (New York: Macmillan, 1977). Baumer's analysis of both historicism and the increasingly pessimistic evaluation of history in the early twentieth century is in many respects a description of the cultural context out of which Huxley was writing. The various problems of what I refer to as "ideological historicism" are identified and carefully examined in Isaiah Berlin's *Historical Inevitability* (London: Oxford University Press, 1957). The inconsistencies present within the narrower definition of historicism (both forms are defined in this chapter) are catalogued and examined in Rolf Gruner's article "Historicism: Its Rise and Decline" in *Clio* (Fall 1978).

A comprehensive survey of the methodological problems associated with historicism and philosophy of history can be found in R. F. Atkinson's *Knowledge and Explanation in History: An Introduction to the Philosophy of History* (Ithaca: Cornell University Press, 1978) and Maurice Mandelbaum's *The Anatomy of Historical Knowledge* (Baltimore: The Johns Hopkins University Press, 1977). The broad spectrum of positions adopted by those philosophers who created a systematic philosophy of history is surveyed in Bruce Mazlish's *The Riddle of History* (New York: Harper & Row, 1966) and Patrick Gardiner's *Theories of History* (New York: The Free Press, 1959). Finally, a useful analysis of the structural principles involved in philosophy of history can be found in Hayden White's *Metahistory: The Historical Imagination in Nineteenth-Century Europe* (Baltimore: The Johns Hopkins University Press, 1973).

4  Rolf Gruner, "Historicism: Its Rise and Decline," *Clio*, 8, No. 1 (Fall 1978).

5  Harvey Gross, *The Contrived Corridor: History and Fatality in Modern Literature* (Ann Arbor: The University of Michigan Press, 1971), pp. 6–7.

6  Huxley, *Letters*, p. 384.

7  Ibid., p. 383.

8  Huxley's rejection of general laws in history throughout the interwar period and his preference for what he called historical "undulations" (discussed later in this chapter) are in accord with much current thinking on the subject of verifiability and explanation in history. Chapters one and four of R. F. Atkinson's *Knowledge and Explanation in History* and chapter seven of Maurice Mandelbaum's *The Anatomy of Historical Knowledge* (see note 4 above) review the problems associated with law explanations. Huxley's position is, by and large, in accord with their conclusions. I am much indebted to Edward Hallett Carr's discussion of causation in history in chapter four of *What is History?* (London: Macmillan, 1961).

9  A good analysis is Hume's theory of causality and its implications for historical explanation can be found in Atkinson's *Knowledge and Explanation in History*, pages 144–45.

10  *Knowledge and Explanation*, p. 25.

11  Huxley's remarks on the various interpretations of the eighteenth century can be found in *The Olive Tree*, pp. 135–38.

12  Huxley, *Letters*, p. 37.

13  Ibid., p. 155.

14  Jerome Meckier, *Aldous Huxley: Satire and Structure* (London: Chatto & Windus, 1969), p. 73.

15  Sanford E. Marovitz, "Aldous Huxley and the Visual Arts," *Papers on Language and Literature*, 9 (Spring 1973): 174.

16  M. H. Abrams, *Natural Supernaturalism* (New York: W. W. Norton, 1971), p. 117.

17  Huxley, *Letters*, p. 155.

18  Jerome Buckley, *The Triumph of Time: A Study of the Victorian Concepts of Time, History, Progress and Decadence* (Cambridge: Harvard University Press, 1966), p. 85.

19  Huxley, *Letters*, p. 604. Huxley continues this examination of *Brave New*

*World* and Orwell's *Nineteen Eighty-four* in the first chapter of *Brave New World Revisited.*

20  Sir Herbert Read, *The Contrary Experience* (London: Faber, 1963), p. 11.

21  Despite the strictures of Richard Gilman, who argues in *Decadence: The Strange Life of an Epithet* (New York: Farrar, Straus and Giroux, 1979) that the term "decadence" has no deterministic meaning, a number of writers have felt the need for such a term to describe the kind of cultural drift involving a pervasive decline in moral, political, and aesthetic values coupled with a prevailing neurasthenia and a very intense sense of a broad social departure from previous standards of behavior. Gilman's reservations are in many respects justified; but his absolute repudiation of the word is unnecessary. Huxley, conscious of what he regarded as the cultural debility and waning moral energy of European society after the Great War of 1914, preferred the word "deteriorationist" (*Limbo*, 262) and various other synonyms to express his sense of being well along on "the descending road of modern history." While the narrator of *Limbo* is not Huxley, the novels and essays of the interwar period provide ample evidence of his essentially "deteriorationist" perspective. A useful examination of this concept can be found in Jerome Buckley's "The Idea of Decadence," chapter five of his *The Triumph of Time* (see especially pp. 83–93).

22  Peckham's theory of romanticism is gradually developed through a series of four essays, which can be found in *The Triumph of Romanticism* (Columbia: The University of South Carolina Press, 1970). The final two essays, "The Dilemma of a Century: The Four Stages of Romanticism" and "Romanticism: The Present State of Theory," are most applicable to Huxley. Peckham's emphasis on role-playing and the mask is especially pertinent to satires like *Antic Hay* and *Those Barren Leaves*, where many of the characters consciously adopt masks and roles to confer identity upon themselves. More important, Peckham's concept of "Negative Romanticism," the negation of "all value and meaning" (*Triumph*, p. 41) is very close to Huxley's theory of "new" or "reverse" romanticism discussed above. Finally, Peckham's typology of romantic stances or personae (ibid., pp. 41–45) is fully congruent with Huxley's satirical gallery of romantic hedonists, Byronic egotists, spurious visionaries, dandies, and Bohemians in the interwar novels from *Crome Yellow* to *After Many a Summer Dies the Swan*. Peckham's identification of romanticism with cultural crisis and a radical break with previous metaphysical and psychological certainties, and his categorization of romanticism into four historical phases (ibid., pp. 47–55), are to varying degrees dramatized in Huxley's satires, where Peckham's "Analogism" and "Transcendentalism" are roughly equivalent to Huxley's "new" or "reverse" romanticism. Peckham's treatment of the mask and identity in "The Dilemma of a Century" can be usefully supplemented by John A. Lester, Jr.'s, essay on "The Mask" in part three of his *Journey through Despair, 1880–1914; Transformations in British Literary Culture* (Princeton: Princeton University Press, 1968).

23  Peckham, *Triumph*, p. 45.

24  Ibid., p. 46.

## Chapter Two: The Green Heart of England

1 Keith M. May, *Aldous Huxley* (New York: Barnes and Noble, 1972), p. 23. A similar emphasis on the "Peacockian" element in Huxley's satire pervades much of the recent criticism on Huxley's early novels. In a letter written in 1921, Huxley described *Crome Yellow* as embodying "the essential Peacockian datum—a houseful of oddities." Huxley's critics have, with ample justification, followed his lead regarding the tone and setting of the early novels. I am simply suggesting that the "Peacockian novel" (*Letters*, p. 202) merges with the more ambitious "novel of social history" (ibid., p. 383) as early as 1921. The first traces of the latter can be found in the theme of history and Denis Stone's romantic subjectivity.

2 Richard Gill, *Happy Rural Seat: The English Country House and the Literary Imagination* (New Haven: Yale University Press, 1973), pp. 141–44.

3 Gill, *Happy Rural Seat*, p. xiv.

4 Huxley, *Letters*, p. 202.

5 In *Crome Yellow* Scogan rejects realism and its attempt to mirror the "social plenum" (*CY*, 102). Huxley's letters offer a more precise indication of his intentions as a satirist preoccupied with "the present days of the collapse . . . of the social system" (*Letters*, p. 243—see also p. 224).

6 George Woodcock, *Dawn and the Darkest Hour: A Study of Aldous Huxley* (London: Faber and Faber, 1972), p. 82.

7 Harold H. Watts, *Aldous Huxley* (New York: Twayne, 1969), p. 46. Watts, however, does make the parenthetical observation that Crome also "functions as the Royal Palace of older drama or Fairy Tale."

8 Peter Bowering, *Aldous Huxley: A Study of the Major Novels* (New York: Oxford University Press, 1968), p. 34.

9 Percy Bysshe Shelley, *Complete Poetical Works of Percy Bysshe Shelley*, ed. Thomas Hutchinson (London: Oxford University Press, 1960), p. 422.

10 A useful examination of Voltaire's philosophy of history can be found in chapter three of Bruce Mazlish's *The Riddle of History*.

11 Mark Girouard, *Life in the English Country House: A Social and Architectural History* (New Haven: Yale University Press, 1978), p. 303.

12 Peter Firchow, *Aldous Huxley: Satirist and Novelist* (Minneapolis: University of Minnesota Press, 1972), p. 56. Peter Bowering also claims that Wimbush's studies reveal an earlier "pattern of order and stability" (*Aldous Huxley*, p. 44).

13 Huxley, *Letters*, p. 224.

14 Milton Birnbaum, *Aldous Huxley's Quest for Values* (Knoxville: The University of Tennessee Press, 1971), p. 66.

15 Huxley's examination of Piranesi's *The Prisons* is a meditation on history, contemporary culture, and "acedia or spiritual confusion." The essay can be found in *Themes and Variations* (see especially p. 216).

16 In the essays and fiction of the interwar period, Huxley employed Shelley's *Adonais* as a touchstone for romantic Prometheanism. In *Adonais* Shelley defined the archetypal visionary poet in terms of both Greco-Roman and

Judeo-Christian myth, drawing upon the myths of Actaeon, Dionysus, Cain, and Christ. Like Dionysus, whose power and fecundity became for Shelley an essential aspect of the creative artist, Lypiatt conceives of painting and poetry as a matter of inspiration and power. Shelley also linked the Promethean artist to Actaeon and his death-inducing vision of naked divinity, to Cain and his guilt-ridden life as social outcast, and finally to Christ as a martyred prophet of a new redemptive order. Similarly, Lypiatt acts out the conventional romantic drama of the avant-garde visionary, redemptive prophet, and social martyr. *Adonais* also comes very close to recommending suicide, a theme of obvious pertinence to Lypiatt's self-destructive egoism and his final suicide.

17  Huxley, *Letters*, p. 353.

18  Huxley's examination of what he regarded as the explicitly religious element in the valley of the Gondo episode in the sixth book of Wordsworth's *Prelude* can be found on page 99 of *Do What You Will*.

19  Byron's quest for the *"one* word" finds its most intense evocation in stanza xcvii, Canto III, of *Childe Harold's Pilgrimage*; see his *Poetical Works* (London: Oxford University Press, 1970), page 223.

20  May, *Aldous Huxley*, p. 61.

21  Lawrence Brander, *Aldous Huxley: A Critical Study* (London: Rupert Hart-Davis, 1970), p. 128.

22  Woodcock, *Dawn and the Darkest Hour*, p. 127.

23  Firchow, *Aldous Huxley*, p. 82.

24  Meckier, *Aldous Huxley*, p. 74.

25  This theory of history is examined in chapter two of E. H. Carr's *What is History?* Carr refers to it as the "bad King John" theory, where historical events are explained by, or traced back to, the actions of a single individual.

26  I am using Edward Engleberg's definition of the *Kunstlerroman* in "James and Arnold: Conscience and Consciousness in a Victorian 'Kunstlerroman,'" *Criticism*, 10 (1968): 93–114.

27  May, *Aldous Huxley*, p. 62. However, May, in an interesting analysis of *Those Barren Leaves*, goes on to observe that Chelifer's autobiography is "a very important part of what Huxley wishes to say" (p. 66). He argues that the "tone" of Part II is what unites it with the novel as a whole. This is certainly true; but I would argue that the theme of Chelifer's narrative is equally important.

28  A reproduction of the Grien etching can be found in Richard Ellmann's *Ulysses on the Liffey* (London: Oxford University Press, 1972), following page 158.

## Chapter Three: The Descending Road of Modern History

1  Samuel Hynes, *The Auden Generation: Literature and Politics in England in the 1930s* (New York: Viking, 1977).

2  Ibid., p. 187.

3 Bernard Bergonzi, *Reading the Thirties: Texts and Contexts* (Pittsburgh: The University of Pittsburgh Press, 1978), p. 56.

4 Hynes, *The Auden Generation*, p. 25.

5 Ibid., p. 63.

6 May, *Aldous Huxley*, p. 81.

7 Carr, *What is History?*, p. 39.

8 Huxley, *Letters*, p. 155.

9 Ibid.

10 Rampion's comparison of Spandrell with Stavrogin can be found on page 564 of *Point Counter Point*. A recent attempt to assess Spandrell's role, including Rampion's relationship to Spandrell, is James Quina's "the Mathematical-Physical Universe: A Basis for Multiplicity and the Quest for Unity in *Point Counter Point*" in a special issue of *Studies in the Novel* (Winter 1977) commemorating the fiftieth anniversary of the publication of *Point Counter Point*. See especially page 435, where Quina examines Rampion's view of Spandrell.

11 Meckier, *Aldous Huxley*, p. 125.

12 Bowering, *Aldous Huxley*, p. 91.

13 Woodcock, *Dawn and the Darkest Hour*, p. 153. See also Charles M. Holmes's *Aldous Huxley and the Way to Reality* (Bloomington: Indiana University Press, 1970). Holmes maintains, while offering no full argument, that the "inspiration for Spandrell is Baudelaire" (p. 65). Donald J. Watt in "The Criminal-Victim Pattern in Huxley's *Point Counter Point*," *Studies in the Novel* (Spring 1970) also observes that Spandrell is "in all likelihood, Huxley's modern replica of Baudelaire" (p. 49). Huxley's conception of Baudelaire is clearly an element within Spandrell's characterization, but only Milton Birnbaum has recognized, if only in passing, that Spandrell "is devoted to both a masochistic and sadistic demonstration of what he feels are the world's illusions" (*Aldous Huxley's Quest*, p. 124). James Quina stresses Spandrell's wider role (see note 10 above).

14 Woodcock, *Dawn and the Darkest Hour*, p. 160.

15 Sigmund Freud, "Contributions to the Psychology of Love," *The Standard Edition of the Complete Psychological Works of Sigmund Freud*, trans. James Strachey (London: Hogarth Press, 1964), 2, 170. Huxley's letters, essays, and novels prior to the publication of *Point Counter Point* (1928) are filled with references to both Freud and the corrupt state of contemporary European culture. In a letter to Julian Huxley in 1918, he connected "the spirit of Romanticism" with a broad cultural tendency to call "your whims and passions by holy names." More important, he observes of Alfred de Musset: "Alfred's spiritual sadisme, his enjoyment of pain for its own sake was justified by a religious philosophy which said that pain was the great purifier. Their [the romantics] happiness was intense and their misery equally piercing" (*Letters*, p. 155). The "spiritual sadisme" of de Musset resembles the sadistic spirituality of Spandrell, while Huxley views both figures as broadly representative of a cultural phase. In *Those Barren Leaves*,

which appeared three years before *Point Counter Point,* Cardan laments that "Too much light conversation about the Oedipus complex, and anal eroticism is taking the edge off love" (*Those Barren Leaves,* 38). Mary Bracegirdle applies Freudian analysis to her dreams in *Crome Yellow* (chapter seven), much as Huxley does to his prejudices in a 1927 letter to Julian Huxley (*Letters,* p. 290). Huxley was clearly familiar with the main tenets of Freudian psychology, including both sadomasochism and the Oedipus complex, those "Freudian 'complexes' for which family relationships are responsible" (ibid., p. 351). The reader should also consult "The Substitutes for Religion," published in *Proper Studies* the year before the appearance of *Point Counter Point,* where Huxley notes: "Defined in psychological terms, a fanatic is a man who consciously overcompensating a secret prurience." He adds that their influence "in the modern world is great" (*Proper Studies,* 220). Spandrell's idealistic fanaticism is in essence rooted in a "secret prurience" and at the same time is broadly representative of his society.

16  Wilhelm Stekel's account of the symptoms and genesis of this condition can be found in *Sadism and Masochism: The Psychology of Hatred and Cruelty,* 2 vols., trans. Louis Brink (New York: Grove Press, 1963). Stekel refers to "the prostitute complex" on page 362 (vol. 1), but his examination of this condition extends throughout the entire study. Freud uses a similar label, namely "love for a prostitute," on page 166 of "Contributions" (see note 15 above). Huxley, of course, is not describing the evolution of such a neurosis in clinical detail, but his account of Spandrell's psychological history includes all of the salient features, and he uses the term "masochistic prostitutions" (*Point Counter Point,* 301) to describe Spandrell's sexual behavior.

17  Ford Madox Ford, *Parade's End* tetralogy, volume one, *Some Do Not . . .* (London: Bodley Head, 1963), p. 223.

18  Ibid., p. 135.

19  Freud, "The Economic Problem of Masochism," *Complete Works,* 2, 169–70.

20  Huxley, *Letters,* p. 384.

21  Woodcock, *Dawn and the Darkest Hours,* p. 160. Peter Bowering also finds Spandrell "not an entirely unsympathetic figure" (*Aldous Huxley,* p. 91).

22  Peter Firchow discusses the suicide scene (*Aldous Huxley,* p. 110), but he regards Spandrell as an example of what he calls "Christian diabolism" (p. 108).

23  Freud, "The Economic Problem of Masochism," *Complete Works,* 2, 169.

24  Huxley, *Letters,* p. 243.

25  Northrop Frye, *Fearful Symmetry: A Study of William Blake* (Princeton: Princeton University Press, 1947), pp. 407–8). James Quina explores Huxley's use of Blake in *Point Counter Point* in his article on Rampion's "mode of consciousness" (see note 10 above).

26  Huxley was evidently familiar with F. H. Bradley's *Appearance and Reality,* especially the famous ninth and tenth chapters on the self. Huxley's repeated

employment of the burrow motif and his attack on the idea of a persisting self, especially in *Eyeless in Gaza,* owes something to Bradley's concept of the "finite centre" and his systematic analysis of the ontological basis of human identity—a concept that, as does Huxley, he vigorously repudiates.

27 Anthony Beavis's moral reformation closely resembles the ethical progress of George Eliot's self-renunciatory heroines, who surrounded by a similar cast of egoists, espouse an ethic of self-sacrifice rooted in a selfless devotion to the social good. Like Anthony, they demonstrate a pronounced aversion to egosim, a belief in the necessity of emotional involvement in the lives of others, and an optimistic faith in their ultimate good will that is remarkably similar to Miller's belief that if treated decently, people will respond in a positive way.

28 The most important of Blake's references to the states can be found in *Milton* (plate 32) and *Jerusalem* (plate 31). Both references are usefully annotated in Stevenson's and Erdman's edition (see note 29 below).

29 Anne Kostelanetz Mellor, *Blake's Human Form Divine* (Berkeley: University of California Press, 1974), pp. 219–20. See also W. H. Stevenson's discussion of the states on page 688 of *The Poems of William Blake* (London: Longman Group, 1971), edited by Stevenson and David Erdman in the Longman's Annotated Poets series.

30 Jerome Meckier has discussed Huxley's use of Keats and Wordsworth. His emphasis with regard to Blake is different from mine (see especially *Aldous Huxley,* pp. 150, 193).

31 Huxley satirizes Wordsworth's theory of memory and poetry in chapter four of *Those Barren Leaves,* where Mary Thriplow "spontaneously" associates past and present in a parody of Wordsworthian aesthetics (see pp. 45–48).

32 Huxley's criticism of romanticism is, throughout the novels of the interwar period, one of the unifying themes of his work, particularly when it is linked to his assessment of history. Too much has been made of Huxley's "life-worshipping phase," a tendency that has encouraged critics to read *Point Counter Point* as a pendant to *Do What You Will.* Keith May in "Accepting the Universe: The Rampion-Hypothesis in *Point Counter Point* and *Island,*" *Studies in the Novel* (Winter 1977) takes a more flexible position (see especially p. 422).

33 H. Robert Huntley, *The Alien Protagonist of Ford Madox Ford* (Chapel Hill: The University of North Carolina Press, 1970), p. 25.

34 Ibid., p. 9.

35 Huxley, *Letters,* pp. 604–5. I discuss Huxley's exchange with Orwell in more detail in chapter four.

36 May, *Aldous Huxley,* 109.

37 Huxley, *Letters,* p. 344.

38 Ibid., p. 345.

## Chapter Four: History and Ideological Historicism
### in *Eyeless in Gaza*

1   Huxley, *Letters*, p. 356.

2   Ibid., p. 376.

3   Ibid., p. 391. The reference to "Wellsian Progress" can be found in an earlier letter to T. S. Eliot in April, 1934 (ibid., p. 380).

4   The essay entitled "Variations on a Philosopher" appears in the 1943 collection *Themes and Variations*, alongside the other major essays involving history and art. To my mind, the historical explorations comprising this volume represent Huxley's best work as an essayist. "Variations on a Baroque Tomb" and the essays on El Greco and Piranesi are especially important in relation to Huxley's philosophy of history. I have, however, used the more readily available *Collected Essays* in citing these works. See pages 217–18 and 233 there for Huxley's discussion of holism.

5   Huxley, *Letters*, p. 383.

6   Huxley makes this link when he observes that "Sorel" has been "influential in the modern world" because of Mussolini's interest in his work (*The Olive Tree*, 14).

7   Neil McInnes, in an article on Sorel in volume seven of *The Encyclopedia of Philosophy* (New York: Macmillan, 1967), notes that Mussolini regarded Sorel highly. However, he also notes that "despite tenacious legend, Sorel had no influence over either fascism or communism" (*Encyclopedia*, p. 497).

8   Huxley, *Letters*, p. 384

9   Staithes shows little enthusiasm for the Marxist concept that the complexities of the cultural superstructure are wholly traceable to the economic foundation of its society. As a Sorelian elitist, Staithes shows the same uneasy contempt for the lower classes as Everard Webley in *Point Counter Point*. Huxley tended to eschew such holistic explanations throughout *Ends and Means*, and as the reference to Babbitt suggests, Staithes regarded the lower classes as essentially bourgeois, a staple of Huxley's own political philosophy as early as *Do What You Will*.

10  An interesting account of Huxley's relationship with Nancy Cunard can be found in chapter three of part two of Sybille Bedford's *Aldous Huxley: A Biography* (New York: Alfred A. Knopf/Harper & Row, 1974). Bedford's evocation of this "tragic figure" has much in common with Huxley's rendering of Myra Viveash in *Antic Hay*. It has often been noted that Myra Viveash was modeled on Nancy Cunard, but Lucy Tantamount and Mary Amberley also seem to be variations on this personally important as well as culturally representative figure.

11  The very close conjunction of love and creativity is a central theme of Shelley's *Prometheus Unbound* and Blake's *Jerusalem*. The clearest, most representative statement of the romantic insistence on an almost organic connection of love and the creative imagination is Wordsworth's *The Prelude*, especially Book Fourteen, lines 206–209 (1850 version). Huxley was

certainly aware of this, and what he found repugnant in 1923 had become a self-evident necessity by 1936.

12  This pairing of Erasmus and Luther with Huxley's praise of the former is a favorite theme. A typical instance occurs in *The Olive Tree* (pp. 36–38).

13  See note 26 for chapter three above.

14  Blake's best description of the constricting subjectivity of what he calls the "cavern'd man" is in the opening of *Europe: A Prophecy*.

## Chapter Five: Conclusion: *After Many a Summer Dies the Swan*

1  Huxley, *Letters*, p. 434.

2  Ibid., p. 437.

3  Ibid., p. 441.

4  Ibid., p. 440. Huxley's use of "parable" marks a movement away from the novel of social history and his avowed aim of creating a "paradigm" of cultural life toward a more symbolic satire, simplified in plot and less mimetic in its depiction of society. This tendency, however, was present in Huxley's satire from the outset, as a comparison of *Crome Yellow* and its more grotesque variant, *After Many a Summer Dies the Swan*, suggests.

5  These quotations can be found on pages 316, 318, 329, and 320 of Donald Watt's *Aldous Huxley: The Critical Heritage* (London: Routledge and Kegan Paul, 1975).

6  Bowering, *Aldous Huxley*, p. 142.

7  K. Bhaskara Ramamevity, *Aldous Huxley: A Study of his Novels* (New York: Asia Publishing House, 1974), p. 82.

8  Mann's remark was directed at *Time Must Have a Stop*, but it is representative of the increasingly negative reaction to Huxley's rejection of human existence on the level of historicist experience. Mann's letter is reprinted in Watt, *Critical Heritage*, p. 346.

9  Huxley, *Letters*, p. 428.

10  Ibid., p. 445.

11  Huxley's repugnance for the new destructive "social patterns" and their accompanying "neurasthenia" characteristic of European society in the final years of the interwar period is best conveyed in the chapter "War" in *Ends and Means* (see especially pp. 123–25). However, the quotation is from *Letters*, p. 444.

12  Huxley, *Letters*, p. 440.

13  Ibid., p. 449.

14  Ibid.

15  Ibid., p. 450.

16  Ibid., p. 449.

17  Ibid., p. 351.

18  The "cyclopean gazebo" can be found on page 215 of the *Collected Essays*, significantly in a discussion of the Zeitgeist, "historical pressures," and the "water-tight compartments" in which most people immure themselves.

19 Bowering, "'The Source of Light': Pictorial Imagery and Symbolism in *Point Counter Point*," *Studies in the Novel*, 9 (1974): 389.
20 Samuel Edwards, *Peter Paul Rubens* (New York: David McKay, 1973), p. 194.
21 David E. Stannard, *The Puritan Way of Death: A Study in Religion, Culture and Social Change* (New York: Oxford University Press, 1977), p. 189.
22 Ibid., p. 180.
23 Ibid., p. 194.
24 Stekel, *Sadism and Masochism*, 1, 277.
25 Fritz Stern, ed., *The Varieties of History from Voltaire to the Present* (New York: Random House, 1973), p. 17.

# Bibliography

## The Works of Aldous Huxley

Unless otherwise noted, all editions are published in London by Chatto & Windus.

| NOVELS | FIRST EDITIONS | EDITIONS USED |
|---|---|---|
| *Crome Yellow* | 1921 | 1969 |
| *Antic Hay* | 1923 | 1969 |
| *Those Barren Leaves* | 1925 | 1969 |
| *Point Counter Point* | 1928 | 1963 |
| *Brave New World* | 1932 | 1956 (New York: Random House) |
| *Eyeless in Gaza* | 1936 | 1972 |
| *After Many a Summer Dies the Swan* | 1939 | 1939 (New York: Harper & Brothers) |
| *Time Must Have a Stop* | 1944 | 1944 |
| *The Devils of Loudon* | 1952 | 1952 |

| SHORT STORIES | | |
|---|---|---|
| *Limbo* | 1920 | 1920 |
| *Two or Three Graces* | 1926 | 1926 (New York: George H. Doran) |
| *Brief Candles* | 1930 | 1930 |

| ESSAY COLLECTIONS AND POLITICAL PROSE | | |
|---|---|---|
| *On the Margin* | 1923 | 1926 |
| *Along the Road* | 1925 | 1925 |
| *Jesting Pilate* | 1926 | 1926 (New York: George H. Doran) |
| *Essays New and Old* | 1927 | 1927 (New York: George H. Doran) |
| *Proper Studies* | 1927 | 1927 |

| | | |
|---|---|---|
| *Do What You Will* | 1929 | 1929 |
| *Music at Night* | 1931 | 1960 |
| *The Olive Tree* | 1936 | 1936 |
| *Ends and Means* | 1938 | 1938 |
| *Themes and Variations* | 1950 | 1950 (New York: Harper & Brothers) |
| *The Doors of Perception and Heaven and Hell* | 1954 and 1956 | 1961 (Penguin) |
| *Collected Essays* | 1958 | 1958 (New York: Harper & Brothers) |

## Criticism and Reference

Abrams, M. H. *Natural Supernaturalism: Tradition and Revolution in Romantic Literature.* New York: W.W. Norton, 1971.

Adams, Robert Martin. *After Joyce: Studies in Fiction After Ulysses.* New York: Oxford University Press, 1977.

Atkinson R. F. *Knowledge and Explanation in History: An Introduction to the Philosophy of History.* Ithaca: Cornell University Press, 1978.

Avineri, Sklomo. *The Social and Political Thought of Karl Marx.* London: Cambridge University Press, 1969.

Bate, W. J. *John Keats.* Cambridge: Harvard University Press, 1964.

Baumer, Franklin L. *Modern European Thought: Continuity and Change in Ideas, 1600–1950.* New York: Macmillan, 1977.

Beaty, F. L. *Light from Heaven: Love in British Romantic Literature.* DeKalb: Northern Illinois University Press, 1971.

Bedford, Sybille. *Aldous Huxley: A Biography.* New York: Alfred A. Knopf/Harper & Row, 1974.

Beja, Morris. *Epiphany in the Modern Novel.* Seattle: University of Washington Press, 1971.

Berghahn, V. R. *Germany and the Approach of War in 1914.* New York: St. Martin's Press, 1973.

Berlin, Isaiah. *Historical Inevitability.* London: Oxford University Press, 1957.

Berlin, Isaiah. *Vico & Herder: Two Studies in the History of Ideas.* New York: The Viking Press, 1976.

Birnbaum, Milton. *Aldous Huxley's Quest for Values.* Knoxville: The University of Tennessee Press, 1971.

Bottomore, T. B. *Classes in Modern Society.* New York: Pantheon Books, 1966.

Bowering, Peter. *Aldous Huxley: A Study of the Major Novels.* New York: Oxford University Press, 1968.

Brander, Lawrence. *Aldous Huxley: A Critical Study.* London: Rupert Hart-Davis, 1970.

Buckley, Jerome Hamilton. *The Triumph of Time: A Study of the Victorian Concepts of Time, History, Progress, and Decadence.* Cambridge: Harvard University Press, 1966.

Camerson, Kenneth Neill, ed. *Romantic Rebels: Essays on Shelley and His Circle.* Cambridge: Harvard University Press, 1973.

Camerson, Kenneth Neill. *Shelley: The Golden Years.* Cambridge: Harvard University Press, 1974.

Canary, Robert H., and Kozicki, Henry, eds. *The Writing of History: Literary Forms and Historical Understanding.* Madison: The University of Wisconsin Press, 1978.

Carr, Edward Hallett. *The Twenty Years Crisis, 1919–1939.* London: Macmillan, 1954.

Carr, Edward Hallett. *What is History?* London: Macmillan, 1961.

Craig, Gordon A. *Europe Since 1815.* New York: Holt, Rinehart and Winston, 1966.

Craig, Gordon A. *Germany, 1866–1945.* New York: Oxford University Press, 1978.

Dunlop, Ian. *The Shock of the New.* New York: American Heritage Press, 1972.

Edwards, J. R. *British History, 1815–1939.* New York: Humanities Press, 1970.

Erdman, David V., and Stevenson, W. H. *The Poems of Blake.* New York: W.W. Norton, 1971.

Firchow, Peter. *Aldous Huxley: Satirist and Novelist.* Minneapolis: University of Minnesota Press, 1972.

Friedrich, Carl J. *The Age of the Baroque, 1610–1660.* New York: Harper & Brothers, 1952.

Frosch, Thomas R. *The Awakening of Albion: The Renovation of the Body in the Poetry of William Blake.* Ithaca: Cornell University Press, 1974.

Frye, Northrop. *Fearful Symmetry: A Study of William Blake.* Princeton: Princeton University Press, 1947.

Fussell, Paul. *The Great War and Modern Memory.* New York: Oxford University Press, 1975.

Gardiner, Patrick. *Theories of History.* New York: The Free Press, 1959.

Gay, Peter. *Style in History.* New York: Basic Books, 1974.

Gill, Richard. *Happy Rural Seat: The English Country House and The Literary Imagination.* New Haven: Yale University Press, 1973.

Gilman, Richard. *Decadence: The Strange Life of an Epithet.* New York: Farrar, Straus and Giroux, 1979.

Girouard, Mark. *Life in the English Country House: A Social and Architectural History.* New Haven: Yale University Press, 1978.

Gross, Harvey. *The Contrived Corridor. History and Fatality in Modern Literature.* Ann Arbor: The University of Michigan Press, 1971.

Honour, Hugh. *Romanticism.* New York: Harper & Row, 1979.

Huxley, Aldous. *Letters of Aldous Huxley.* Ed. Grover Smith. London: Chatto & Windus, 1969.

Jack, Ian. *English Literature, 1815–1832.* New York: Oxford University Press, 1963.

Jones, Howard Mumford. *Revolution & Romanticism.* Cambridge: Harvard University Press, 1974.

Kuehn, Robert E., ed. *Aldous Huxley: A Collection of Critical Essays.* Englewood, N.J.: Prentice-Hall, 1974.

Larrain, Jorge. *The Concept of Ideology*. Athens: The University of Georgia Press, 1980.

Leff, Gordon. *Tyranny of Concepts: A Critique of Marxism*. University: University of Alabama Press, 1969.

Lester, John A., Jr. *Journey Through Despair, 1880–1914: Transformations in British Literary Culture*. Princeton: Princeton University Press, 1968.

Mandelbaum, Maurice. *The Anatomy of Historical Knowledge*. Baltimore: The Johns Hopkins University Press, 1977.

May, Keith. *Aldous Huxley*. New York: Barnes and Noble, 1972.

Mazlish, Bruce. *The Riddle of History: The Great Speculators from Vico to Freud*. New York: Harper & Row, 1955.

Meckier, Jerome. *Aldous Huxley: Satire and Structure*. London: Chatto & Windus, 1969.

Mellor, Anne Kostelanetz. *Blake's Human Form Divine*. Berkeley: University of California Press, 1974.

Miliband, Ralph. *Marxism and Politics*. New York: Oxford University Press, 1977.

Mowat, Charles Loch. *Britain Between the Wars, 1918–1940*. Chicago: The University of Chicago Press, 1955.

Nicholls, A. J. *Weimar and the Rise of Hitler*. London: Macmillan, 1968.

Nisbet, Robert. *History of the Idea of Progress*. New York: Basic Books, 1980.

Peckham, Morse. *The Triumph of Romanticism*. Columbia: The University of South Carolina Press, 1970.

Roberts, John. *Europe, 1880–1945*. London: Longmans, Green and Co., 1967.

Stannard, David E. *The Puritan Way of Death: A Study in Religion, Culture, and Social Change*. New York: Oxford University Press, 1977.

Stern, Fritz, ed. *The Varieties of History from Voltaire to the Present*. New York: Random House, 1973.

Taylor, A. J. P. *English History, 1914–1945*. London: Oxford University Press, 1955.

Taylor, A. J. P. *The Struggle for Mastery in Europe, 1848–1918*. London: Oxford University Press, 1957.

Thody, Philip. *Aldous Huxley: A Biographical Introduction*. New York: Charles Scribner's Sons, 1973.

Trilling, Lionel. *Sincerity and Authenticity*. Cambridge: Harvard University Press, 1972.

# Index

JACKET DESIGNED BY MIKE JAYNES
COMPOSED BY THE COMPOSING ROOM, KIMBERLY, WISCONSIN
MANUFACTURED BY THOMSON-SHORE, INC., DEXTER, MICHIGAN
TEXT AND DISPLAY LINES ARE SET IN PALATINO

Library of Congress Cataloging in Publication Data
Baker, Robert S., 1940–
The dark historic page.
Bibliography: pp. 243–246.
Includes index.
1. Huxley, Aldous, 1894–1963—Criticism and
interpretation. 2. History in literature.
3. Historicism. 4. Satire, English—History and
criticism. 5. Social history in literature.
I. Title.
PR6015.U9Z5617     823'.912     81–70004
ISBN 0-299-08940-1     AACR2